The GOSPEL of the KINGDOM

HOPE FOR THE CHURCH AND THE WORLD

Kingdom Secrets to Restoring Nations Back to God

ABRAHAM JOHN

The Gospel of the Kingdom: Hope for the Church and the World
Kingdom Secrets to Restoring Nations Back to God

Copyright © 2019 by Abraham John

Published by Abraham John

The Kingdom Network
www.TheKingdomNetwork.org
Email: mim@maximpact.org
1-800-580-5020

ISBN: 978-1-948330-05-3

Printed in the United States of America

Unless otherwise indicated, all Scriptures are from the New King James Version®. Copyright © 1982 by Thomas Nelson. Used by permission.

Scripture marked (KJV) is from the King James Version of the Bible, and in public domain.

Scripture quotations marked (ESV) are taken from the ESV® Bible (The Holy Bible, English Standard Version®). ESV® Text Edition: 2016. Copyright © 2001 by Crossway, a publishing ministry of Good News Publishers. The ESV® text has been reproduced in cooperation with and by permission of Good News Publishers. Unauthorized reproduction of this publication is prohibited. All rights reserved.

Scripture quotations marked (NLT) are taken from the *Holy Bible,* New Living Translation, copyright © ©1996, 2004, 2007, 2013, 2015 by Tyndale House Foundation. Used by permission of Tyndale House Publishers Inc., Carol Stream, Illinois 60188. All rights reserved.

Scripture quotations marked (TLB) are taken from The Living Bible copyright © 1971 by Tyndale House Foundation. Used by permission of Tyndale House Publishers Inc., Carol Stream, Illinois 60188. All rights reserved. The Living Bible, TLB, and The Living Bible logo are registered trademarks of Tyndale House Publishers.

Scripture quotations marked (NIV) are taken from the Holy Bible, NEW INTERNATIONAL VERSION®, NIV® Copyright © 1973, 1978, 1984, 2011 by Biblica, Inc.® Used by permission. All rights reserved worldwide.

All *emphases* or additions in parentheses within scriptural quotations are the author's own.

All rights reserved. No part of this book may be reproduced or transmitted in any form or by any means, electronic or mechanical, including photocopying, recording, or by any information storage and retrieval system, without permission in writing from the author. Please direct your inquiries to info@thekingdomnetwork.org

Contents

Preface	5
Introduction	9
Part I: The Gospel of the Kingdom	**17**
Chapter 1: Kingdom Alignment	19
Chapter 2: The Kingdom of Heaven Is Near	31
Chapter 3: Enter the Kingdom	43
Chapter 4: Seek the Kingdom	47
Chapter 5: See the Kingdom	57
Chapter 6: The Kingdom Prayer	61
Part II: Eternal Perspective	**77**
Chapter 7: God and Jesus as Kings	79
Chapter 8: The Origin of the Kingdom	87
Chapter 9: The Creation of Lucifer	91
Chapter 10: The Fall of Lucifer	109
Part III: The Present Earth	**123**
Chapter 11: The Diluvian Age	125
Chapter 12: The Creation and Fall of Man	129
Part IV: Kingdom of Darkness	**135**
Chapter 13: Origin of the Present World—Kingdom of Darkness	137
Chapter 14: The Seven Mountains of this World	157

Chapter 15: The Mystery of Great Babylon—the Counterfeit Church 169

Part V: Restoration of the Kingdom **181**
    Chapter 16: The Restoration of Man 183
    Chapter 17: Arrival of the Kingdom 191
    Chapter 18: Understanding Salvation 201
    Chapter 19: The Process of Salvation, Part I 209
    Chapter 20: The Process of Salvation, Part II 235
    Chapter 21: Discipling Nations with the Gospel of the Kingdom 247

Preface

The Big Why

A couple of years ago, I joined a local business group that trains people to grow their businesses and make them profitable. On the first day of the meeting, the person in charge shared on how to identify the "Big Why" of each one's business.

He said that most businesses fail within a couple of years after their start-up, and most people fail in their lives because they do not have a "why" that is big enough. To know your company's "big why" in the business world is to know the purpose of its existence. He said it had to be something different and bigger than to make money. It had to serve a good cause or solve a problem that exists in our world.

Before we delve into understanding the gospel of the kingdom, we need to understand the Big Why of our life. What is our Big Why? Our Big Why refers to the reason God created this planet and put us here in the first place. If we do not understand that, then we will not understand anything else about life, God, the earth, the Bible, or the church.

What was in the mind of God when He decided to create this planet that we live on, and then create mankind to inhabit it? In both the Old Testament and the New Testament, we see a common thread or theme. It is that our God is a King and He has a kingdom.

When I ask people why God created us and this planet, they usually answer that He did it because God is love and He wanted a family, or because He wanted people who would glorify or worship Him. Those are three of the most common religious answers, and you have probably heard them all before.

But if our God wanted a family, why didn't He create us and keep us with Him in heaven? That's what families do; they want to be close to each other and be together as much as they can. You might spiritualize this and say that God is closer than the air we breathe, and I understand that. Still, we live on two different planets: God is in heaven and we are on the Earth.

Sometimes I jokingly say that I would like to have a family like God has and keep them on a different planet, telling them, "I love you; now enjoy your life out there and I will visit you once in a while, especially when you sing enough songs to make me happy." If I did that, I wouldn't have a family for very long, right?

If God created man to worship Him, then why didn't He say anything about that to the first couple, Adam and Eve? Did He just forget to mention the most important reason for which He created them, the purpose of their lives? That doesn't sound like a smart Creator to me!

We are God's family. He is our Father. I have a family, but that is not the reason for my existence; that is part of my function, not my purpose. God was not lonely before He created us.

Two Fundamental Truths

The entire Bible and our lives hang on two fundamental truths. The first is that our God is a King. Our King has a kingdom, and He wants to see it established on planet Earth. That is the simple definition of the gospel of the kingdom. To accomplish that purpose, He created a species in His image and likeness and entrusted them with that task. That is the Big Why for God creating this planet and then mankind.

Every other doctrine in the Bible fits under that one BIG doctrine. If we do not establish that as the foundation, then nothing else will work well for us. That is the reason the church has not been effective for hundreds of years and has turned into a religious entity—Jesus never intended for His church to become a religion!

The second fundamental truth is that the species God entrusted to accomplish that task failed in their mission, or fell from their position. They were deceived by an enemy kingdom, which stole everything God had given to them. To restore everything we lost because of that failure—or Adam's fall—God came up with a plan called salvation. Salvation is all about restoring mankind to their original intent. Once you are saved, you are supposed to go back to where you fell from, and you didn't fall from heaven!

If we do not understand and keep those two fundamental truths close to our hearts, the enemy will continue to deceive and steal everything God has given us. This book is written to end this menacing situation that's been continually acted out for generations, to empower the body of Christ to rise up and become everything God created us to be, and to keep the enemy where he belongs: under our feet!

The Key to a Meaningful Life

There is nothing new that God is trying to do on this planet; His plan remains the same for all eternity. We think we are waiting on God to move, in truth He has been waiting on us for generations. When we align ourselves with His plan and purpose, and what He has been doing, then for the first time, life will become meaningful. If not, no matter what else we do, sooner or later we will get tired and become fed up with it.

The whole Bible is about a King, His kingdom, His royal family, and His plan for planet Earth. Just think and meditate for a few minutes on what you just read. Take a pen and a journal and write everything you believed prior to this about the reason for our existence and that of the earth (and everything else religion has taught you). Write down every question and conflict that may arise in your heart.

Unless we boldly confront the lies that have been rooted in our minds and hearts for generations, nothing will change for the better. There will probably be many more conflicts and questions that will arise in your mind before you see all the answers, but the Holy Spirit will help you through all of it, so please read on.

Introduction

The Lie of the Great Escape

Are you happy with the direction your nation is headed? Do you sense in your spirit that something is missing from the current church system? Is what we are experiencing now all there is to God and spirituality?

The church has done a great job of creating an escapist mentality in most Christians. What I mean by that is most people believe they do not belong on this earth and they are just passing by. They are waiting to die and go to heaven or for Jesus to come and take them *home*. They have no idea why God put them here, so they are looking for the sweet by-and-by, a future time in which they will enjoy life. They are waiting to escape from the very inheritance their Father has given them (Matthew 5:5).

That is one of the most horrendous lies the devil has perpetrated into the church: that we don't belong here. As long as you believe that the devil has full reign over every aspect of our society, he will continue to wreck havoc. He will steal everything God has given you and use it to build his kingdom. Many people waste their precious life and their potential in the time between their salvation and the rapture because they fail to grasp the fact that they have a purpose to fulfill here on earth.

Something has gone wrong with our understanding of Christianity and how we live it. I asked Jesus one day, "Lord, how come all the churches you mentioned in the book of Revelation and the ones Paul started have disappeared from the face of the earth? You said you will build Your church and the gates of hell shall not prevail against it? Then why isn't there a trace of those churches today, except some of the letters Paul wrote to the believers?" Do you know what He said? "Son, they were wonderful churches, but they failed to continue to administer My kingdom into the society and the nation in which they existed."

God did not intend for His church to contain itself in a building or a worship service on a Sunday morning. Jesus mentioned the church only two times in the four gospels, but He mentioned His kingdom more than a hundred and twenty times. We do the opposite — we preach about the church a hundred and twenty times, and mention the kingdom only two or three times at the most!

We are Supposed to Administrate the Kingdom

Jesus preached and taught about the kingdom more than any other subject, but no one has trained us to live in a kingdom. Kings think differently than ordinary citizens think. King's children are raised differently than common children. People who live in a kingdom think and function differently than people who live in a democratic society. *A kingdom has the same components as a democratic nation, but it functions differently.*

Paul said we are ambassadors of Christ. An ambassador is someone who represents a government and lives in a foreign country. They represent their home country in that foreign country. The place, or the office, they work in is called an embassy. The church is the embassy of God's kingdom on the earth. If you are a believer in Christ, you are an ambassador. Your citizenship is in heaven and you have been sent to earth to represent His kingdom here.

The church is supposed to be the agency that administers God's kingdom on earth. The church is not a building or a choir, or any of the kinds of pictures that often come to people's minds when they think of the church. We have trained people to preach, sing, and conduct weddings, funerals, and baptisms; but we have failed to teach them about the kingdom of God and how to live in it.

I spent five precious years of my life in seminaries, but there was not even a single class about the kingdom of God. Most believers, and even ministers,

INTRODUCTION

live way below what God ever intended for them. We have more preachers, churches, and mission organizations on the earth today than in all other times combined, but still more than half of the world is dying and going to eternity without Christ. We have more believers with the mindset of a beggar instead of that of sons and daughters of the King of Kings. But in the first century, twelve men reached the entire known world in their lifetime with the gospel of the kingdom.

Everything we see with our natural eyes is temporal. The kingdom of God is more real than the world we see and live in. It has everything we need for our lives and more. There is no limit to its resources. God's kingdom rules everything in this universe (Psalm 103:19).

The culture of His kingdom is righteousness, peace, and joy in the Holy Spirit. There is joy unspeakable and peace that surpasses all understanding. Love transcends every form of human knowledge. People on this earth are starving for true love, joy, and peace. They will only find that in the kingdom of God.

The Kingdom Should Be Political

Everything Jesus did with His disciples was symbolic of how a kingdom operates. He selected twelve disciples. In Scripture, the number twelve represents divine government. Then He sent out seventy followers to witness about Him because there were seventy Gentile nations on the earth during Jesus' time. (Some translations say seventy-two because there was a dispute about how many nations actually existed at that time.) The number seventy-two equals six times twelve.

Additionally, in the Old Testament time, it took a minimum of seventy people to form a nation. When Jacob and his children moved to Egypt, they were seventy in number. When the day of Pentecost came, there were 120 people in the upper room. Twelve times ten is 120. The number 120 represents the dominion and influence of a kingdom.

In Jesus' time, the Sanhedrin (the Jewish religious governing body) had 120 members. In Daniel 6:1, we read that King Darius appointed 120 leaders to govern the provinces of his kingdom. Then he appointed three governors over them, and Daniel was one of those three. Out of the twelve disciples, Jesus had Peter, James, and John as His inner circle leaders. Through this, we begin to get an understanding of how kingdoms operate.

Every kingdom (and most nations) have three types of top-level leaders: king, elders, and governors. In the kingdom of God it is the Father, the Son, and the Holy Spirit. In the U.S. we have a president, vice president, and secretary of state. In India, we have a president, vice president, and prime minister. The church also has three top levels of leadership: apostles, prophets, and elders.

Many of the terms Jesus and Paul used in their teachings were political, not religious or spiritual. King, kingdom, *ekklesia* (the Greek word for church), apostle, ambassador, commonwealth, general assembly, covenant, treaty, nation, world, judge, Lord, elder, and many more are all political words.

Living in Kingdom Authority

Most believers do not want a kingdom because it is ruled by a king. They think that all kings do is give orders. That is their comparison between a kingdom and the democratic government they live in. Those who live in a free society may not want a kingdom because they don't want to be told to do anything. Why? Because they think they are *free* and no one can tell them what to do. That is a demonic mentality. Lucifer does not like to submit to authority either. Everything in the kingdom of God works according to the principle of authority and submission.

Adam surely had an opinion and freedom of choice in the garden, even though he was living in a kingdom, —but we know what happened when he chose to operate independently of God. The kingdom of God works a little differently than the kingdoms of men. When the Israelites asked for a king, they said they wanted a king just like the Gentile nations around them (1 Samuel 8:1-7). The understanding about kingdoms most believers have is based on Gentile kings and their kingdoms, not on God's kingdom.

How did we miss the most important subject of the Bible (the kingdom of God) for so long? There are many answers to that question, but the vital

INTRODUCTION

part we need to focus on is gaining an understanding of how the kingdom of God is supposed to work now and how our lives fit into it.

I believe this book will revolutionize your life and how you live it for the rest of the time you have left. May the Lord use this to bring the change that is needed in the body of Christ before it is too late, especially for the United States.

What Kingdom Expansion Should Look Like

God never intended for life on earth to be any different than life in heaven. Our God is a King, and it is the nature of kings to expand their territories to new regions. He created the earth to be an extension of His kingdom. His plan was to see His will done on earth as it is in heaven. He still has the same plan, and He will never back away from that plan.

It is also the nature of kings and kingdoms to colonize. When they colonize, the same culture, language, and way of life will be brought to the new country that is being colonized. When the British came to India, they brought their culture, language, and way of life. Indians drink tea in the morning and afternoon because it is the custom of England.

At that time, the king and queen of England wanted to see the people in India following the same system as in Britain: to speak the same language, eat the same food, dress as they did, and so on. That is what it means when we pray, "Thy kingdom come and Thy will be done on earth as it is in heaven."

Crisis Mode

God wanted the culture, way of life, language, economy, food, and customs in heaven to come to earth. He is still waiting for that dream to be accomplished. Right now the earth is not working as God intended. Nations are in crisis mode. People everywhere are looking for solutions to their problems but they are not finding any. They are frustrated, angry, and don't know what to do.

If we look around, we see that every system of this world is going through some form of crisis or transition. Every nation is facing a crisis. Crisis is not a bad thing. If we look at it from God's perspective, we see that it is a huge opportunity in disguise. Below are seven benefits of a crisis.

- Crisis is a sign that something is out of alignment.
- Crisis is a sign that you have been ignoring a problem for too long.
- Crisis is an opportunity to bring the necessary change.
- Crisis is not the end, only a time for a new beginning.
- Crisis forces you to learn new information, habits, and skills.
- Crisis is a forerunner of new seasons.
- Crisis is an opportunity for promotion.

If you are going through any crisis personally, know that it is not the end, but the beginning of something new. *There is only one agency that can solve the problems our planet has, and that is the kingdom of God through the church.* Any human government, the United Nations, or any other political or humanitarian organization cannot solve the problems we have. We have been trying to do this for thousands of years; at least by now we should be ready to admit that these means are not working, but for some reason we keep trying the same old thing and keep getting the same old results.

Is the blood of Jesus sufficient enough and powerful enough to reverse every form of evil and every curse that was initiated by the entrance of sin to the planet? I believe so.

The Missing Gospel

Jesus came with the solution for every problem we would ever have. He came with a kingdom, but we failed to tell people about it. We have limited Him to just escaping to heaven when we die. Jesus and the apostles preached the gospel of the kingdom continually. I grew up in church, and for more than twenty-five years of my life I never heard a message about

INTRODUCTION

the kingdom of God. Following is evidence of Jesus preaching the gospel of the kingdom.

> And Jesus went about all Galilee, teaching in their synagogues, preaching the *gospel of the kingdom*, and healing all kinds of sickness and all kinds of disease among the people (Matthew 4:23).
>
> Then Jesus went about all the cities and villages, teaching in their synagogues, preaching the *gospel of the kingdom*, and healing every sickness and every disease among the people (Matthew 9:35).
>
> And this *gospel of the kingdom* will be preached in all the world as a witness to all the nations, and then the end will come (Matthew 24:14).
>
> Now after John was put in prison, Jesus came to Galilee, preaching the *gospel of the kingdom* of God (Mark 1:14).
>
> But He said to them, "I must preach the *kingdom of God* to the other cities also, because for this purpose I have been sent" (Luke 4:43).

This book is a humble attempt to explore the gospel Jesus and the apostles preached. I believe that after reading this, you will have a better understanding of what the kingdom is and how to live your life within it.

Though this book is very basic, I did not repeat many of the things I already wrote in the other Kingdom Secrets series books. I highly recommend you read the free book *ReDiscovering the Lost Kingdom* that we offer on our website before you read this one. Please visit www.thekingdomnetwork.org to download your free copy. Thank you.

-Abraham John

Part I: The Gospel of the Kingdom

Chapter 1: Kingdom Alignment

When most people think of the kingdom, they think of power, healing, or some sort of miracles. Yes, power is part of the kingdom, but that is not all there is in a kingdom. What is the purpose of all the miracles, healings, and signs that took place in the Bible? These things happened to bring something back into alignment that was out of order. If your body is sick, that means it is out of alignment; it is not functioning as it is supposed to function, so God intervenes and manifests His power to bring your body back into alignment.

What is kingdom alignment? God intended that everything on earth work in alignment with heaven. When something on earth is not in alignment with heaven, it will not work properly. Being aligned with heaven means that we will see the manifestation of the will and the plan of God in each aspect of our life. Being out of alignment means something is out of order, or out of place.

Broken Relationships

When Adam fell, seven levels of relationship were affected. These seven areas of relationship were broken. They fell out of alignment with heaven and no longer functioned as God wanted.

1. The relationship between man and God
2. The relationship between heaven and earth
3. The relationship between man and other men (or women)
4. The relationship between man and the animal kingdom

5. The relationship between man and nature
6. The relationship within man himself (the alignment of spirit, soul, and body)
7. The future relationships between different nations

When man's relationship with God was broken, it also affected every other aspect of creation, so shouldn't the restoration of man's relationship with God also affect every other aspect of creation that was broken? Jesus came to restore all those levels of relationship, not just take us all to heaven. He finished His work and is now seated at the right hand of God. What can you think of on earth or in your city that is in alignment with heaven?

Loss of the Kingdom Government

Ever since man lost God's kingdom, it has been the plan of the devil to deceive us by offering us a substitute for everything God ordained, so we will be sufficiently distracted *and never look for our country of origin*. It is the plan of God to rule the earth with His kingdom, and be our King. Deceived by the enemy, man has rebelled against God's plan and will from the very beginning.

Ever since we lost the kingdom government, the enemy (with man's partnership) came up with different forms of government, but so far none of them have worked. If you look at any country on earth, you will see that its major problem is its government. The very thing that people set in place to solve their problems creates more problems than it solves.

God never intended for any wicked person to be in a position of authority or to rule. This is happening because we gave the devil our dominion, and then he appointed his lieutenants to rule over the righteous. There is nothing more vexing or unbearable under the sun than the righteous being governed by the wicked.

The only form of government that will work for us is the government of God, which is the kingdom of God. We haven't given God a chance yet. Ever since He put us here, we have been telling Him not to rule over us.

He has been waiting patiently for us to willingly come to Him and invite Him to be our King, to rule over the earth and us.

The Enemy's Substitutes

Ever since man lost relationship with God, the enemy has come in with a substitute called religion. People everywhere are dissatisfied with religion. Religion will never work because it was never meant to be the solution. One simple definition of religion is doing the same thing again and again, and expecting a different result. I know it is the definition of insanity, but there is nothing more insane than being religious!

Ever since man lost the economy of God, it's been the plan of the enemy to substitute it with a different form of economy based on money. Money is not part of the kingdom economy. In fact, the monetary system of this world depends on the kingdom economy.

It is not God's will for you to spend the majority of your life doing something other than what you were created to do, just to make money. If you do, you are serving money. That is the purpose of the world's system: to make you depend on it so you are not free to do what God has called you to do.

Ever since man lost his purpose, the enemy came up with an educational system to train people to depend on this world's system and never fulfill their God-given purpose. Once we are stuck in the world's system of survival, it is very difficult to get free from it. This world's education system is based on getting a job and working to make a living and trying to survive. *God didn't create you to survive, but to live a life of significance.*

True education is supposed to help you discover your purpose and develop your gifts and talents. Today's system is a counterfeit to kingdom education. The main focus of today's education is to give you a degree so that you can find a job that will pay you some money.

We lost kingdom family life too. God's original design for man and woman is to become one and to fulfill their God-given purpose as one. Ever since the fall, men and women began fighting against each other for dominance and control instead of becoming the greatest blessing they were meant to be. Family life has become terribly painful for many.

We live in a world that is trying to eliminate gender differences. God's intent was for a husband and wife to function as one flesh. Individualism, selfishness, and pride have hindered the plan of God for man and woman.

We no longer follow God's design for marriage either, but marry just to satisfy the lust of the flesh. As a result, divorce has become rampant, even in the church, because there is no deep connection between the spirits of men and women; it is only maintained on a superficial level between the two bodies.

Loss of the Kingdom Culture

Ever since we lost the kingdom culture, a superstitious culture began to develop on earth, which divided people and caused them to fight each other over their cultural differences. People in every nation think their culture is superior to every other, which creates pride and arrogance in people. When we are born again, we all become citizens of the kingdom and become part of the same country and culture.

Sadly, most people do not become free from their natural culture; they bring it into the kingdom and start imposing it on others. As kingdom of God citizens, we are supposed to teach people about kingdom culture and how to live in it.

There was only one language in the beginning, but since we lost the kingdom language, thousands of languages have emerged and confusion was birthed as a result. The language of the kingdom is faith. *We are only supposed to speak faith-filled words once we come into the kingdom.* The kingdom of God is governed by the words we speak.

Nineteen Years of Transition

God is doing a new thing on the earth today and He wants us to come into alignment with what He is doing. Has any major event taken place in the body of Christ in the last nineteen years? Other than some of our prominent leaders going to be with the Lord, no. We have been playing the same tune and singing the same songs for nineteen years, just waiting and wishing for something to happen.

Since the year two thousand—for nineteen years—the body of Christ has been in a period of transition. We are transitioning from preaching the gospel of salvation to the gospel of the kingdom. Here and there a few people are beginning to capture what God has been trying to do from the beginning. We have been the most passive body of people on the planet. Jesus is *not* a passive Person. We are supposed to be active and involved in everything good that is happening around us. God is always moving. We do not know how to come into alignment with His move.

How come countries like South Africa, Zimbabwe, the United States, and many other countries where Christians are a majority have been overtaken by chaos? The church doesn't have much influence over what's happening in those countries, and we've had no real and practical solutions to offer. We tell people to come to church, but the church is still filled with people who are looking for solutions, and not finding any there.

In all these nations, the Lord is doing a new thing. Believers are being awakened to a new sound—the sound of the gospel of the kingdom. It's happening now only at a grassroots level. Soon it will become a wildfire that will consume and make level everything in its path.

We Need a New Mindset

If we preach and demonstrate the gospel of the kingdom, we can solve every problem in these countries within ten to fifteen years. That's good news to me. People will run to church when we solve problems for them. We are supposed to solve the economic problems by manifesting kingdom economy. We are supposed to eliminate disease by manifesting kingdom agriculture and kingdom health. *It is possible!* What we need is a different mindset. People everywhere are looking for something different, whether they are new or seasoned believers.

- People are searching for a lost country.

- People are looking for a government that functions.
- People are looking for a lost kingdom.
- People are looking for a viable and dependable economy.
- People are looking for something meaningful.
- People are looking for something that satisfies their souls.
- People are looking for their purpose.

Mankind's purpose is to establish and expand God's kingdom here on earth. Because man lost his original purpose, we have been trying to replace it with something different. Nothing has worked so far, and nothing ever will. People keep trying to feel fulfilled through entertainment, sports, sex, money, and every other gimmick they can imagine; and even though these things are destroying them left and right, people keep searching for fulfillment through these means.

Sometime I wonder how a person can suck smoke into their lungs and exhale it through their nose and feel good about it, or find some satisfaction from it. These are all signs that something is broken inside. Something is out of alignment.

Imagine that you are trying to escape from the very place God sent you to fulfill your purpose. Imagine that you think it's an inconvenience for you to live your life in the place of your inheritance. This earth is your inheritance from your heavenly Father.

Until you discover and fulfill what God created you to do, nothing will satisfy. It doesn't matter how much (or how little) money you have. Whatever kind of status we keep, nothing can substitute our original assignment.

Kingdom Alignment

Any area of our life that is not in alignment with God's kingdom will not function the way it is supposed to function. Any aspect of our society, nation, or government that is not in alignment with God's kingdom will not work properly. It doesn't matter how many resources we pour into something or how much a person is educated, it will all end up wasted.

What is kingdom alignment? Kingdom alignment is having an understanding of God's original intent for creating something and aligning ourselves to that intent. Almost everything on this planet right now is misaligned and not functioning the way it is supposed to function. Just take a look at any area and you will see what I am talking about.

The more I travel and encounter believers from all over the world, the more I am perplexed because people are broken inside and outside, yet they hide it behind a religious mask or by speaking *Christianese*, which they have become accustomed to using. Inside, they are crying out for help—and sadly, some of them end their lives prematurely. Others die of various diseases and sicknesses. That is not God's will.

Nobody taught us what salvation really is, where Adam fell from, and what he lost when he disobeyed God. Most of us are repeating old behaviors, singing the same songs, and speaking in the same Christian clichés that have been handed over to us by the religious spirit. We do this like parrots, just repeating what we have been told without thinking. We do not recognize that these traditions and methods are not producing good fruit. We fail to consider why it is not working.

In our lifetime, we will witness the deaths of our loved ones and friends. I am not sure if there is an adult who has not witnessed a funeral yet. Most of those precious ones were not planning to die when they did. They had dreams that were not realized; they lived lives of continual waiting for something to change in the church. They hoped they were going to witness the rapture in their lifetime. Most of them went to the grave without seeing the fulfillment of the dreams God had placed within them.

My question to you is this: do you want the same thing to happen to you? Or do you want a different result? Do you want your children and grandchildren to have a different outcome than what you have had? If so, we need to change the way we do things. *In order to change the way we do things, we need to change the way we think.* To change the way think, we need to go back and unfold the belief systems that have been passed on to us and see if they are all truly biblical. Just because preachers preach from a pulpit or through a screen doesn't mean everything they are saying is true.

Misconceptions about the Kingdom

If our belief system is truly scriptural then we will reap the outcome the Word says we should. In most cases, this is not happening. What God promised in the Scriptures, we do not see manifesting in our lives. We question God, asking Him why He is not doing what He promised to do.

The problem is never with God. We will reap the harvest of what we believe and speak. *If we don't like the results we are getting, then it's time to change what we believe.* To be honest with you, much of what we believe as Christians is not scriptural. Let me share a few examples.

We have been taught that salvation is about going to heaven when we die. Nobody taught such things in the Bible. Nobody asked anybody in the New Testament if they wanted to go to heaven when they died. Most evangelism today is done by scaring people about hell. Nobody did that in the preaching found in the New Testament.

We have been taught that when we are born again, we will enter the kingdom, which is synonymous with going to heaven. That is not what Jesus said. He said that unless you are born again, you will not *see* the kingdom (John 3:3). There is a huge difference.

Another lie we were taught is that God created man to worship Him, and that worship means singing. Nowhere in the Bible does it say such a thing! The word *worship* appears 190 times in the Bible, and not even once is it mentioned in relation to singing.

We were taught that God created man to live in heaven; that we will go to heaven when we die and sing hallelujah for all eternity. Again, nowhere in the Bible does God say this. If we die today, or get raptured, we will wait in heaven until we come back to earth to rule and reign with Christ. That waiting period in heaven is our retirement, or rest (Revelation 22:5). I can't find a single verse that says humans are doing anything in heaven.

We believe the church's primary mission is to evangelize the world. But Jesus told us to go and *make disciples of all nations* (Matthew 28:19). That is not the same thing. If the evangelism we do is not geared toward discipling a nation, then we are not doing it for the right reason.

Another lie we believe is that our job is to plunder hell and populate heaven. God did not tell anyone in the Bible that this was their job. God created man to rule and populate the earth. The first command was to be fruitful and fill the earth (Genesis 1:28-30).

We have been singing that this world is not our home, and that we'll fly away, or to take the whole world, but give me Jesus. Those songs are not scriptural. Nobody in the Bible sang such songs. This world is our home (1 Corinthians 3:22). We are not supposed to give it away, but reign over it.

We have been taught by tradition that for God to show up in a service, we have to sing two fast songs and three slow songs. No such formula is used in the New Testament either.

We have been taught that God dwells in the praises of His people. That is not New Testament theology. Under the new covenant, we are His temple and He dwells in us.

These are just some of the lies we have been taught, and ideas we have been brainwashed into believing by the religious spirit. If you don't believe me, read your Bible for yourself and find out the truth.

Believers in Bondage

Jesus offered people salvation, healing, and deliverance all in one package. Whenever people had an encounter with Jesus, they were made whole. Religious leaders separated the benefits of salvation and began to offer people each one individually and for different *prices*. As a result, we have an abundance of believers in our churches today whose spirit is saved, but their body and mind still remain under bondage to various ailments, their culture, and the oppression of the enemy. They are emotionally and financially broke and trying to hang on until something happens.

THE GOSPEL OF THE KINGDOM

This has to change if we are going to give a true witness of what Jesus did for us on the cross. Either He shed His blood and died for all the sin of the world or He did not. We know that He did. When sins are forgiven, every consequence that came because of sin must leave as well: sickness, curses, poverty, and bondages are some of the consequences of sin. Once we are saved, the next step should be to save our town, city, state, and then the whole nation. Only the gospel of the kingdom has the power to do that.

Jesus preached the gospel of the kingdom wherever He went. Then He healed the sick and cast out demons. The gospel of the kingdom includes the salvation of souls, physical healing, and deliverance from demonic oppression and every evil consequence that sin brought upon humanity and this world.

During the nineteenth and twentieth centuries, the church went to the four corners of the earth, preaching the gospel of salvation. Their main goal was to take people to heaven when they died. As a result, we have more than a billion souls in the church who are waiting for the rapture. They have no clue what to do now or how to get involved in what is happening in their nations.

They only have a limited understanding of what salvation is all about. They heard that Jesus came to take everyone to heaven and that He is the way to heaven. In truth, Jesus and His apostles never asked anyone if they wanted to go to heaven. Jesus never said He was the way to heaven either. He said He was the way to the Father (John 14:6).

Jesus' primary mission was not to take everyone He met to heaven. His primary goal was to bring heaven (His kingdom) to earth, so that life in heaven could manifest on earth. As it is in heaven, so shall it be on earth.

So why did Jesus and the apostles preach the gospel of the kingdom? And why don't very many people preach it these days? What is the gospel of the kingdom? What's the difference between the gospel of salvation and the gospel of the kingdom? We will explore all of these questions.

The gospel of the kingdom has the power to bring everything into alignment. That is why Jesus instructed his followers to go into all the world and preach the gospel to every creature (Mark 16:15). Every creature needs to hear the gospel, not just humans. The gospel of the kingdom affects every aspect of our society, not just the souls of people.

Anything that was broken because of sin can be mended by the gospel. That is why it is called the *good news*. Let's discover this amazing news together and spread it all across the world!

In 2007, there were about 36.6 million non-religious people in the United States. These were people who said they were not affiliated with any religion. Now the Pew Research Center has determined that there are nearly sixty million non-religious people in the US.[1] This is an increase of about nineteen million in only twelve years. That is startling! This is the result of all the ministries, churches, TV, and radio channels that claim they are preaching the gospel. That is the result we get? Something is not right somewhere.

Let us explore and find out what Jesus, our Lord, preached and taught while He was on the earth. You don't need to believe me, but believe what Jesus said and did. Are you ready?

---

1. Benjamin Wormald and Benjamin Wormald, "America's Changing Religious Landscape," Pew Research Center's Religion & Public Life Project, September 07, 2017, accessed June 06, 2019, https://www.pewforum.org/2015/05/12/americas-changing-religious-landscape/.

Chapter 2: The Kingdom of Heaven Is Near

Coming Out of the Dark

The Messiah, the Savior of mankind for whom the whole world waited for more than four thousand years, the Seed of the woman who would crush the head of the serpent, God Almighty in human form appeared on this planet. The Word that became flesh, born of a virgin woman, finally manifested on earth.

Heaven, earth, and the angels rejoiced at His birth. All creation may have sung for joy to see their Creator made flesh. How many of us have wished that God would speak to us face-to-face or that we could hear His audible voice? Wouldn't it be wonderful to know and hear what God has to say to us? To know what He wants and expects from us? To know what is important to Him and finally be able to get on with our life the way He wants us to? That is exactly what happened with the coming of Jesus.

There was a fight going on between God and man since the time of Adam's fall. For some reason, God said one thing, and man heard and did the very opposite. There was a communication gap between God and man. God eventually became so tired of man's rebellion that He stopped speaking and did not send any prophets for almost four hundred years.

This had happened once before—during Eli's time. The Bible says there was no widespread revelation before the call of Samuel (1 Samuel 3:1). After the book of Malachi, there was a silent period of 400 years. There was no recorded communication between God and man during that period. It is known as the Dark Age.

Then an extraordinary thing occurred: God, who seemed unapproachable and difficult to please, finally took our form so that we could relate and hear from Him on our level. Now we could know exactly what He thought of us and wanted from us, and find out why He put us here in the first place!

Most of us live our life by just winging it, thinking we are doing everything to the best of our ability, trying to do the right thing and hoping that God is pleased with us. By the time we realize that what we have been doing isn't working, it's often too late to change anything. I want to tell you the good news. God made life simple and easy, but we have made a mess out of it.

The Father's Message

I have wished I were there in Israel when Jesus walked on earth, to hear Him speak, see the miracles He did, and ask Him questions about life on this earth. But thank God for the writers of the gospels who captured most of it and wrote it down for us so we can know exactly what He said and did.

Whether you ever heard God's audible voice before or whether you have seen Him face-to-face, I am going to share exactly what God Almighty told mankind when He appeared on earth, without altering or adding anything to it.

Jesus waited for thirty years to begin the work His Father gave Him to do. Finally, the day arrived and He got ready to go out and tell humanity what God in heaven wanted to communicate with them. I want you to imagine this with me for a minute. Imagine you are Jesus getting ready for the first day of work. Prior to that He might have been asking, "Father, what is the message You want me to tell mankind?"

Remember, this is happening after four hundred years of silence from God. There is no recorded evidence of God speaking to anyone during those years. The fact that Jesus would come in this way was prophesied in the Old Testament. The prophet Isaiah wrote:

THE KINGDOM OF HEAVEN IS NEAR

> Who has believed our report? And to whom has the arm of the Lord been revealed? For He shall grow up before Him as a tender plant, and as a root out of dry ground (Isaiah 53:1-2a).

Jesus was a royal root out of four hundred years of dry ground. He is also called the Branch. After those long years of silence, God was about to speak with mankind through His Son. What did God Almighty have to say to us?

People in those days were weary, tired, and broken. The Jewish nation lived under Roman oppression and did not have the freedom to do what they wanted. Everything about their lives was restricted and controlled by the Roman authorities, so whatever Jesus was to tell them had to impress them to make any difference in their lives.

I've heard the old saying, "The first impression is the best impression." He might have thought, "What I am going to tell them first should be the most important message." Jesus woke up early that morning, freshened up, and got ready. I can imagine He might have been a little nervous, wondering what people would think about Him and if they would receive what He was going to tell them. How would they respond?

The Holy Spirit came to His aid and He went out and began to preach. The first sentence that came out of His mouth is recorded in the gospel of Matthew. Let us read it together as if we are hearing it from Jesus Himself in person for the first time.

> From that time on Jesus began to preach, "Repent, for the kingdom of heaven has come near" (Matthew 4:17 NIV).

After hearing what Jesus said, many people might have thought and said, "What? Repent? What is that? Another kingdom is coming? We are already tired of being under this Roman kingdom. We don't have food; we need freedom; we are sick; and we are tired. We don't need another utopian philosophy. We need the kingdom of Israel to be restored. We do not need any kingdom from anywhere else."

I noticed He didn't come and say, "I can't believe you are not praying more and reading the Torah every day. I love you. You all need to be more spiritual and practice more spiritual disciplines. How come you don't have music groups in every village to praise Me?" He didn't say any of those things.

You might have heard the words *repent* and *kingdom* before. If you have been a part of any religion or religious church, I am sure you've heard the word *repent* many times before. Let's think about that word for a minute. What does *repent* mean, and why did Jesus say we needed to repent? You might have been taught by religious leaders that we need to repent to go to heaven, or even to receive Jesus, or to join a particular form of religion or church. But Jesus did not preach any of those things.

Good News Coming

Jesus was very specific and clear, as always, but the religious spirit twists and turns what He said, so we won't get the same result He said we would get for doing what He told us to do. Read that again. The religious spirit twists and turns what Jesus said, so we won't get the same result He said we would get for doing what He told us to do. May Jesus give us discernment to see through this in every instance as we read God's Word.

Jesus said to repent because something was near, or at hand. He said to do it because a kingdom was "about to" arrive on this planet. That was the most important message Jesus had to communicate with humanity on the first day of His ministry. How on earth did we miss that?

The purpose, or the result, of repentance is not to leave this planet, *but to benefit from the kingdom that was about to arrive.* That was, and still is, a revolutionary and mind-boggling statement.

Jesus said that something good was about to arrive here on this planet. Something different, and something that every human needs. Something every person had been waiting for and could not live without was finally about to arrive. That's good news! The gospel is called the *good news* of the kingdom.

Jesus did not say we needed to repent to join a church, go to heaven, or change from one religion to another. He never said any of those things. He was very specific and kept it simple:

Repent because a kingdom is coming to a place near you. If you do not repent you will miss it.

Why do we need to repent because of the arrival of a kingdom? What does the kingdom of heaven have to do with repentance? What is the kingdom of heaven? And why is it coming to earth? I have heard from many religious leaders that Jesus came to take us all out of here. He came to give anyone who believes in Him a passport to escape this planet. A get-out-of-jail-free card! Have you heard such things before?

Instead, Jesus said that He was bringing heaven down to earth, and that before it came and once it arrived, if we wanted to benefit from that kingdom, we needed to repent. That is the complete opposite of what I have heard preached and what I also preached in my early years of ministry.

Heaven Is Coming to Earth

What is a kingdom? And what is the kingdom of heaven? In the days of the Old Testament, there were only kingdoms on earth. Every country was ruled by a king. The people who heard Jesus speak were familiar with kings and kingdoms, but they had never heard of the *kingdom of heaven*.

A kingdom is a country or a territory ruled by a king. A kingdom is a king's domain. Our God is a King. Every king needs a kingdom. Our God has a kingdom, called the kingdom of God, and it is ruled from a place called heaven. Because God lives in heaven, it is called the kingdom of heaven.

Why was it necessary for the kingdom of heaven to come to earth? Why would He say it was near if it was going to happen thousands of years later after His second coming? Was He trying to fool them? Why wasn't anyone preaching the kingdom-near, or at-hand, message after the day of Pentecost? Why is this the most important message Jesus had to convey to us? You will find the answers to all of those questions in this book.

Captive by a Pseudo-king

God created our planet to be an extension of His kingdom. He wanted life here to be representative of life in heaven. He wanted earth to be a reflection of heaven. He wanted earth to be a colony of heaven. That was his original idea and plan. Sadly, the species He created to accomplish that task was deceived and taken captive by a pseudo-king and his kingdom.

This rebel king who took us captive has used us to establish his kingdom on earth instead of God's. God had to temporarily withdraw His kingdom and wait for the right time to restore His original plan for mankind and the earth. That plan was to restore His kingdom and once again establish it on the earth through us.

Every kingdom has a culture, language, economy, educational system, and a form of government. The culture of the rebel kingdom that took us captive is made of pride, hatred, selfishness, greed, cheating, mutating, and murdering anyone who doesn't submit to its will.

The language of this kingdom is called lying. In fact, its ruler is called the father of all lies. The economy of his kingdom is comprised of greed, covetousness, and poverty.

The purpose of his educational system is survival and slavery, and no one gets to fulfill their God-ordained purpose.

This king does all of this by injecting venom into humans and taking over their minds and thoughts. He corrupts the original software by installing malware called "S-I-N."

The acronym for sin is Satanic Information Network. Anyone who has been infected by this malware loses the ability to think correctly. It affects their function and productivity. It alters and corrupts their view of themselves, the world around them, and God Himself.

The purpose of the malware is to make humans slaves to this king and his kingdom, so he can use them to accomplish his evil intent on earth. You might ask who this rebel king is: It is no other than Satan. His very name means "adversary."

The True King and Kingdom

On the other hand, the true King and His kingdom work opposite to this rebel kingdom.

His kingdom also has a culture, economy, educational system, and government. His culture is made of righteousness, which is doing things the right way because you are in right standing and relationship with the King. Peace, joy, and contentment are some of the attributes of His culture. His economy is made of abundance, sharing, and contentment. Nobody needs to have an unmet need.

In His government, everyone gets to play a role in governing the whole kingdom. His educational system is based on equipping you to fulfill your purpose by helping you discover your calling, and by identifying and developing your gifts, talents, and skills.

What It Means to Repent

The word *repent* means to change the way we think. In order to change the way we think, we need to cleanse and renew our minds by rooting out that malware and its viruses. We must completely delete it and reinstall the original software by which we are supposed to function and operate.

Many people confused the word *repent* with confessing our sins. Confessing sins is the first step of the road to repentance, and not the end. It is part of it. If *repentance* means only confessing sins, then Jesus wouldn't have used such a word. He would have just said, "Confess your sins."

To repent means to reboot the entire system by deleting every infected area of our mind. Every mindset that hinders us from thinking the way God thinks of us and from seeing ourselves the way God sees us has to go. The existence of anything that causes us to think of ourselves less than what God thinks of us, shows we are infected by that malware called sin.

Any time we function lower than the way God functions is an indication that we are affected by malware in that area. Those areas need to be rebooted. It's an ongoing process. The more we repent or change the way we think, the more we understand this kingdom and enjoy God's benefits from it.

We are created in God's image and likeness and we are supposed to function like God functions. We are supposed to speak like God speaks and rule and reign like God reigns. We were created to live in and expand His kingdom here on earth.

When the Messiah, the Savior of this world came, the first thing He told us to do was repent, or reboot our system by deleting the software of the enemy's kingdom and downloading the original operating system called the "Word."

The kingdom that Adam lost was coming back to earth. We will learn more about how we lost the kingdom and why God is bringing it back, later in this book. We need to begin at the beginning right now: To benefit from that kingdom's return, we need to change the way we think and operate. That's what repentance means and that is the reason Jesus asks us to do it.

The Kingdom At Hand

Now, let's look at the word *near* or the phrase "at hand." Exactly what does that mean? There are two words that are used in Greek for our English word *near*. One means something that is physically close to a place or a location. The other means near in time, like something that is going to happen very soon. The word Jesus used for *near* was something that was physically near.

After the day of Pentecost, we don't read about anyone preaching about a kingdom being near or at hand again. That is because in the time between the resurrection and the day of Pentecost when the Holy Spirit arrived on earth, something dramatic or important had happened on this earth. We will discuss more about this later.

The Most Important Message

When the Father decided to send His Son to earth to save humanity, He gave Him a message to convey. It was the most important message God wanted to share with us. The Father did not tell His Son to share how much He missed us all or how He was longing to see us all in heaven. No. He did not say anything like that.

THE KINGDOM OF HEAVEN IS NEAR

Jesus preached one message, day and night, from the first day of His ministry to the last day He was on earth after His resurrection, and that message was about the kingdom of God. One night, Nicodemus, a Jewish religious leader, came to see Him to show appreciation for what He was doing. Jesus shared the message of the kingdom with him, too (John 3:1-6).

On the first day of His ministry, He began with:

> From that time Jesus began to preach and to say, "Repent, for *the kingdom of heaven* is at hand" (Matthew 4:17).

On the last day of His ministry:

> To whom He also presented Himself alive after His suffering by many infallible proofs, being seen by them during forty days and speaking of the things pertaining to the *kingdom of God* (Acts 1:3).

The book of Acts begins and ends with the message of the kingdom.

> Then Paul dwelt two whole years in his own rented house, and received all who came to him, *preaching the kingdom of God* and teaching the things which concern the Lord Jesus Christ with all confidence, no one forbidding him (Acts 28:30-31).

The church age began with the preaching of the kingdom of God, and it will end with the preaching of the gospel of the kingdom:

> And *this gospel of the kingdom will be preached* in all the world as a witness to all the nations, and then the end will come (Matthew 24:14).

How many times have you heard the kingdom of God preached in the last several years? Preachers often use the phrase "the kingdom" or "the kingdom of God" flippantly. That doesn't mean everything they do and say has anything to do with the kingdom of God. We hear a lot about revival and the rapture, but not much about the kingdom of God—the subject that Jesus and the Father held to be most important.

Why the message of the kingdom? Why did the Father not have anything more important to tell us? That is what we are going to find out in this book. The message of the kingdom is important to God, and should continue to be important to us in this day and age.

To understand why the message of the kingdom is important to God, we need to understand who God is. Most people will say these days that God is love, based on what it says in John 3:16 and 1 John 4:16. Keep in mind that those verses were written thousands of years after mankind was created. What kind of understanding did mankind have about God prior to those verses being written?

In all those thousands of years, what was the primary revelation of God predominant among humans? How did they relate with God? There is one predominant thread of revelation about God that has been going on from the beginning of the Bible to its end. That is the revelation that our God is a King with a kingdom.

And that was the first message Jesus preached. It was about a kingdom coming to earth. Then He selected twelve disciples to be with Him and sent them out to preach about it. Let's find out what He told them to preach.

Tell Them the Kingdom Is Coming!

Jesus selected twelve disciples to train and sent them out to preach. It is important to notice what He told them to preach about. He didn't send them to preach about Himself or revival.

> And as you go, preach, saying, *"The kingdom of heaven* is at hand." Heal the sick, cleanse the lepers, raise the dead, cast out demons. Freely you have received, freely give (Matthew 10:7-8).

He told them to go and heal the sick, cleanse the lepers, raise the dead, cast out demons, and tell the people that the kingdom of heaven was near. Why?

Why didn't He tell them to preach about God, the love of God, or even the fact that He (Jesus) had arrived? Why did He tell them to announce the arrival of the kingdom? It is because mankind lost a kingdom, and God was about to restore it.

The disciples didn't go around preaching, "Come to Jesus and He will give you peace or heaven." That might surprise and irritate some of us who have been drenched in the religious gospel for so long. Peace is a by-product of receiving the kingdom Jesus offers, because peace is a vital part of its culture.

The disciples didn't go around saying "Come to a church that we are going to start." Or, "Believe in Jesus so you can all go to heaven." No. Compare that to what the religious leaders of our day have been preaching and what we heard when we were born again.

The reason we do not see the same results they saw when we preach, is because **we do not preach the same message they preached**. It's that simple.

Chapter 3: Enter the Kingdom

> For I say to you, that unless your righteousness exceeds the righteousness of the scribes and Pharisees, you will by no means enter the kingdom of heaven (Matthew 5:20).

The second thing Jesus said about His kingdom was to give instruction for how to enter it. First, He spoke of its imminent arrival, and second, He told us what to do to enter it.

I was talking to a friend about the kingdom of God and he said that he thought the kingdom was something like a euphoric experience or feeling. That was his understanding of the kingdom. If the kingdom of God were some kind of pie-in-the-sky feeling or excitement, how would you enter it? When I travel to another country, there is always a port of entry. In most places, we are required to fill out a form for immigration and customs.

If the kingdom of God is not a place, why would Jesus say that we had to do something or we couldn't enter it? In every country, you enter through one of its ports of entry: airport, seaport, or by land. If we try to enter through any other way, we will be considered an illegal immigrant.

The Righteousness of the Pharisees

The above scripture says that unless our righteousness exceeds the righteousness of the Pharisees, we shall not enter this kingdom. The Pharisees were one of the most religious Jewish sects in Jesus' time. They would swallow an elephant in an attempt to filter a mosquito. That means they followed the letter of the Law to its fullest extent. By doing so, they lost the whole purpose behind the Law, which was to show grace and mercy to the people.

They believed that their righteousness was based on their works, including how they looked and what they said. They gave tithes to the temple on everything they possessed. They would not walk by a leper, fearing they would become unclean. They lived and died the Old Testament Law like no one else could. Then Jesus came along and said our righteousness has to *exceed* theirs to enter His kingdom. What does that mean? Do we have to do more righteous works than they did? Do we have to follow the Law more strictly than they did? Do we have to wear holy robes to become holy?

None of these suggestions will answer our problem. Jesus very clearly said that we need to seek "His kingdom and His righteousness." The answer is right there. He said we could not enter the kingdom if we depended on our own righteousness earned by doing good works. If it were so, Scripture would contradict itself, because the Bible says our righteousness is like filthy rags before God (Isaiah 64:6).

The only righteousness that exceeds the righteousness of the Pharisees is the righteousness of God Himself! How do we receive that? God bestows His righteousness freely upon everyone who believes in the Lord Jesus. We cannot enter the kingdom based on our works, the way we look, or by the good long prayers we pray.

Faith, Not Good Works

The Bible says that no one is justified by the works of the law. And if anyone still depends on the works of the law, he is under a curse (Galatians 3:10; Romans 3:20, 28; and Philippians 3:9).

> But now the righteousness of God apart from the law is revealed, being witnessed by the Law and the Prophets, even the righteousness of God, through faith in Jesus Christ, to all and on all who believe. For there is no difference (Romans 3:21-22).

ENTER THE KINGDOM

It is very difficult to accept the fact that God will declare a sinner righteous because He believes in Christ. Our natural mind does not accept that, and we tend to add stuff to it in order to feel better about ourselves. Our fallen human nature tends to try to look good before others and do good things to feel better and be accepted by other people. The whole religious system of the world is geared toward one thing: encouraging people to do good things so they can escape the wrath of God, or the gods they believe in.

The Bible is the only book that teaches righteousness by faith. It teaches that God accepts a person not based on their *work*, but on their *faith* and faith alone. Therefore, it is difficult for people to believe and receive the free gift of God.

Most people are ignorant of the fact that God has already accepted them, and all they need to do is believe it (Romans 5:8, 10). Jesus came to declare the acceptable year of the Lord (Isaiah 61:1-2). What does that mean? Jesus came to declare that God was not angry with people and that He accepted them and loved them for who they are, not based on their works.

This is because all of humanity, except Adam, became sinful not by their choice. As the Bible says, *because of one man's disobedience, everyone became a sinner*, and so because of the obedience of one man, God declared everyone righteous (Romans 5:18).

So if you want to enter the kingdom, do not boast of your personal achievements or performance, but receive the free gift and walk in it.

> For by grace you have been saved through faith, and that not of yourselves; it is the gift of God, not of works, lest anyone should boast (Ephesians 2:8-9).

Jesus did the work for us and paid the price for our freedom, and what a liberty God has provided for us! Does that mean we do not need to do anything good because we are freely declared righteous? God forbid. Good works are a foundational teaching of the Bible. The heart and reason behind what we do is what matters now.

We do not do any good works to be accepted by God; we do good works because we are righteous, and accepted by God. Righteous people do righteous works. Good works are the natural fruit of our relationship with God. Righteous works do not make an unrighteous person righteous—ever. In the Pauline epistles, it is interesting to see how often Paul encourages both leaders and believers to be involved in good works. (See also Romans 2:10; Romans 13:3; 1 Timothy 2:10; and many others.) Our good works are inextricably linked to our purpose and calling.

> For we are His workmanship, created in Christ Jesus for good works, which God prepared beforehand that we should walk in them (Ephesians 2:10).

There are six other principles Jesus mentioned in reference to entering His kingdom. You will find them in the book *ReDiscovering the Lost Kingdom* that you can download from our website for free.

Chapter 4: Seek the Kingdom

I thought by now that Jesus would have had something more exciting to tell us, like falling under the Spirit, prophesying, or even promises of the rapture; but He had only one subject to talk about, and that was His kingdom.

Instead of teaching people how to prophesy or heal, Jesus gave a stern warning to those who followed after the gifts without knowing the purpose for which they were given. The gifts were given to help accomplish His will (Matthew 7:21-23).

The next step Jesus gave us was to seek His kingdom and His righteousness first, promising that all the things we needed in our life would be provided. It is recorded in Matthew 6:

> But seek first the kingdom of God and His righteousness, and all these things shall be added to you (Matthew 6:33).

As I mentioned before, the majority of the people on earth are worried about their livelihood and spend most of their lifetime trying to make money to meet those needs. Jesus, our King, says that if we seek His kingdom and His righteousness first, what we need for our livelihood will be added to us as a bonus. To be honest, that is the best good news we could hear and preach!

What if someone promised you that they would take care of your basic needs: food, shelter, and clothing, for the rest of your life? Would that not make you free to live and fulfill your purpose? For most of us, the majority of our time is spent making money to provide shelter, food, and clothing.

What if that someone is God? That is exactly what Jesus is doing. He is saying, "Seek My kingdom first, and all the things you are looking for will be given to you so you can really focus and spend your time on the real reason God put you here.

Unfortunately, the majority of Christians will not discover God's kingdom because they are stuck in a religion, or a denomination. They are stuck in the culture of the pseudo-king I mentioned earlier, working hard to make enough money to pay for their livelihood.

You may ask how someone can discover the kingdom, or why the majority of Christians missed the message of the kingdom for so long. Let me be honest with you; the devil hates the message of the kingdom. As long as the church keeps preaching about revival, the end times (which we have been doing for so long), faith, and the rapture, the devil will not bother us much, nor will he lose much. The moment you talk about the kingdom of God, you will get his reaction. He doesn't want to see it manifest on the earth or lose an inch of this planet to another kingdom.

The Spirits of the World

Satan has different spirits; some are more powerful than others. He has his levels of authority in his kingdom, as we read in Ephesians 6:12. Two of those powerful spirits are the religious spirit and the spirit of this world (1 Corinthians 2:12). When people are deceived by either of these spirits, they will never discover the kingdom of God. These spirits are the antithesis of the Holy Spirit.

When the religious spirit is operating in a person, it makes them feel as though they are spiritual in practicing Christian duties, keeping the law, and speaking *Christianese*. They will look pious on the outside, but inside they are like a whitewashed tomb. Their religiosity will not benefit them or others. Remember the story of Nicodemus, the religious leader and teacher of Israel? How is it that he didn't know anything about the kingdom of God as a religious leader? That is exactly what Jesus asked him. (John 3:1-10). The religious spirit had blinded Nicodemus. We will look at more about the religious spirit and its symptoms in another chapter on the process of salvation. I will say this here, if you are a Christian and have no clue about the kingdom of God, then you have been deceived by this spirit. I was for a long time.

The spirit of this world works opposite to the religious spirit (Ephesians 2:1-2). This spirit will offer you all the fun, money, and entertainment you want. Its mission is to keep you busy and distracted. The moment you are done with one event or form of entertainment, it will offer you the next. Something new will always arrive on the market, or the new season of something you enjoy will come on.

When one distraction is over, there will be another. It will keep you blinded and busy, enjoying this world and its glitter so you will never understand the kingdom of God. It will make you feel like you are in the kingdom of God because of all the fun you are having and the fact that you are going to church every Sunday.

How the Spirit of This World Works

There were several people who came to Jesus and said they wanted to follow Him. One of them came and said that first he wanted to go and bury his father and then he would return and follow Him. That meant he wanted to wait until his father was dead, receive his inheritance, and make his life secure. Then he would follow Jesus (Luke 9:57-60).

Jesus did not fall for that offer. He was not on a mission to create followers. He told him "Let the dead bury their own dead, but you go and preach the kingdom of God" (Luke 9:60).

Do you know what we do today? We let people do anything they want and live any lifestyle they choose, as long as they show up on Sunday morning. *We care about numbers.* Jesus will not change His priority, which is to seek His kingdom and righteousness *FIRST*.

Another person came and asked Jesus what he should do to inherit eternal life. Jesus told him to keep all the commandments. He said that he was keeping them and had been since he was a youth. Jesus told him to go and sell all that he had and give the money to the poor. He went away sorrowful because he had great possessions (Matthew 19:16-22).

The spirit of this world influenced both of those individuals. They were stuck with the things of this world. They wanted the kingdom of God as an addition to everything else they had. That won't work with this kingdom; either you are all about the kingdom or you have nothing to do with it. There is no middle ground.

Pride Keeps Us from the Kingdom

The third reason people do not discover the kingdom of God is because of pride and self-reliance. Do you remember the first line of the Beatitudes? "Blessed are the poor in spirit, for theirs is the kingdom of heaven" (Matthew 5:3). The word *poor* doesn't refer to someone without any money. It means someone who is humble, needy, and hungry for God. That is the first condition necessary to receive the kingdom—admitting that you need help. To be honest with you, that is the most difficult thing for some people to admit because they are full of themselves and full of pride. They will not enter the kingdom of God. That is why Jesus said:

> And again I say to you, it is easier for a camel to go through the eye of a needle than for a rich man to enter the kingdom of God (Matthew 19:24).

Why did Jesus say it was difficult for rich people, or those who thought they were rich, to enter the kingdom of God? It is very difficult for them to admit their need for a Savior, or that they need help from someone else. They depend on their own self. They would rather do everything by themselves or not do it at all. You need to experience deliverance from the above-mentioned spirits before you can enter and experience the kingdom of God.

Kingdom Seeking

Do you remember the first thing Jesus told us to do? It was to repent or change the way we thought. The second was how to enter His kingdom.

Matthew 6:33 tells us what we need to seek first. Ever since we lost our original kingdom—the one we were supposed to live in and establish here—our hearts have been searching for a place, or a country.

The majority of the people on this planet believe that if they move to a developed country or better community, their lives will be different and better. But if you live in a developed country, you know that it is failing its citizens. Citizens are not happy and are not fulfilled because of migration, failed governments and economies, corruption, high taxes, and pollution. These are grave concerns in most countries.

People all over the world are moving from one country to another, one city to the next, from one house to a bigger house, but they still feel empty and broken. They know deep down in their hearts that something is missing, but they are unable to articulate it because there is nothing they have seen or know that compares to it.

Sex, money, fame, position, luxury, religion, fun, spiritual experiences—none of these will satisfy that longing. There is only one thing, and it is a place (a kingdom) that will fulfill that longing. That place is the kingdom of God.

That is why Jesus came and told us to seek His kingdom first before we seek anything else. He didn't say to seek a better church, a better community, or a religion. Once we rediscover His kingdom, that longing in our hearts for a place will end. For the first time, we will feel at home. His kingdom is not a physical place right now. It begins as an awakening we experience in our spirit through Jesus Christ.

Why didn't Jesus tell us to seek *Him* first? Or to repent so we can receive Him, or to join His church? Because Jesus understood that we were created to live in a kingdom.

We are Not to Worry

Jesus preached an entire message prior to making the statement in Matthew 6 about seeking first His kingdom and his righteousness. His primary message was not to worry about life—what we should eat, drink, and wear.

Why would Jesus care about us worrying or not worrying? That is our personal stuff. Why would God get involved in our personal life and care about what we eat, what we wear, and where we live?

Know that we are His children. In the same way any parent cares about their children and their well-being, Jesus wants us to live a worry-free life because He knows the cause and effect that worrying will eventually bring to our mind and body. Jesus told us to look at the birds of the air and the lilies of the field to learn how they live. They do not worry or gather food for the next day. They do not have banks and credit cards, but they live happily and do what they are supposed to do.

I have never seen a bird that is worried about their next day. Jesus said, "Your heavenly Father takes care of them" (Matthew 6:26). He said, "*Your* heavenly Father." They have a God, but we have a heavenly Father. Our Father feeds and takes care of innumerable creatures, but most of His children don't trust Him to take care of them.

Worry is a symptom of fatherlessness. How much more will our heavenly Father take care of us because we are more precious than all other creatures? He said the Gentiles (those who don't believe in God and do not have a Father) worry about those things. We have a Father who loves us.

Then He made a powerful statement, He said, "Seek first the kingdom of God and His righteousness and all these things shall be added to you" (Matthew 6:33). We have read and heard many sermons about this, but that has not stopped us from worrying, because we never took the time to sit and learn what Jesus really meant by this and then implemented it in our lives. When we get the revelation of what He said, we will stop worrying.

Seeking the Kingdom Should Take Care of Your Needs

He said that if we seek His kingdom and His righteousness first, then everything we need in our life: food, clothing, shelter—everything we are worried about in our life—will be taken care of. Does that sound wonderful to you? It should, because life on earth is short. Your life is more precious than just living to make some money to pay bills and retire.

SEEK THE KINGDOM

What does it mean to seek the kingdom? When I was growing up, I was taught that to seek the kingdom meant to share and preach the gospel to other people. Now I understand that this is far from the truth. I know hundreds or even thousands in Third World countries who do that, but still lack the basic essentials in their lives.

If Jesus wanted us all to go and *preach*, then He would have told us to go and preach the gospel and all of those things shall be added unto us. I know countless ministers and believers around the world who are sharing and preaching the gospel and their daily needs are not met. Recently, I talked with someone who told me that the majority of the body of Christ are financially broke and do not have the resources to fulfill their vision. Many are tithe-giving and mission-sowing believers.

They live a life that is inferior to people who do not believe in God, or even people who worship idols and serve them. I don't believe that anyone who serves the King of all kings and Lord of all lords has to be poor and beg for their livelihood. That does not represent a benevolent King, or a prosperous kingdom. If He feeds the birds and the lilies, and none of them go hungry for even a day, we had better believe that He has a better plan and cares for you and me.

What It Means to Seek the Kingdom

I don't believe it is God's will for His children to be in debt for the majority of their life, working to make the people in the world rich. The devil has enticed the church with the things of this world and the church has lost its mission and significance. If you look at the standard of living between the church and the world, it is almost the same.

There are sick, poor, depressed, and hopeless folks in the church, and divorce is rampant. Addiction, lying, cheating, adultery, and pornography are common in the church today—even among leaders. The only evident difference is that we speak *Christianese*, and the world has no idea what we are talking about when we do. That does not represent a kingdom life!

To seek something does not mean to preach about it. If a king ruled America, it would be called the "Kingdom of America." If the president of India asked me to seek the Kingdom of America, I wouldn't think he meant I should start preaching about America in India. The word *seek* means to start searching, explore, and then find what we are looking for. If the president of India wanted me to find America, then he or she wanted me to see what life was like in America, and how that kingdom operated, the culture, economy and the condition of the people living in that country.

Jesus said to "seek first His kingdom." Kingdom means a land or territory ruled by a king. The word *kingdom* is made up of two words: king + dom (dominion) = kingdom. In this regard, we need to seek a kingdom that is ruled by Jesus. *To seek the kingdom means to forsake the culture, principles, and concepts (the world system) of the country in which you are born and live in now, and seek and learn the culture, principles, or laws by which the kingdom of God operates and then live accordingly.*

When we do what Jesus said, what we need for our life will be added to us as a bonus. That is good news to me. Why don't we preach this more? Most people are working to meet their basic needs and they are not happy.

A kingdom is made up of a king, government, people, economy, territory, culture, language, education, military, industries, media, and agriculture. For the proper function of a kingdom the above factors have to work in unison. The kingdom of God has all of these factors and we are commanded to seek it *first*.

Seek to know what the kingdom of God is, and how it works and operates, and you will have everything you need in your life: houses, cars, food, clothes, and much more will all come *seeking* you when you are in the kingdom of God. Man was created to live in God's kingdom. When we find the kingdom of God and discover and operate in it according to the laws by which the kingdom of God operates, everything we need will be added to us.

It is upsetting to see people in the church and in the world look the same, act the same, and have the same kinds of problems. I get tired of hearing church talk and not seeing any evidence of kingdom living in the lives of the people. I've noticed that sometimes people in the world live a better quality of life than people in the church. When I wondered why, God opened my eyes to the truth about His kingdom and living in it.

Sign of the End

Whenever Christians hear about a tragedy or calamity, they often say that Jesus is coming soon and that whatever happened is the sign of the end time. Unless the kingdom of God is established, as long as the earth remains, there will be famine, wars, and disasters that take place. It is true that there are many signs of the end times, but there is only one sign that will usher in the end of this age.

Jesus specifically told us what to do for the end to come, and that is to preach the gospel of the kingdom of God in every nation. How do we preach the gospel of the kingdom unless we know what it is? We are not trained on the subject. God in His mercy helped me write this book to equip the body of Christ to preach the gospel of the kingdom.

> And this gospel of the kingdom will be preached in all the world as a witness to all the nations, and then the end will come (Matthew 24:14).

Chapter 5: See the Kingdom

Although we all have heard the familiar phrase "born again," very few of us know why Jesus told us to be born again. Again, the religious spirit teaches that we need to be born again to go to heaven. I used to tell people that they needed to be born again so they could go to heaven, because that is what the religious leaders taught me. One day I opened my Bible and read John 3. Jesus didn't say anything about going to heaven or joining a church in John 3. When I realized that, I became very curious. Do you remember that I promised you earlier to tell you exactly what Jesus said without altering or adding anything to it? That's what I will continue to do. Whether you believe it or not is up to you.

Losing Spiritual Vision

Instead of speaking about heaven, Jesus said that unless we are born again, we will not *see* the kingdom of God. According to Jesus, the reason we need to be born again is to *see* His kingdom.

> Jesus answered and said to him, "Most assuredly, I say to you, unless one is born again, he cannot see the kingdom of God" (John 3:3).

Why do we need to be born again to see His kingdom? When Adam fell, he lost the ability to *see* God's kingdom. Instead, he began to see things that God never intended for him to see about himself, about God, and about his surroundings.

THE GOSPEL OF THE KINGDOM

The Bible says that when Adam and Eve ate the fruit of the tree that God told them not to eat, "then the eyes of both of them were opened" (Genesis 3:7). What does that mean? Were they blind before? No, they were not. Sin twists the way we see both God and ourselves.

Before they ate the fruit they could see God and they could see the spirit world, just like we see the natural world; but once they ate the forbidden fruit their spiritual eyes were closed and their carnal eyes were opened. The eyes God never wanted to be closed could no longer see spiritual things.

When we are born again, God opens our eyes back up and we are supposed to see His kingdom. Most of us don't recognize it because we were taught that we need to be born again to go to heaven when we die.

If you remember when you were born again, you should have felt peace and joy in your heart. You were brought to the kingdom of God and you experienced its culture in your heart and spirit. Peace and joy are elements of that culture.

Seeing the Calling

When you were born again, God put a picture of your future in your heart in the form of a vision or a dream. That is what it means to *see His kingdom*. God gives you vision for the part, or the aspect, of His kingdom that He wants to manifest through *you* on earth. He put that in your spirit in the form of a picture. We are supposed to follow that vision from the moment we are born again. That is the call of God on your life.

When you were saved, you were also called. When God calls you, He puts a picture of that calling in your spirit. He calls you to do something in His kingdom. If you are saved, you are called as well.

> Who has saved us and called us with a holy calling, not according to our works, but according to His own purpose and grace which was given to us in Christ Jesus before time began (2 Timothy 1:9).

Citizens of Heaven

You were brought into the kingdom of God. When you were naturally born, you became a citizen of your country. When you were born again, you became a citizen of heaven.

Though I was born in India, I now live in the United States because my assignment for the kingdom is connected to the US. In the same way, though you are a citizen of heaven your assignment is connected to planet Earth.

Why do we need to see His kingdom? *Because what we see is what we manifest.* Vision is very important. If our vision is not right, nothing else will work. That is why Jesus said that if our eye is good, then our whole body will be full of light. If our eye is not good, then our whole body will be full of darkness (Matthew 6:22-23).

How do we establish God's kingdom on earth? First, we need to receive a revelation of the kingdom of heaven. We have to see it in our spirit. Once we see it, then we can manifest it.

God's desire is to see His will done on earth as it is in heaven. How do we know His will in heaven? We understand what it is through revelation in our spirit. We are the only agents through which God can accomplish this task.

That is the reason we need to be born again—to see God's kingdom and receive a glimpse of His will. God's will is how He operates His kingdom in heaven: how things are done in His kingdom. We are supposed to duplicate that on earth. To know more about seeing and entering the kingdom, please read the book, *Seeing, Entering, and Manifesting the Kingdom*.

Chapter 6: The Kingdom Prayer

Do you know that even Jesus have a prayer request? When the disciples asked Jesus to teach them how to pray, He had only one prayer request. That was for His kingdom to come and for His will to be done on earth as it is in heaven. Why didn't Jesus ask them to pray for more churches to be planted and for more souls to reach heaven? He did not mention any of those things in His prayer.

Jesus never *taught* His disciples how to heal the sick, cast out a demon, or prophesy in a classroom setting. Instead, He taught these things through practical lessons. One thing He taught them was how to pray. Most born-again believers do not pray the Lord's Prayer. They think it is a religious prayer. It is not a religious prayer, but a kingdom prayer. Everything related to our lives is included in the Lord's Prayer. It covers the spiritual, physical, and social aspects of our lives. I did not understand this for a long time.

Only One Prayer

Why didn't Jesus teach us how to pray to heal the sick or various types of sicknesses? Why didn't He teach us to pray for prosperity or how to cast out different kinds of demons? Jesus taught us to pray only one kind of prayer. In that single prayer He included everything we need in our life.

God created us with seven fundamental needs. He made plans to meet those needs through His kingdom. When one of those needs is not met, we will feel unfulfilled. The kingdom prayer (the Lord's Prayer) is laid out in a way that addresses each of those needs. This prayer is the key to meet all of those needs and live successfully in His kingdom.

The first man had all these needs, and God met each of them through His kingdom. Since Adam lost the kingdom with the fall, those needs weren't met anymore. Since then, mankind has been trying to meet those needs on their own without God and His kingdom. And we created a big mess as a result!

With the coming of Jesus, God our Father decided to restore His kingdom back to us. With the restoration of His kingdom, we were privileged to have all of those needs met through His kingdom once again.

Seven Needs Met through the Kingdom Prayer

With the help of the Holy Spirit, I am going to show you how God has included those seven needs in the kingdom prayer Jesus taught us. We gave that prayer to the Catholic Church, and they recite it every time they meet. As a result, they became the most powerful church politically, financially, organizationally, and in real estate—though they veered off doctrinally—in all of history.

What happened to us is this: We got the doctrines right (at least we think we do), but messed up in how we function, or operate. We've fragmented into millions of pieces and lost our effectiveness. If we had really gotten all the doctrines right, we wouldn't be fragmented the way we are. Catholic churches function and operate correctly as an organization. If they received the proper doctrines, and if we receive the correct way to function, then we would win this entire earth for Jesus our King in no time. That is God's will and plan.

Below are our seven fundamental needs:

1. Place: A country or community where we are happy
2. Power: Government that serves righteousness, justice, truth, and mercy
3. Purpose: Significance
4. Provision: Food and Shelter

5. Person: Fulfilling Relationship
6. Protection: Safety
7. Pleasure: Happiness

Below you will see how God made plans to meet our seven fundamental needs through the Lord's Prayer, the perfect kingdom prayer:

> "In this manner, therefore, pray:
>
> Our Father in heaven,
> Hallowed be Your name.
> Your kingdom come.
> Your will be done
> On earth as it is in heaven.
> Give us this day our daily bread.
> And forgive us our debts,
> As we forgive our debtors.
> And do not lead us into temptation,
> But deliver us from the evil one.
> For Yours is the kingdom and the power and the glory
> forever. Amen.
>
> (Matthew 6:9-13)

1. Place: A country or community where we are happy

> "Our Father in heaven."

By saying "our" and not "my," we indicate a community or family and not individualism. In the next line, "Your kingdom come," we are asking God to restore to us the place or country where we originally belonged, which we lost. Heaven is a place and it's a kingdom. We want His kingdom to come and His will to be done on earth as it is in heaven. People who dwell in His kingdom are happy because peace and joy are part of its culture.

2. Power: Government that serves righteousness, justice, truth, and mercy

> "Your kingdom come."

When God's kingdom comes, His government also comes. We cannot separate His kingdom from His government. His kingdom *is* the government.

3. Purpose: Significance

> "Your will be done on earth as it is in heaven."

God's will is His purpose. He has a will and plan for each of us. His desire is for His will to be done, not just in our lives, but on the entire planet.

4. Provision: Food and Shelter

> "Give us this day our daily bread."

Adam's provision was included in the garden. When we discover His kingdom, our provision will be added to us too.

5. Person: Fulfilling Relationships

> "And forgive us our debts, as we forgive our debtors."

Forgiveness is the key to an enduring and fulfilling relationship. God decided to forgive our sins and restore us to Himself as His children. Then He asked us to forgive one another. If you have been in any relationship for any period of time, you will realize that unless you are willing to forgive, that relationship won't last long. Through this prayer, Jesus is giving us the key to fulfilling relationships.

6. Protection: Safety

> "And do not lead us into temptation, but deliver us from the evil one."

This refers to protection. We need His protection every moment of our life. Our enemy walks around like a roaring lion to see whom he may devour.

7. Pleasure: Happiness

> "For Yours is the kingdom and the power and the glory forever. Amen."

It should give us the greatest pleasure imaginable to know the King, and know that the kingdom and the power and the glory belongs to our Father, and on top of that, to have the privilege of living in His kingdom. It should be a greater joy than watching or experiencing any form of entertainment.

A Closer Look at the Lord's Prayer

I want to explain a little bit more about the mysteries hidden in the Lord's Prayer. We no longer need to pray for His kingdom to come anymore because, according to Mark 9:1, the kingdom of God already came with power on the day of Pentecost. Now we need to pray for its manifestation and administer it to execute the will of God *on earth as it is in heaven.*

Our Father in Heaven

The prayer starts with "*our* Father in heaven," not "*my* Father in heaven." It talks about a community or family, telling us that God has more than one child on this planet. The first thing God wants us to know about prayer is that it is a family business, not a religious ritual. We need to keep that in our mind as we learn about His kingdom. Sometimes we get so focused on ourselves that we forget that God has other children. He has a big family.

Even though God is a King, we relate to Him as a Father. Why does God want to relate to us as a Father? The root of most of the problems that exist in this world today have been caused by fatherlessness and father wounds. Many people have grown up without a father figure in their lives or with emotional wounds that were inflicted by their fathers or their father figures. Children are supposed to inherit their identity, value, purpose, and destiny from their father.

One of the main responsibilities of parenting is to represent and reveal God to our children, and then to guide them to have a personal relationship with Him. God knew the challenges fathers would face and how the enemy would attack them in an effort to confuse children about their identity, value, and purpose. He Himself decided to relate to each human being as their Father.

Once we discover our heavenly Father, we discover our true identity, value, purpose, and destiny. The majority of us did not get what we were supposed to receive from our fathers. Once you accept God as your heavenly Father, He is the only One who has any right to have any opinion about us, and His is the only opinion we should believe.

Another responsibility of a father is to protect, provide, and teach his children. Children look to their fathers to protect them, provide for them, and teach them life's lessons. Most children feel secure and safe when they are with their father, or when their father is at home. At least, they are supposed to feel that way.

The enemy knew that if he could distort the fathers and wound them, then they would not be able to portray God to their children; and in turn, the children would never want anything to do with God. It is generally accepted in both Christian and therapeutic communities, that most children view God based on the experience they have with their earthly father while growing up.

Hallowed Be Your Name

After we have a revelation of our Father, the second thing He wants us to know about is His name. He wants His name to be made holy on the earth and in our lives. What does *holy* mean? The holiness of God is a combination of many of His attributes. Holy means pure.

God is pure in all of His dealings with us. It also means without any defilement or blemish. His love, faithfulness, and compassion toward us is wholly pure. He wants our lives to be a reflection of His holiness. He wants us to be pure in all of our dealings because we represent Him on earth. The Bible says that without holiness no man can see God (Hebrews 12:14). Jesus said, "Blessed are the pure in heart, for they shall see God" (Matthew 5:8). Holiness in not an outward expression we obtain by wearing a particular style or color of clothing. Our inner holiness will reflect itself in every aspect of our lives.

What is in His name? Why is God so particular about His name?

We know God and His nature and character through His names, which are revealed in the Word. Everything He does toward us or for us is a revelation of one of His names. Every miracle in the Bible is a manifestation of one of His names. If He provides for you, that provision is the manifestation of His name, Jehovah-Jireh. If He heals you, that is a manifestation of His name, Jehovah-Rapha. Jesus said in His high priestly prayer:

> I have manifested Your name to the men whom You have given Me out of the world (John 17:6a).

Jesus also said that whatever we ask the Father in His name, He will do it for us. (See also John 14:13-14; 15:16; and 16:23-24, 26.) For every need you have, there is a name of God through which you can access the provision He has for that in His kingdom.

Your Kingdom Come

It is interesting to note that most Christians are waiting to go to heaven, when God's desire and purpose is to bring heaven down to earth so His kingdom can be made manifest here. That is His priority. What does it mean to pray for "God's kingdom to come"? What does it look like practically? God never intended for our lives to be any different on earth than in heaven. He wants us to have the same quality of life right now. Does everyone experience that? No.

God created man to live in His kingdom. He knows that man cannot survive without His kingdom, and He wants to give it to His children. He also wants us to depend on His kingdom while living on earth, not on this world. He wants us to influence earth with heaven. The earth is limited, and His kingdom is unlimited. Earth is natural, and His kingdom is spiritual. We are both natural and spiritual at the same time. We are a spirit living in a body.

God is the Creator and the original Owner of the planet. He created it to extend His kingdom, but it was taken over by the enemy, and God has been in the process of reclaiming it ever since. That is why He told us to pray for His kingdom to come here once again. We are the only agents through which that vision can materialize. Jesus came and taught us the principles and mysteries of His kingdom and how to administer and operate it.

We have not fully gotten hold of God's vision yet. Most of us don't even pray the prayer He taught us to pray. This prayer must be prayed by all of God's children worldwide. Imagine more than a billion saints across the world praying that prayer. Do you know why the Roman Catholic Church has the influence they have? They don't speak (at least most) in tongues and roll on the floor, but they pray that prayer almost every time they meet.

When we pray for His kingdom to come, we are praying for His rule—His system of operation, His dominion—to come to earth and to every area of our lives; for His kingdom to come in our personal lives, family, finances, and more. We are praying for kingdom economy to come to our finances, for kingdom family to come to our marriages, for kingdom agriculture to come to our world and our eating habits, and for kingdom culture to come to our way of doing things. Each area of our life needs to come under the influence of His kingdom.

Your Will Be Done on Earth as It Is in Heaven

Every king has a will and a plan and wants to see it accomplished in his kingdom. God is a King, and His will is accomplished in heaven, as He wants it to be. But on earth, there has been opposition, and someone else's will is being accomplished instead. Right now in most parts of the earth, Satan's will is accomplished instead of God's. Some people say that God's sovereignty rules everywhere. That is partially true. He has the final say on everything, but if that were entirely true, then He would not have told us to pray for His will to be done here on earth as it is in heaven, because it would already have been made manifest.

You and I are part of the team God has ordained to see His will accomplished on earth as it is in heaven. The church is supposed to be teaching and training people about how to do that, instead of teaching them to sing. We need to learn what God's will is and how He does it in heaven, and copy that on earth. God has a will and plan for every area of our lives. When we deviate from that, we will encounter enormous problems.

There is no poverty, lack, or sickness in heaven because it is not the King's will to have them in heaven. They did not originate in heaven; they are the works of the devil. That is why the Bible says the Son of God was manifested to destroy the works of the devil (1 John 3:8).

As I mentioned earlier, God put man in Eden originally where His will was done as it was in heaven. Then it was man's task to duplicate, expand, and make the entire earth like Eden: to cause the entire earth to be filled with God's kingdom and glory. (See Numbers 14:21; Psalm 72:19; and Habakkuk 2:14.) We failed in that task; and through Jesus, God has restored that kingdom to us. Then He gave an assignment to the church: go and preach the gospel of the kingdom and fill the earth with the knowledge of His glory.

The Word of God is the revealed will of God. Whatever the Word says we are, that is what we are; and whatever the Word says we should have, that is what we should have. Whatever the Word says we should do, that is what we should be doing.

Give Us This Day Our Daily Bread

In a kingdom, it is the king's responsibility to take care of the citizens, to make sure everyone has enough to eat and that they are protected. If a citizen of a kingdom is poor, it affects the reputation of the king. God our King guarantees our daily provision, so we should not be worrying about it. The only thing you and I need to make sure of is that we are citizens of His kingdom. You could be a member of a church and not be a citizen of His kingdom.

Most people think that because they go to church on Sunday morning they are automatically citizens of God's kingdom—what a sad dilemma! The first requirement for becoming a citizen of God's kingdom is to become a child of the King. Whatever we need for our daily life is called "bread" in the Bible. There are different kinds of bread. I will mention a few of them here:

Natural Food

First, we all need physical bread, or food, every day. God is faithful and is committed to providing that for us. He feeds the birds and animals in the forest, so how much more will He take care of His own children?

> He causes the grass to grow for the cattle, and vegetation for the service of man, that he may bring forth food from the earth, and wine that makes glad the heart of man, oil to make his face shine, and bread which strengthens man's heart (Psalm 104:14-15).

Jesus promised to provide everything we needed as long as we are seeking His kingdom first. He promised to provide food and all the other basic provisions we needed in our lives. If anyone out there is lacking the basics, that means they are not seeking His kingdom first.

Healing

Healing is also called "bread" in the Bible. There are many viruses and sicknesses that our bodies fight each day, keeping us safe from them. If it were not for our immune system—which is God's healing system in our body—we all would have died. We need healing every day of our lives.

Jesus called healing "the children's bread":

> And behold, a woman of Canaan came from that region and cried out to Him, saying, "Have mercy on me, O Lord, Son of David! My daughter is severely demon-possessed." But He answered her not a word. And His disciples came and urged Him, saying, "Send her away, for she cries out after us." But He answered and said, "I was not sent except to the lost sheep of the house of Israel." Then she came and worshiped Him, saying, "Lord, help me!" But He answered and said, "It is not good to take the children's bread and throw it to the little dogs." And she said, "Yes, Lord, yet even the little dogs eat the crumbs which fall from their masters' table." Then Jesus answered and said to her, "O woman, great is your faith! Let it be to you as you desire." And her daughter was healed from that very hour" (Matthew 15:22-28).

Financial Bread

We need money as long as we live on this earth. Money is also called "bread" in the Bible.

> Cast your bread upon the waters, for you will find it after many days (Ecclesiastes 11:1).

The word "bread" here refers to financial investments.

God is faithful to provide us with the money we need. One of the best examples is when Peter wanted to pay taxes. Jesus told him to go and cast a hook in the water, and in the mouth of the first fish would be a piece of money to cover the tax for both of them. (See Matthew 17:27 and 2 Corinthians 9:10.)

Spiritual Bread

Just like our body needs food to survive, our spirit needs spiritual food for its nourishment and growth. Jesus is called the Bread of Life (John 6:48).

In the same way we eat natural food every day, we need to eat the Word every day.

Emotional Bread

We all have emotional needs too. Our heavenly Father is faithful to meet our emotional needs. His love, acceptance, and comfort keep our souls emotionally healthy. God is a Shepherd, meeting our physical, emotional, and spiritual needs daily. (See Psalm 23 and Psalm 51:12.) We constantly need favor, ideas, wisdom, solutions, and guidance. We need to thank God each day for providing us with our *daily bread* in all the previously mentioned areas of our lives.

And Forgive Us Our Debts as We Forgive Our Debtors

Everything in God's kingdom flows through relationship. Walking in love and forgiveness is imperative for living in God's kingdom. We are commanded to forgive others as He forgives us. If we do not forgive others, God will not forgive us our sins; it is that important. God forgiving our sins is conditional on us forgiving others. That sounds a little scary to me. Jesus taught about forgiveness more than once. (Some examples are found in Matthew 18:21-35 and Mark 11:25-26.) There will be some people in your life who are hard to forgive. Whenever you pray this prayer, mention their names and release forgiveness from your heart.

And Do Not Lead Us into Temptation

Every sin originates with a temptation. The enemy is lurking to tempt us every chance he gets. Our great-great-grandparents, Adam and Eve, were tempted and fell into transgression, and sin entered the world. Jesus was tempted by the enemy, but He overcame it. We are supposed to follow the footsteps of our Lord and overcome temptations. We are prone to be tempted, and we need the grace of God each day to walk in victory.

The evil one will set snares on our way to trap us in his net. We read in Psalm 91:

> Surely He shall deliver you from the snare of the fowler (Psalm 91:3a).

This is a promise from our heavenly Father to deliver us from those snares.

But Deliver Us from the Evil One

The Bible says the enemy is walking around like a roaring lion to find whom he may devour (1 Peter 5:8). We need to ask God daily to deliver us from the evil one, who is Satan, and his works. What are his works? Poverty, debt, curses, sicknesses and diseases, strife, offenses, delays, stealing, fear, deception, and lies are some of his works. If any of these works are operating in your life, ask the Lord to remove and deliver you from the works of the evil one. He will do it if you ask Him. The Word says, "For the Son of God was manifested to destroy the works of the evil one" (1 John 3:8). I have paraphrased the Lord's Prayer and mentioned it below, so that you can pray it every day before you start your day. If you do, you will notice the difference.

For Yours Is the Kingdom and the Power and the Glory Forever!

The kingdoms of this world, with their power and glory, belong to our God. (See Psalm 22:28 and Revelation 11:15.) The enemy stole that from Him through man; and when Jesus was tempted, the devil offered Him the world, its kingdoms, and its glory (Luke 4:5-7). Since the enemy took it from us, God wants to restore it through us. That is why Jesus died for our sins. We have been taught that Jesus died to recruit and take a bunch of people to heaven. As the Bible says, sin came through man, and salvation from sin also came through a Man, Jesus Christ (Romans 5:12-17).

If there is any area of your life that is not in alignment with the kingdom of God, you have the right and opportunity now to bring it back into alignment, whether it is in your finances, health, family life, children, your community and nation, or anything else. As a kingdom ambassador, this is your responsibility.

There has been reconciliation between heaven and earth and the things in heaven and things on earth through the blood of Jesus. (See Ephesians 1:7-10 and Colossians 1:19-22.) Whenever you see something that is not in alignment with God's will, you need to release kingdom authority by commanding (decreeing and declaring) that thing to come back into alignment. That is part of the assignment of preaching the gospel of the kingdom.

Praying the Lord's Prayer in Our Lives Today

I would encourage you to pray the Lord's Prayer whenever you can. If you are part of an *ekklesia*, when you come together, pray this prayer as a group. I have paraphrased the prayer for you below. You are free to personalize it as the Holy Spirit leads you:

Our Father in heaven, hallowed be Your name.

Let Your name be made holy in our nation, in my family, and in the whole earth. Thank You for giving us Your kingdom. Help us to administer it effectively on earth. Teach us how to tap into your kingdom resources to solve problems on this earth.

Let Your kingdom rule and dominion come into my life, my family, and my nation.

Let Your kingdom economy, culture, education, and health come to this earth, in my life, nation, and family.
Your will be done on earth as it is in heaven.
Give us this day our daily, physical, financial, spiritual, and emotional bread.
And forgive us our debts,
As we forgive our debtors.
(If there is anyone you need to forgive, say their name and release forgiveness from your heart.)

And do not lead us into temptation,
But deliver us from the evil one.

THE KINGDOM PRAYER

Thank You for protecting us from evil, curses, offenses, jealousy, strife, sickness, ignorance, lack, and poverty. For Yours is the kingdom and the power and the glory forever. Amen.

I hope by now you have enough evidence to see the importance of the gospel of the kingdom. The *gospel* of the kingdom simply means the *good news* of the kingdom. In order to understand why the message of the kingdom is the most important subject to Jesus, we need to go back to the beginning. We need to understand who God is and what He has been trying to accomplish on earth. Only then will we understand His heart.

When you don't understand how something started, it is like watching a movie from its middle without understanding where it began and why it was made. If we do not understand the beginning, we won't understand the middle nor the end. Nobody taught us clearly why God created this planet and put mankind in it to manage it.

To be honest, almost every church, ministry, and organization out there focuses on the middle. They do not teach the people about the beginning and why God created us. They do not understand or start with the Big Picture. They are just focused on one or two of the spiritual habits, disciplines, gifts, programs, or benefits like prayer, healing, blessings, or evangelism.

I know of a ton of organizations out there that focus on discipleship. All they do is focus on spiritual disciplines and developing new habits. But everything we do as believers should start with the Big Why. Why did God begin all this in the first place, and what happened to it? Unless we understand the Big Picture, we will be like people watching a movie from the middle, leaving us pretty clueless about the whole story.

We have often heard the story of Adam and Eve, the fruit they ate, the snake, the church, the rapture and revival, but nobody taught us the why! That is what we are going to learn about in this book. Then we will understand the gospel of the kingdom.

THE GOSPEL OF THE KINGDOM

You might be wondering why the message of the kingdom was so important to Jesus. Why haven't we seen it until now? What does it have to do with us today? If Jesus had come to earth in our day and time, He would have preached the same message. Everything about our life and walk with Him is connected to His kingdom.

To find out why the message of the kingdom is the most important message to Jesus, we need to travel back in time. For Jesus, this kingdom message did not begin when He arrived on earth during the Roman occupation. It began many, many years before that. How do we know what happened so long ago? It's in the Bible. Everything we need to know about His kingdom and His purpose is clearly written in the Bible. Unfortunately, because of the influence and deception of the religious spirit, most of us have missed it.

Let's take a journey into God's Word and find out why the message of the kingdom is important to God and why it should be important to us too. Then we will come back and pick up where we left off. To understand His kingdom, we need to know who God is, first of all.

Part II: Eternal Perspective

Chapter 7: God and Jesus as Kings

To understand the gospel of the kingdom, we need to understand who our God is. One of the things we have to keep in mind is that our God is a Creator and a King. Before He ever became a Savior or Redeemer, we know Him to be a King. When you come to Him, come to Him as you are coming to a king. There are plenty of references in the Bible that show us God the Father and Jesus as Kings.

Our God is a King.

The Lord is *King* forever and ever (Psalm 10:16a).

For the *king*dom is the Lord's, and He rules over the nations (Psalm 22:28).

For the Lord Most High is awesome; He is a *great King* over all the earth (Psalm 47:2).

For God is the *King of all the earth*; sing praises with understanding (Psalm 47:7).

He is also called the King of glory (Psalm 24:8).

Jesus was born King:

> Where is He who has been born King of the Jews? For we have seen His star in the East and have come to worship Him (Matthew 2:2).
>
> Now to the King eternal, immortal, invisible, to God who alone is wise, be honor and glory forever and ever. Amen (1 Timothy 1:17).

There were many people in the Old Testament who witnessed God as King on the earth throughout their lifetime. Why don't we see this in our day? Did God cease from being a king? Let us find that out.

> For unto us a Child is born, unto us a Son is given; and the government will be upon His shoulder. And His name will be called Wonderful, Counselor, Mighty God, Everlasting Father, Prince of Peace. Of the increase of His government and peace there will be no end, upon the throne of David and over His kingdom, to order it and establish it with judgment and justice from that time forward, even forever. The zeal of the Lord of hosts will perform this (Isaiah 9:6-7).

These verses describe one of the most famous prophecies about our Lord Jesus Christ. The first thing it says about Him is that the government will be upon His shoulder. How does government rest upon His shoulders? He is the Head of the church, and we are His body on this earth. The shoulder is part of the body, which means *the government of this earth is supposed to be on the shoulders of the church.*

Why Is the Kingdom not in the Government?

For some reason, we made this verse part of our eschatology, which refers to something that is going to take place sometime in the future. But this is not correct according to what these verses actually say. That is what religion does. It steals from us what we should have now and gives us a false hope that someday things are going to be better. But faith says, "Now!"

From the phrase, "from that time forward, even forever," we understand that the fulfillment of that particular prophecy began from the time a Son was given. It says that of the increase of His government and peace, there will be no end. That means it is eternal. We all know the Son spoken of here is Jesus. He came two thousand years ago and He is going to order His government with judgment and justice from that time forward, even forever. It literally began two thousand years ago, but we have not grasped what it really means yet. Below are the verses from the New Testament that prove its fulfillment.

> He will be great, and will be called the Son of the Highest; and the Lord God will give Him the throne of His father David. And He will reign over the house of Jacob forever, and of His kingdom there will be no end (Luke 1:32-33).

The above verses are the announcement about the birth of Jesus to Mary through an angel.

When the wise men from the East came to see Jesus, they came looking for the King who was born in Bethlehem. How did they receive the revelation that Jesus was a king? They saw His star in the East. When He died, He died as a king too. The inscription on the cross was "King of the Jews." When the governor asked Jesus if He was the King of the Jews, He did not deny it. He said, "It is as you say" (Matthew 27:11).

How do we witness to others of Jesus as a king? Believers need to be involved in the political arena of their nations. We have been avoiding politics for too long. Because of that, the unrighteous have taken over governments all over the world. There is no righteous justice system in the world anymore. People with money make their own rules. Any wicked person with money can do almost anything they want anywhere in the world.

Isaiah said the government shall be upon the shoulders of Jesus, not on the shoulders of the devil. Church leaders should encourage believers to get involved in politics, both locally and in the central government of their nations. Otherwise, how do we witness to others that Jesus is King? We do not witness for Him after we die or in eternity. We are called to be His witnesses on this earth right now.

One of the main reasons this world is in chaos is because there are not very many people witnessing about Jesus as King.

> When *the righteous are in authority,* the people rejoice: but when the wicked beareth rule, the people mourn (Proverbs 29:2 KJV).

We have had enough mourning and groaning going on for a long time because the righteous have been avoiding politics and government for that long. It is time for change. Whenever I meet someone from any country, they are always complaining about how badly the government in their nation is doing, and they talk against their leaders. Just speaking negatively about your government is not going to change anything for the better!

The only way to change anything is if we have witnesses for Jesus in those governments. We need believers in positions of influence so we can make gains in the kingdom causes that we are striving for. We must find out why we do not have any influence in government and come up with a solution.

One of the popular messages of the last few years in the US was telling Americans to go back to their roots; that message is dying out as I write this book. America cannot go back to her roots. We need a new strategy.

How to Take Our Countries Back

There were fifty-six men who signed the Declaration of Independence. Out of the fifty-six, fifty-four of them were known to be Christians and attended some form of church. That meant their moral and ethical value system was based on Judeo-Christian ethics. That is why this country was established the way it was. How many people do we have in our government now who are a witness for Jesus?

If we are going to take this country back, we need believers in positions of government—at both the state and national levels—who will witness Jesus as a king.

Again, we are not here to take over governments, but like Joseph and Daniel did, we need to have people witnessing in high places. Everyone God used in the Old Testament is a type of Christ: Moses, Joseph, David, Daniel, and Esther. Every single person God used, manifested Christ through their life and their mission on earth. We have received the real deal, and today there are fewer witnesses for Jesus than ever in world governments.

God has anointed many people with His power to be a witness in government, but they have avoided it, thinking it is not God's will for them. The enemy has deceived us to stay out of this most important aspect of our nation, so he can have free reign without any hindrances.

Every government on earth should belong to Jesus because there is no authority, natural or spiritual, except His. Why should we give the authority God gave us to the devil, and then complain about what he is doing with it? Paul calls people in governmental authority "ministers." Did you know that? In Romans 13 he mentioned it two times. I was really surprised when I read this.

> For he is the *minister of God* to thee for good (Romans 13:4a KJV).

> For this cause pay ye tribute also: for they are God's ministers, attending continually upon this very thing (Romans 13:6 KJV).

I am a minister of the gospel. I preach the gospel to groups of people. You can be in charge of the finance in the government of your nation and you are also a minister of God. You preach the gospel through your influence, your skills, and your decisions. The same Holy Spirit is working through us, but in different manifestations.

Each believer is anointed to manifest at least one aspect of Jesus. When we all come together as a body, we have the fullness of God (Ephesians 4:13). Church, this has to happen! It *must* happen if Jesus is going to return to the earth. He is not coming for a church that is crying and whining like a baby to get them out of the earth. He is coming for a victorious church.

Every person God used in the Old Testament was a type or shadow of Christ. That means they were representing or foreshadowing Christ who was to come. Abraham was a prophet, Joseph was a prime minister, and David was a king. Esther was a queen, Moses was a deliverer, and the list goes on. They were all witnesses of the Messiah. Jesus is all of them and more. Jesus said every scripture testifies of Him.

> You search the Scriptures, for in them you think you have eternal life; and these are they which *testify of Me* (John 5:39).

The Everlasting Kingdom

Nowhere in the Bible do we read that Jesus' reign or kingdom comes only during the millennium, or that His kingship starts once this current world system ends. That is another misunderstanding the deceiver brought to the church, trying to tell us that His physical kingdom and reign will be here on the earth only in the millennium — but He is a King forever and ever, and His kingdom is from generation to generation. Throughout the Bible, it says God and Jesus' reign is for *now and forever.*

In the Old Testament, we read about a heathen king who lived more than four thousand years ago who had a powerful revelation about the kingdom of our God. I pray that the church will finally understand this revelation. The church keeps preaching that the kingdom of our God is going to come at some point in the future that nobody knows. Please read what this king said in the following verse:

> And at the end of the time I, Nebuchadnezzar, lifted my eyes to heaven, and my understanding returned to me; and I blessed the Most High and praised and honored Him who lives forever: For His dominion is an everlasting dominion, and His kingdom is from generation to generation" (Daniel 4:34).

This says that when the understanding was returned to the king, he had a revelation about God's kingdom, whose dominion is an everlasting dominion. His kingdom is from generation to generation, not just during the millennium. I think that when this realization dawns on believers worldwide, they will come to the same understanding.

> Then to Him was given dominion and glory and a kingdom, that all peoples, nations, and languages should serve Him.

GOD AND JESUS AS KINGS

> His dominion is an everlasting dominion, which shall not pass away, and His kingdom the one which shall not be destroyed (Daniel 7:14).

> To make known to the sons of men His mighty acts, and the glorious majesty of His kingdom. Your kingdom is an everlasting kingdom, and Your dominion endures throughout all generations (Psalm 145:12-13).

You may say, "Brother, that is Old Testament. Show me some verses in the New Testament that say Jesus' kingdom and reign is for now and forever." I am glad you asked that. Here you go!

> He will be great, and will be called the Son of the Highest; and the Lord God will give Him the throne of His father David. And He will reign over the house of Jacob forever, and of His kingdom there will be no end (Luke 1:32-33).

> Now to the King eternal, immortal, invisible, to God who alone is wise, be honor and glory forever and ever. Amen (1 Timothy 1:17).

> If anyone speaks, let him speak as the oracles of God. If anyone ministers, let him do it as with the ability which God supplies, that in all things God may be glorified through Jesus Christ, to whom belong the glory and the dominion forever and ever. Amen (1 Peter 4:11).

> To Him be the glory and the dominion forever and ever. Amen (1 Peter 5:11).

> To God our Savior, who alone is wise, be glory and majesty, dominion and power, both now and forever. Amen (Jude 1:25).

> And from Jesus Christ, the faithful witness, the firstborn from the dead, and the ruler over the kings of the earth. To

> Him who loved us and washed us from our sins in His own blood, and has made us kings and priests to His God and Father, to Him be glory and dominion forever and ever. Amen (Revelation 1:5-6).

All these verses tell us that Jesus' kingdom and dominion is everlasting. It was here before we were born, and it will be here after we die. Now we are going to journey back in time to understand the Master Plan that God the King has for planet Earth and why He created us.

Chapter 8: The Origin of the Kingdom

A Tale of Two Kingdoms

Many years ago in eternity past, there existed a kingdom. The Great King who ruled this kingdom called His senior associates who were close to Him for a very important meeting in His magnificent palace. His associates came to the meeting, knowing the King had something serious to share with them. Otherwise, He would not have called them together. They knew that whatever He was going to share with them would take place just as He said.

The subject of the meeting was nothing more than the expansion and prosperity of His kingdom. He said, "Everything I have is unlimited and never stops growing. I have purposed to expand My majestic kingdom to a new part of the universe and to create a new planet." He shared what was in His heart, and everyone who attended the meeting unanimously agreed to carry out the plan. They knew that whatever He planned would excel, and nothing withstood His counsel.

This King and His kingdom worked a little differently than those with which we are acquainted on earth. He had no opponent and His kingdom had no beginning or end. He had (and continues to have) no lack of anything, and He does not depend on anyone to do anything. He does what He wills and His counsel stands forever, and no one can ever thwart His purpose.

THE GOSPEL OF THE KINGDOM

The uniqueness of this meeting was that the King's only Son was specially called in and seated next to the Father. It was very clear that His Son was going to be a key player in this new venture the King was planning to undertake. The Son paid keen attention to everything His Father said regarding this new planet. He delighted in this new responsibility His Father was planning to entrust to Him. The King said to His Son, "My beloved Son, I want You to design this planet and bring it into existence as I speak it forth." The Son said to His Father, "Yes, Father, I am here to do Your will. My Spirit will bring into existence everything You speak."

> For by Him (the Son) all things were created that are in heaven and that are on earth, visible and invisible, whether thrones or dominions or principalities or powers. All things were created through Him and for Him. (Colossians 1:16).
>
> All things were made through Him (the Son), and without Him nothing was made that was made (John 1:3).

The King said this planet would be called *Terras* and would be like no other planet He had created before. This one would be one of the most beautiful that He had created so far. The King declared this, saying, "One of the specialties of this planet is that everything in it will praise and sing to Me. They will declare my works forever and ever. It will be filled with My knowledge and glory. This planet will resemble My kingdom here in heaven in every way. My will, will be done on this planet, just as it is done here in heaven.

"I am going to give this planet to none other than my close associate, Lucifer, to manage, since he is the worshiping prince and has a spirit of excellence and is full of wisdom. He will be in charge of My wealth, business, and development. He and his echelons of angels, spirits, and other living creatures that assist him will inhabit this planet and ascribe glory and honor to Me. Since he is in charge of the wealth and wisdom regarding the universe, I have given him permission to come in to My presence from this planet whenever the sons of God come to see Me. I will also create other spirit beings to serve him in this kingdom."

THE ORIGIN OF THE KINGDOM

This King is like no other king, and has a very special way of doing things. When He declares something, it takes existence from that moment on, and nothing can stand in His way or annul what He has said. The universe trembles at His voice, and millions of angels stand ready to execute His orders.

The King declared His words, and His Son brought this special planet into existence. It was made by Him and for Him and through Him, though it was going to be given to Lucifer to manage. The King paid very special attention to this planet, and everything in it was made by wisdom, understanding, and knowledge (Proverbs 3:19).

He laid its foundation on water and covered the atmosphere with water to protect it. It was one of the most beautiful places in the universe, and light shone from one end of the planet to the other. The atmosphere was specially protected by clouds and water. It did not need a sun or moon to give light. The brightness and glory of Lucifer illuminated it from one end to the other, for his name meant, "the light bearer."

Then that special day came when the King laid the foundation of this great planet. It was a great day of celebration. The sons of God were shouting for joy.

> To what were its foundations fastened? Or who laid its cornerstone, when the morning stars sang together, and all the sons of God shouted for joy? (Job 38:6-7).

The King made a special throne for Lucifer in the northern part of this planet (Isaiah 14:13). His throne was located in the span between this planet and heaven. Lucifer brought all the angels and other spirit beings that worked under him and made arrangements to praise and worship the King from this planet. It was a time of great joy and jubilation like no other time on earth and in heaven. The King rejoiced at His handiwork as He saw His kingdom expanded to another level, and made sure everything exactly represented His kingdom in heaven.

One of the qualities of a good king is that whenever he does something in a foreign country, he will replicate everything to match what is in his kingdom. He will make sure that everything exactly represents the system and rules where His kingdom exists. His intention of expanding His kingdom is that those who see the work should know Him and His popularity must increase.

This is the story of the first earth we read about in Genesis 1.

> In the beginning God created the heavens and the earth. The earth was without form, and void; and darkness was on the face of the deep. And the Spirit of God was hovering over the face of the waters (Genesis 1:1-2).

The earth became dark, void, and flooded with water. How and why? We are going to find that out. First we are going to see how God created Lucifer and what his life was like where he was before his fall. Let us go to the biblical account of the above-mentioned meeting and find out more details. Only then will we understand why God created us and put us here on this planet.

Chapter 9: The Creation of Lucifer

The Bible begins with: "In the beginning God created the heavens and the earth" (Genesis 1:1). That means the heavens and the earth were created at the same time—in the beginning. If the earth was created one million years after the heavens were made, then they were not created in the beginning. We also understand from the Bible that man has been on this earth only a little more than six thousand years.

In the record of the six days of creation we read about in Genesis, we do not see God creating the earth or water because they were already in existence. If this is so, when and how did they get there?

The Bible says God's works and His ways are perfect. He never creates anything that is empty, shapeless, or chaotic. But then we read: "The earth was without form, and void; and darkness was on the face of the deep. And the Spirit of God was hovering over the face of the waters" (Genesis 1:2). What could have caused the earth to be in that state? Why was the earth covered with water? In Genesis, we read that God looked at what He created and said, "It is good." The condition of the earth we see in verse 2 is anything but good!

If the heavens and the earth were created at the same time and the earth is as old as the heavens, was it ever inhabited by anyone other than humans? If Lucifer fell from heaven to earth in eternity past, this earth had to be in existence then. Why did he fall to Earth and not any other planet?

Scientists and archeologists have been discovering fossils and other items that are thousands and millions of years old—long before man was created. Where did these fossils come from? Who were these creatures, and what happened to them? What kind of living situation did they have? In Genesis

1:3-31, God was only rearranging and restoring the earth, making it habitable for the human beings He was planning to create.

Where do the fossils of dinosaurs and other animals come from? Were these all just stories that archeologists made up? Some believe that dinosaurs lived before the flood of Noah. If that's true, they are saying that either God is a liar or Noah was a disobedient crook, because God told Noah to bring into the ark "every living thing of all flesh…male and female" (Genesis 6:19-20). We do not see God asking him to exclude dinosaurs. So every creature that was alive *before* the flood, also existed *after* the flood.

> On the very same day Noah and Noah's sons, Shem, Ham, and Japheth, and Noah's wife and the three wives of his sons with them, entered the ark—they and every beast after its kind, all cattle after their kind, every creeping thing that creeps on the earth after its kind, and every bird after its kind, every bird of every sort. And they went into the ark to Noah, two by two, of all flesh in which is the breath of life. So those that entered, male and female of all flesh, went in as God had commanded him; and the Lord shut him in (Genesis 7:13-16).

I hope you noticed the word *every* repeated four times to make sure that *every creature* God created was brought onto the ark. There is no evidence in the Bible that says the dinosaurs jumped out of the ark before the flood ended and committed suicide or were eaten by some other animals, or by Noah and his family. They did not have to eat the dinosaurs because God told Noah to collect enough food for them and for the animals, and, most importantly, man only started eating animal meat *after* the flood. (See Genesis 6:21-22 and 9:3-4.)

The Earth's Inhabitants

God created the earth for habitation. The Bible says:

THE CREATION OF LUCIFER

> For thus says the Lord, who created the heavens, who is God, who formed the earth and made it, who has established it, who did not create it in vain, who formed it to be inhabited: "I am the Lord, and there is no other" (Isaiah 45:18).

This verse is talking about the original earth when God made it. There were inhabitants on this earth. I believe the earth was inhabited by other beings before the creation of human beings. If there were inhabitants on this earth, who were they, and what happened to them?

If humans were the first inhabitants, how did demons come to live here before man? Why did God allow Satan and demons to enter animals before the fall of man or before sin entered the earth? Why did God tell Adam to *subdue* the fish of the sea, the fowl of the air, and every creature that creeps on this earth? How were they in any danger to Adam's existence? Why did he have to *subdue* them if there was no *rebellion*? These are some of the questions I want you to think through with me, and I will try to answer them in this chapter.

Only when we understand who Lucifer was, where he lived, and what his responsibilities were, will we understand his dealings with people on this earth today as our enemy. *Ignorance of our enemy and how he operates can destroy us.* In two different accounts, the Bible gives us a glimpse of how Lucifer was made, where he was, his qualities, abilities, responsibilities, and how he fell. We are going to look at those scriptures and learn a little bit about this magnificent creature God created.

I believe the earth was inhabited by Lucifer and his associates. The earth was his kingdom. There is a multitude of evidence in the Bible to prove it, which I will share with you. Their original purpose was to rule the earth, worship God, and expand His kingdom here. That is why I believe that after their fall, God created us to fill that place; we were created to rule the earth and expand His kingdom. God gave similar qualities and responsibilities to both Lucifer and human beings.

Traditionally, the church has been teaching that Lucifer was created to worship God and that he was in heaven before he fell. The church also teaches that after Lucifer fell, God created human beings in that place to worship Him. But if Lucifer fell from heaven and we were created to replace him for worship, why were we not put in heaven?

The teaching we have received is only a fraction of the truth. If the devil can convince the church that their greatest responsibility on this earth is to worship (or sing to) God, then he has somewhat succeeded in his mission, because as long as he can make the church busy inside its four walls, singing about "I, me, and mine," it will not be a threat to his kingdom.

While we do our "churchy" stuff, the enemy will come through the back door and steal everything. We are going to see *how* and *why* God created Lucifer and what his responsibilities were. Please read on.

The Kingdom of the Enemy

Whenever the Bible talks about Satan, though he has access to heaven, almost all of his time and operations are in relation to earth and its inhabitants. The only incident that we read where God had a conversation with Satan is in the book of Job. When the sons of God came to meet God, Satan also showed up. God asked him where he had been? He replied saying he was roaming to and fro on the earth (Job 1:6-7)) His function is connected to our planet.

The Bible says that he has a kingdom (Matthew 12:26). If he has a kingdom, he is a king, and he has a throne. I am sure he was not ruling with God side-by-side in heaven. There is no way that could have ever happened. If he was not in charge of worship, then what was his responsibility? When did he become a king, where was he ruling as a king, and where did his kingdom exist?

We read in Revelation that Jesus said to the church in Pergamos the following lines,

> And to the angel of the church in Pergamos write, "These things says He who has the sharp two-edged sword: 'I know your works, and where you dwell, where Satan's throne is. And you hold fast to My name, and did not deny My

faith even in the days in which Antipas was My faithful martyr, who was killed among you, where Satan dwells'" (Revelation 2:12-13).

Jesus is saying that Satan's throne was in Pergamos and that he dwelt there. That is quite interesting. Pergamos was an ancient city located in the Anatolia region close to the present-day Bergama, Izmir province of Turkey. What was so special about this city that made Satan choose it to establish his throne and live there?

Pergamos was one of the most influential cities of its day. It was the center for politics, commerce, religion, the arts, and technology for all of Asia Minor. It was also a center for pagan worship and was famous for the great altar of Zeus. That is the reason Satan chose this particular city to be the base of his operation. He knew that if he could influence Pergamos, he could control the entire region of Asia Minor.

That does not mean his throne is still in Pergamos. In our time, he might choose one of the more influential cities in this world. It was normal at that time for nations to change the location of their capital based on who ruled it. Satan changes with the times.

You may not believe or understand everything I say right away. The only thing I ask is that you not stop reading. In the end, everything will make sense. I will explain in more detail as we go further into the topic. Now let's look at the passage of Scripture that talks about Lucifer from Ezekiel.

> Son of man, take up a lamentation for the king of Tyre, and say to him, "Thus says the Lord God: 'You were the seal of perfection, full of wisdom and perfect in beauty. You were in Eden, the garden of God; every precious stone was your covering: the sardius, topaz, and diamond, beryl, onyx, and jasper, sapphire, turquoise, and emerald with gold. The workmanship of your timbrels and pipes was prepared for you on the day you were created. You were the anointed cherub who covers; I established you; you were on the holy mountain of God; you walked back and forth in the midst

of fiery stones. You were perfect in your ways from the day you were created, till iniquity was found in you. By the abundance of your trading you became filled with violence within, and you sinned; therefore I cast you as a profane thing out of the mountain of God; and I destroyed you, O covering cherub, from the midst of the fiery stones'" (Ezekiel 28:12-16).

These verses had an immediate application to the king of Tyre, whose name is not mentioned. Like most scriptures in the Bible, they also have a spiritual application. From them we learn the following: Most of the descriptions of the person (or being) mentioned above clearly show that it is not talking about an ordinary human being.

No king ever lived in the garden of Eden except Adam. No human king ruled from the mountain of God. No one was a seal of perfection, full of wisdom, and perfect in beauty. It also says in verse 14 that this person or being was an anointed cherub. The noun *cherub* appears thirty times in the New King James Version of the Bible. Twenty-nine times it is talking about spirit beings, and one time as the name of a place in Babylon. Cherubs are one type of spiritual being mentioned in the Bible, and they are not human.

Bible scholars believe that this passage describes Lucifer and what happened to him. These verses say that he was the seal of perfection, meaning everything about him and everything he did was perfect. He was full of wisdom and perfect in beauty, covered with every precious stone. He was residing in Eden, the garden of God (which was on the earth). He was anointed by God. He was on the holy mountain of God.

The book of Ezekiel also shows where the garden of Eden is today:

> I made the nations shake at the sound of its fall, when I cast it down to hell together with those who descend into the Pit; and all the trees of Eden, the choice and best of Lebanon, all that drink water, were comforted in the depths of the earth (Ezekiel 31:16).

THE CREATION OF LUCIFER

> To which of the trees in Eden will you then be likened in glory and greatness? Yet you shall be brought down with the trees of Eden to the depths of the earth (Ezekiel 31:18a).

These two verses tell us that the trees of Eden (garden) are now under the earth. I believe this happened during the second flood that we read about in Genesis 6-8. Until then the garden was protected by cherubim with flaming swords (Genesis 3:24).

Though the person here is symbolized as the king of Tyre, from the description we know that no human king was created by God like this one. God does not call a human king an anointed cherub. According to verse 13, Lucifer was in the garden of Eden, and the Bible clearly says the garden of Eden was on the earth.

In God's kingdom there are different types of spirit beings with different responsibilities. There are angels of different ranks, ministering spirits, angels, then seraphim, cherubim, living creatures, and human beings. Of these, cherubim are the closest to God. Their job is to cover and expand God's glory. They know more of God and His glory than any other creature He has made.

The second thing the Bible says in verse 14 is that Lucifer was on the holy mountain of God, walking back and forth in the midst of fiery stones. Where is the holy mountain of God? The first place the phrase *holy mountain of God* appears in the Bible is in Exodus 3:1 when Moses led the sheep he was watching up to the mountain of God and saw the burning bush. Wherever the phrase *holy mountain* or *mountain of God* is mentioned in the Bible, it always refers to a mountain that is on the earth; it is not talking about any mountain in heaven.

The third description given in verse 14 is Lucifer walking back and forth in the midst of the fiery stones on the mountain. We also see this in the book of Exodus. When God came down on the mountain to meet with Moses, the Bible says that under his feet were sapphire stones shining with fire on top of the mountain. Ezekiel 28:13 talks about Lucifer having sapphire stones as his covering.

> Then Moses went up, also Aaron, Nadab, and Abihu, and seventy of the elders of Israel, and they saw the God of Israel. And there was under His feet as it were a paved work of sapphire stone, and it was like the very heavens in its clarity (Exodus 24:9-10).

> The sight of the glory of the Lord was like a consuming fire on the top of the mountain in the eyes of the children of Israel (Exodus 24:17).

God did not bring down a mountain from heaven. These verses are talking about a mountain on earth where God came down to meet with Moses. I will explain more about the location of Lucifer toward the end of this chapter. As we read just a bit ago:

> The workmanship of your timbrels and pipes was prepared for you on the day you were created (Ezekiel 28:13).

The first human God created was Adam, and He did not create any special kings before that. This is the verse that people use to describe that Lucifer was in charge of worship in heaven, but it actually describes much more than that in these verses.

Now we are going to look at the qualities, abilities, and responsibilities Lucifer had when God created him, and the sins he committed before his fall.

The Qualities of Lucifer

He Was Perfect (Ezekiel 28:12)

First of all, he was the seal of perfection, full of wisdom and beauty. Let us do a word study on these and see what they actually mean in the

THE CREATION OF LUCIFER

Hebrew language. The word used for perfect is *kaliyl* meaning, "entire, all, perfect."²

He Was Full of Wisdom and Beauty (Ezekiel 28:12)

The word used for wisdom is *chokmah,* meaning "skill (in war), wisdom (in administration), shrewdness, wisdom, prudence (in religious affairs), wisdom (ethical and religious)."³

If Lucifer's only responsibility was to worship God, then why did he need skill in war, wisdom in administration, and the other qualities mentioned above?

The word *chokmah* can refer to technical skills or special abilities in fashioning something too. The first occurrence of *chokmah* is in Exodus 28:

> And thou shalt speak unto all that are wise hearted, whom I have filled with the spirit of *wisdom,* that they may make Aaron's garments to consecrate him, that he may minister unto me in the priest's office (Exodus 28:3 KJV).⁴

He Was Covered with Nine Precious Stones (Ezekiel 12:13)

Lucifer was covered with nine precious stones. He was in charge of the wealth of God's kingdom. The number nine is a significant number in Scripture. It is the last of the single digits so it represents finality or the conclusion of a matter. It also signifies judgment. In the Bible, there are nine fruits of the Spirit, as well as nine fruits of wisdom.

---

2. Brown, Driver, and Briggs, "Kaliyl - Old Testament Hebrew Lexicon - King James Version," Bible Study Tools, accessed June 10, 2019, https://www.biblestudytools.com/lexicons/hebrew/kjv/kaliyl.html.

3. Brown, Driver, and Briggs, "Chokmah - Old Testament Hebrew Lexicon - King James Version," Bible Study Tools, accessed June 10, 2019, https://www.biblestudytools.com/lexicons/hebrew/kjv/chokmah.html.

4. W. E. Vine, *An Expository Dictionary of Biblical Words*, ed. Merrill F. Unger and William White, Jr. (Nashville, TN: Thomas Nelson, 1985).

The fruit of *chokmah*, wisdom, are many, and the book of Proverbs describes the character of *chokmah* wisdom. In New Testament terms, the *fruit of wisdom* are the same as the fruit of the Holy Spirit.

> But the fruit of the Spirit is love, joy, peace, longsuffering, kindness, goodness, faithfulness, gentleness, self-control. Against such there is no law (Galatians 5:22-23).[5]

Look at what James says about the traits of wisdom:

> But the wisdom that is from above is first pure, then peaceable, gentle, and easy to be intreated, full of mercy and good fruits, without partiality, and without hypocrisy. And the fruit of righteousness is sown in peace of them that make peace (James 3:17-18 KJV).

Musical Instruments Were Built in Him (Ezekiel 28:13)

The Bible says that Satan had "tabrets" or timbrels built into him. When he flew, the air in the atmosphere produced the greatest music ever played in this universe. The four corners of the earth echoed that music and all spirit beings on this earth resonated in harmony and worshiped God.

> "The whole earth is at rest, and is quiet; they break forth into singing (Isaiah 14:7 KJV).

This is why there are more ungodly musicians on this earth than godly ones. The devil steals the gifts and talents from God's children and gives them to his children and uses them to promote his fame. He has a special interest in music.

He Was in Charge of Manufacturing and the Development of God's Kingdom (Ezekiel 28:13)

The word *workmanship* in Hebrew is *melakah*, which means "occupation, work, business." Thayer's Lexicon gives these meanings to the word:

---

5. Ibid.

"property; work (something done or made); workmanship; service or use; public business, political or religious."[6]

The Hebrew word for pipes is even more interesting. It is *neqeb,* which means "groove, socket, hole, cavity, settings," and is a technical term relating to a jeweler's work.[7] This is the only place this particular word is used in the entire Bible. I thought this word represented a musical instrument, but it does not.

He Was Full of Light or Brightness (Ezekiel 28:17)

The earth depended on the brightness of Lucifer for its light. The word used for Lucifer in the Hebrew language is *heylel,* which means "light-bearer" and has the following meanings:

1) The shining one, the morningstar, Lucifer; used of the king of Babylon and Satan (figuratively);[8]

2) The Theological Wordbook of the Old Testament says this: Helel: describing the king of Babylon. [9]

In the New Testament, Paul says that Satan transforms himself into an angel of light (2 Corinthians 11:14). The Hebrew word used for brightness is *yiph`ah,* which means "splendor, brightness, or shining."[10] He was full of light and brightness, and that is why I said that planet Earth did not need any terrestrial light before the creation of man. When he fell, his light became darkness. That is why the Earth became full of darkness and he became the

---

6. Brown, Driver, and Briggs, "Melakah - Old Testament Hebrew Lexicon - King James Version," Bible Study Tools, accessed June 10, 2019, https://www.biblestudytools.com/lexicons/hebrew/kjv/melakah.html.

7. Brown, Driver, and Briggs, "Neqeb - Old Testament Hebrew Lexicon - King James Version," Bible Study Tools, accessed June 10, 2019, https://www.biblestudytools.com/lexicons/hebrew/kjv/neqeb.html.

8. Brown, Driver, and Briggs, "Heylel - Old Testament Hebrew Lexicon - King James Version," Bible Study Tools, accessed June 10, 2019, https://www.biblestudytools.com/lexicons/hebrew/kjv/heylel.html.

9. R. Laird Harris, Gleason L. Archer, and Bruce K. Waltke, *Theological Wordbook of the Old Testament* (Chicago: Moody Press, 2004).

10. Brown, Driver, and Briggs, "Yiph`ah - Old Testament Hebrew Lexicon - King James Version," Bible Study Tools, accessed June 10, 2019, https://www.biblestudytools.com/lexicons/hebrew/kjv/yiph`ah.html.

ruler of darkness. His kingdom is now called the kingdom of darkness. Later on, God created the sun, moon, and stars to light up the earth and sky.

In the new earth and new heaven, there will not be any sun and moon. The glory of Jesus will be its light day and night (Revelation 22:5).

The Abilities of Lucifer

He Was Supposed to Expand the Trade and Business of God Here

> By the multitude of thy merchandise they have filled the midst of thee with violence, and thou hast sinned: therefore I will cast thee as profane out of the mountain of God: and I will destroy thee, O covering cherub, from the midst of the stones of fire (Ezekiel 28:16 KJV).

The Hebrew word used for merchandise in verse 16 is *rekullah*, which means "merchandize, traffic, or trade."[11]

He was in charge of business and the growth of God's kingdom and wealth on the earth. He manufactured products and filled the earth with these products and trade. His job was to transform God's ideas and manifest them here, or to materialize the thoughts of God in this natural world.

He Was Excellent as a Musician and in Business (Ezekiel 28:13, 18)

Refer to points 4 and 5 of the Qualities of Lucifer for more information on this. Lucifer had the ability to produce things (Ezekiel 28:16). The wisdom he had was *chokmah* wisdom, which also means the ability to imagine and make things.

---

11. Brown, Driver, and Briggs, "Rekullah - Old Testament Hebrew Lexicon - King James Version," Bible Study Tools, accessed June 10, 2019, https://www.biblestudytools.com/lexicons/hebrew/kjv/rekullah.html.

He Could Walk and Travel Freely in the Universe (Ezekiel 28:14)

In Job 1:6-7, we read that Satan was roaming around the earth. He had access to heaven and the presence of God.

The Responsibilities of Lucifer

From the above verses we understand that Lucifer was responsible for the business, wealth, development, and worship of God's kingdom on the earth. He was an anointed cherub. The word for anointed in Hebrew is *mimshach,* and this is the only place it is used in the entire Bible. It means "expansion or spread."[12]

It is interesting to note that Lucifer was anointed to cover, spread, and expand swiftly. In other words, the devil was a cherub of expansion. The purposes of God that related to this earth—His glory, wisdom, abilities, and wealth—were all in Lucifer's hands to expand them on earth. That is why whatever the devil and his children do grows and spreads quickly, while we are struggling to grow our ministries and businesses. It's not because we lack ideas, but because we lack the anointing for growth and expansion.

If you watch the media today, you will hardly hear any positive news. All we hear about is the evil that is going on in the world. Music, movies, or any product that supports the devil and his kingdom quickly spreads worldwide, while we store our plans, books, products, and music in a garage or in boxes somewhere. We do not know what it takes to expand and spread, while worldly people can write complete nonsense, and it will spread and become a bestseller. It is the *chokma* wisdom and the *mimshach* anointing of their god (the devil is the god of this world) who works for them.

Lucifer corrupted his anointing and wisdom, and now it no longer accomplishes God's purpose, but his own instead. We can't wait any longer

---

12. Brown, Driver, and Briggs, "Mimshach - Old Testament Hebrew Lexicon - King James Version," Bible Study Tools, accessed June 10, 2019, https://www.biblestudytools.com/lexicons/hebrew/kjv/mimshach.html.

to expand and grow God's kingdom. Since we have come to know their secret now, we can receive that *mimshach* anointing from God and spread out worldwide in Jesus' name.

Lucifer was in charge of the development and growth of God's kingdom. When God decided to do something new, it was Lucifer who executed it. He was in charge of all business, trade, innovation, manufacturing, and marketing in a world that we know very little about, but there are many clues in the verses that we are going to examine below.

He Was the Anointed Cherub that Covers

Cherubim are the closest to God. One of their jobs is to protect or cover God's glory. It is almost like a personal bodyguard, even though God would not need one. Even today, Lucifer does the same job, but instead of protecting God's glory, he covers or blinds us from seeing God's kingdom and His glory.

That is why the New Testament says,

> The god of this world has blinded (covered) the minds of the unbelievers (2 Corinthians 4:4 ESV).

Sometimes he blinds believers from seeing what God has prepared or done for them (Ephesians 4:17-18). If you are blinded to any truth, know that it is not the Spirit of God who hinders you, but the spirit of this world.

He Had Abundance of Business and Trade (Ezekiel 28:18)

Again, Scripture says Lucifer did trade on the earth and increased in wealth and splendor. Trade means he did business on the earth. There were nations and kingdoms that were built by him and his associates, according to Isaiah 14:16-17. There were spiritual beings that were inferior to him in rank here on earth along with Lucifer and animals like dinosaurs and such. In a similar way today, human beings are the spiritual beings and we have scores of animals and other creatures on this earth, which we call the animal kingdom.

The Sins of Lucifer

We have heard that Lucifer fell because of his pride, but there's more to the story. There were four reasons (sins) why he became prideful and fell. I do not think he would have expressed any of these if he was in heaven.

1. Iniquity

> You were perfect in your ways from the day you were created, till iniquity was found in you (Ezekiel 28:15).

Because of his perfection, wisdom, and wealth, he became haughty and crooked. The Hebrew word used for iniquity is *'evel* which means, "Injustice, unrighteousness, wrong; a) violent deeds of injustice; b) injustice (used of speech); c) injustice (generally)."[13] I believe he began to boast about his abilities and perfection, which led to self-exaltation. That is why the Bible says not to think too highly of yourself (Romans 12:3).

2. Violence

The second sin of Lucifer was violence.

> By the abundance of your trading you became filled with violence within, and you sinned (Ezekiel 28:16).

The Hebrew word used for violence is *chamac,* which means "violence, wrong, cruelty, injustice."[14] He increased his wealth greatly through his trade and became greedy and blind to his own destruction. He might have started to treat his subordinates with cruelty like a dictator. In the Old Testament, when God instituted kings to rule Israel, one restriction given was not to multiply gold, silver, and other types of wealth (Deuteronomy 17:17). In Genesis 6:13, we

---

13. Brown, Driver, and Briggs, "'Evel - Old Testament Hebrew Lexicon - King James Version," Bible Study Tools, accessed June 10, 2019, https://www.biblestudytools.com/lexicons/hebrew/kjv/'evel.html.

14. Brown, Driver, and Briggs, "Chamac - Old Testament Hebrew Lexicon - King James Version," Bible Study Tools, accessed June 10, 2019, https://www.biblestudytools.com/lexicons/hebrew/kjv/chamac.html.

read that before the flood of Noah, the earth was filled with violence because of the wickedness of men, which led God to destroy the earth once again.

3. Pride and Corruption

> Your heart was lifted up because of your beauty; you corrupted your wisdom for the sake of your splendor (Ezekiel 28:17).

We all know this part. He became prideful because of his beauty. He was a magnificent creature with extraordinary abilities and beauty that led him to be proud. He corrupted the wisdom God gave him to execute His will on this earth and began to use it to propagate evil in the world. There were kings in Israel who became prideful and departed from God's ways when God blessed them. They followed the path of Lucifer.

4. Defilement

> You defiled your sanctuaries by the multitude of your iniquities (Ezekiel 28:18)

The Hebrew word used for defile is *chalal,* which means, "1) to profane, to defile, to pollute, to desecrate, to begin to profane oneself ritually, sexually; and 2) to be polluted, to be defiled."[15]

We read in 1 Samuel how the sons of Eli despised and defiled the sanctuary of God by stealing the sacrifices and sleeping with women at the door of the tabernacle (1 Samuel 2:17, 22).

Now we have an idea about what kind of being Lucifer was. He was cunning and shrewd in business and had great beauty and wisdom. He could imagine and create almost anything he wanted. Keep in mind that God created this particular cherub with a free will like you and me.

---
15. Brown, Driver, and Briggs, "Chalal - Old Testament Hebrew Lexicon - King James Version," Bible Study Tools, accessed June 10, 2019, https://www.biblestudytools.com/lexicons/hebrew/kjv/chalal.html.

THE CREATION OF LUCIFER

He was in charge of all of heaven's business (wealth) and music related to our universe! Though he sinned, he was still anointed, except his anointing and wisdom was now corrupted. As I mentioned earlier, he wanted to be like God and rule the earth.

You might wonder why I write about Lucifer in a book about gospel of the kingdom. If you do not know where you came from and why you were put here, you will never be able to discover and fulfill your purpose. Your purpose is connected to God's kingdom. Statistics say that more than ninety percent of the people on earth do not know why they are here. So you can imagine the confusion that people in this world are going through.

So how did Lucifer become Satan, or the devil, as we know him today? Understanding this will help us understand why and how the earth we see in Genesis 1:2 became like it was.

God appointed Lucifer to establish and expand His kingdom here on earth. Because of the reasons outlined above, Lucifer messed it up and missed the opportunity he had. God created us in his place and gave the same responsibility to us that He had given to Lucifer. We will learn more about it as we move forward. I will also share with you why God did not give Lucifer a second chance like He did us, as well as why God did not forgive Lucifer as He forgave us.

Chapter 10: The Fall of Lucifer

Imagine in the ageless past, one day Lucifer was flying in mid-air above Earth, enjoying his new planet and the glory that was given to him. He heard countless numbers of angelic beings singing and worshiping the great King day and night. He saw the abundance of blessing and the glory of this great kingdom. He saw the great cities and golden palaces he and other creatures had built. The atmosphere of the earth was as described in the Bible:

> The whole earth is at rest, and is quiet; they break forth into singing (Isaiah 14:7).

Lucifer had four levels of leadership working under him. The first were principalities, which were in charge of nations and territories and were directly responsible to him. Then he had powers. These were in charge of different departments of nations. Then came rulers (they became rulers of darkness after the fall). These were local leaders and authorities working under the powers. And fourthly, he had armies of spirit beings who took care of the day-to-day affairs of the local territories (after the fall they were called spiritual wicked forces in heavenly places (Ephesians 6:12).

For some reason, he was not as happy as he used to be. He had a different feeling he never had before. His heart was not in what he was doing. He began to wonder. *What is in this for me? I have developed and built all these kingdoms and nations. I do not feel like I get the amount of respect and reward that is due to someone like me. I can do these things on my own, and all this planet was given unto me. I am greater than all these angels, and they all respect and obey me. I don't need to be accountable to anyone. What if I declare my dominion over this planet and make it my kingdom? Mine alone! I will receive the worship and adoration that is given to the great King, and all the wealth and glory of it will be mine to enjoy.*

Have you ever asked in your heart, "What is in it for me?" or "Do I get enough reward for what I do?" You might be a preacher, housewife, or an employee of a company. The moment you start self-seeking, you are entering into dangerous territory.

Days and years went by, and when he prepared music to be sung by the angels, he slowly began to put his own name in one or two places. He did not put his name in directly; instead he made up names for himself and inserted them. He is not only known as Lucifer or Satan on the earth today, but is also known by scores of names of false gods and goddesses in every nation. In India alone there are thirty-three million gods and goddesses—and they all have different names! In the United States, we have sophisticated demons, each with their own names; they just work through a different system here.

At first, he did not foresee any danger of doing this. He was in charge of the planet and did not feel he did anything wrong. Plus, the angels and spirit beings didn't know it either. For a while he felt good when he heard the angels singing his name. It brought a special feeling he'd never felt before, and it made him feel better than the other angels. The more he heard his name, the more he wanted to hear it again. Because he didn't sense any immediate reaction from the King, he thought everything was working for his benefit.

When his business grew and merchandise and trade was multiplied, so did his wealth. He began to keep some of it for himself and demand more and more from his associates, becoming a tyrant who ruled them by force and demanded respect. How do I know this? It says so in the Bible, which I explained under the heading *Sins of Lucifer*. He began to use violence to accomplish his evil intent.

As time went by, he became more eager to get praise and he started to insert his name in almost everything that was done on the earth. He began to exalt himself to a new position. He began to insert his qualities and abilities too, and not just his name, and they began to sing his praises in addition to those of the Great King. The angels that were with him were a little scared about this change, but they had no power to question him. They were to submit to him because he was their ruler.

Slowly, he began to feel that he was better than the great King Himself, and that he also deserved to be praised and adored, just like the King. He began to direct the singing and adoration that was only to be given to the King, to himself instead. He desired to have all the wealth and glory of the earth for himself.

The King knew about the change that was taking place in Lucifer, but because He is longsuffering and foreknew what was coming, He waited to see what choice Lucifer would make regarding this. It was not honorable for a benevolent King to interfere with someone's choice or free will.

A Closer Look at the Fall

Now, we are going to look at the passage from Isaiah 14 and see the fall of Lucifer.

> How you are fallen from heaven, O Lucifer, son of the morning! How you are cut down to the ground, you who weakened the nations! For you have said in your heart: "I will ascend into heaven, I will exalt my throne above the stars of God; I will also sit on the mount of the congregation on the farthest sides of the north; I will ascend above the heights of the clouds, I will be like the Most High." Yet you shall be brought down to Sheol, to the lowest depths of the Pit. Those who see you will gaze at you, and consider you, saying: "Is this the man who made the earth tremble, who shook kingdoms, who made the world as a wilderness and destroyed its cities, who did not open the house of his prisoners?" (Isaiah 14:12-17).

Look again at verse 12: "How are you fallen from heaven, O Lucifer, son of the morning!" He was cut down to the ground and he had weakened the nations. How did he get to heaven? Which nations did he weaken, and what ground is the verse talking about? The answer to that question is mentioned in verses 13 and 14, where it says, "For you have said in your heart: 'I will ascend into heaven…I will ascend above the heights of the clouds.'" If he was ascending to heaven, then he was not in heaven. When he fell, he was ascending into heaven. When he fell, to where did he fall? Verse 12 has that answer. It says, "How are you cut down to the ground."

The Hebrew word used for heaven is *shamayim* (shaw-mah'-yim), which means to be lofty, the sky (as aloft; the dual perhaps alluding to the visible arch in which the clouds move, as well as to the higher ether where the celestial bodies revolve)."[16]

The Hebrew word used for "to ascend" is *alah* (aw-law'); meaning "to ascend, intransitively (be high), or actively (mount);"[17]

The Hebrew word used for *ground* is the same as the word used for *earth* in verse 16 or anywhere else in the Bible.

From the above scriptures, it is clear that Lucifer was not in heaven. He was cut down when he was ascending into heaven; and when he fell, he was cut down to the ground, which is the earth. Verse 16 says, "Is this the man who made the earth tremble, who shook kingdoms, who made the world as a wilderness and destroyed its cities?" This verse clearly describes the condition of the earth in Genesis 1:2 and how it became the way it was.

Some say Lucifer was sent to the garden as an angel to minister to Adam and Eve, then later transgressed against God when he tempted them. You cannot prove that from the Bible. If he transgressed while he was in the garden with Adam and Eve, then when was he on the mountain of God as a king on this earth and directing trade? Where do all the other evil spirits come from?

---

16. James Strong, "Lexicon: Strong's H8064 - Shamayim," Blue Letter Bible, accessed June 10, 2019, https://www.blueletterbible.org/lang/lexicon/lexicon.cfm?t=kjv&strongs=h8064.

17. James Strong, "H5927. עָלָה (alah)," Biblehub.com, accessed June 10, 2019, https://biblehub.com/hebrew/5927.htm.

THE FALL OF LUCIFER

Taking the Praise

One day Lucifer called his key leaders and expressed his true feelings to them. They were sympathetic toward what he felt. He told them they had been working for years and it was not fair that only the King got all the praise and glory. They were the ones who built all of those magnificent palaces and cities, after all. They also deserved to be praised. He was ruling this great planet, and he pointed out that he was also a king. He laid out a plan before them to run a coup to dethrone the King and take over the whole universe. Then they would coerce the rest of the angels to side with them. He promised them special positions when he came into power, assuring them that they could rule from the King's palace itself.

Lucifer could go into the presence of God, as we see in the book of Job. He used his access to heaven to influence other angels of God. I believe angels from heaven visited the earth frequently for communication between heaven and earth. One third of them joined in his revolt against God. The angels that joined with Lucifer lost their position, but they are not roaming this earth attacking humans, as many people believe and teach. The Bible says that fallen angels are kept in the abyss for the day of judgment.

The Plot Revealed

The day came and the plot for the revolt was in place. As if they were going to worship the King, they began to ascend into the heavens. But the King knew their plan and exactly what was going to happen. As Lucifer and his cohorts were ascending into heaven, The King called His warrior princes and informed them of the plot. He commanded them to cast Lucifer and his associates down from their positions. Lucifer was not willing to surrender, for he had made up his mind to do his own will, even if he had to fight with the King and His princes.

So a great battle broke out in heaven, and the King and His princes won. Lucifer and his friends were cast down and they fell to earth like lightning. They could never go back to their original position on the earth. In revenge and with great wrath, Lucifer and his associates destroyed all the kingdoms and nations that were on this earth.

THE GOSPEL OF THE KINGDOM

Jesus said,

> I saw Satan fall like lightning from heaven (Luke 10:18).
>
> How you are cut down to the ground, you who weakened the nations! (Isaiah 14:12b).
>
> Is this the man who made the earth tremble, who shook kingdoms, who made the world as a wilderness and destroyed its cities, who did not open the house of his prisoners? (Isaiah 14:16b-17).

The King commanded that all the angels that rebelled with Lucifer should be bound and kept in darkness until the day of judgment. (See 2 Peter 2:4 and Jude 1:6.) These were mighty angels, strong in power and wisdom. They could do great damage if they were released on the earth. Some of them will be released to kill mankind during the end times (Revelation 9:13-15).

There were other creatures on the earth that existed during Lucifer's reign too. They no longer respected the King nor honored His kingdom. They began a new order of worship and gave honor to Lucifer. They began to change the systems on the earth. Great cities and nations were destroyed and darkness filled the earth. The King saw that the earth was no longer the place where His will was done as in heaven. He grieved over the creatures He had made on the earth and decided to destroy everything with a great flood.

God destroyed that world with a flood, and all the creatures that were created to serve Lucifer and his kingdom also perished; their nature had become corrupted by associating with Lucifer. Their bodies perished in the flood, but their spirits did not. Their spirits were disconnected from the King and became evil in nature, and later became evil or unclean spirits (demons). Their spirits began to roam the atmosphere of the earth, looking for habitation. The earth became formless and void, filled with darkness, and covered with water.

The earth was greatly impacted by this revolt, and it marred its beauty and the perfection it once had. Lucifer could not reestablish his kingdom now.

Though he had access, he lost his authority over the earth. So he stayed in the mid-air realm between the earth and heaven. Thus it says in Genesis 1:2: "The earth was (became) without form, and void; and the darkness was on the face of the deep. And the Spirit of God was hovering over the face of the waters."

The King did not totally give up on the earth. He knew His will would be done on the earth again as it was in the beginning. Other angels in heaven looked at Lucifer and began to regret what happened to him, saying, "How you are fallen from heaven, O Lucifer, son of the morning! How art thou cut down to the ground, you who weakened the nations!" (Isaiah 14:12).

Jeremiah saw this earth in the spirit and described about it in Jeremiah 4:

> I beheld the earth, and indeed it was without form, and void; and the heavens, they had no light. I beheld the mountains, and indeed they trembled, and all the hills moved back and forth. I beheld, and indeed there was no man, and all the birds of the heavens had fled. I beheld, and indeed the fruitful land was a wilderness, and all its cities were broken down at the presence of the Lord, by His fierce anger (Jeremiah 4:23-26).

This affected Lucifer more than anything. His nature was completely corrupted and he lost his glory and splendor. He became full of darkness instead. Sin and rebellion entered his being and he became an enemy of the Great King. Everyone associated with him inherited this same nature. He was kicked out of God's kingdom because his nature was corrupted with sin. He and his cohorts waited for another opportune time to take over the earth and pay the King back for what He had done to them. He was not repentant for what he had done, nor was he willing to seek repentance, for his pride made him feel that it was the right thing. His name was no longer Lucifer; it became Satan, which means "adversary."

God did not forgive Lucifer because, first of all, he did not repent. Secondly, Lucifer had known God and His ways in a deeper way than any of us will ever know on this side of eternity. The more we know, the more will be required of us. For some reason, if any angelic beings rebel, there is no excuse for them. They will be condemned to darkness forever.

If Lucifer had been in heaven, he could not have sinned because there is perfection in heaven, and there is no sin. He was in a different realm than heaven where God dwells; he was on the earth in its original form and beauty.

Flooded Earth

God judged the earth and destroyed that world with a flood. It resulted in the destruction of the earth and all that was in it. The archeological findings of fossils and other remnants that are millions of years old are from that civilization only. Satan could no longer establish his kingdom here. The earth is a physical world, and only those with physical bodies can remain on it, so Satan established his kingdom above the earth. That is why the Bible calls him the prince of the power of the air (Ephesians 2:2). He was not allowed in heaven and He could not come back to earth because it was flooded.

When God destroyed the then-inhabited world, all the animals and spiritual beings (they had physical bodies) were destroyed, but their spirits remained on this earth, waiting for physical bodies to reenter. That is why God told Adam to subdue the earth and its creatures. For some reason, God allowed these evil spirits to enter creatures on the earth before the fall of man. They are the evil spirits, or demons, on earth today. The Eden of Lucifer was destroyed by the first flood, and the earth became empty, void, and full of darkness.

The reason the devil and those spirits could not come back to earth was because they needed a physical body (either human or animal) to operate in the physical realm. The earth was covered with water, and there was no physical object that could be seen. Sometimes these spirits can enter into other physical substances besides living organisms.

So they stayed in the second heaven (the invisible realm, spiritual realm, or heavenly places) and made it their abode. They waited until God restored the earth before entering back into physical substances or living organisms.

This is why the devil had access to the earth and the garden of Eden before the fall of man. Though God judged them, He did not sentence them to their eternal punishment yet. As we see in the Gospels, demons requested that Jesus not judge them before the time (Matthew 8:29).

Evil Spirits are Not Angels

I do not believe demons are fallen angels because the Bible says those angels that were fallen, or had sinned, were bound and kept for their judgment.

> For if God did not spare the angels who sinned, but cast them down to hell and delivered them into chains of darkness, to be reserved for judgment (2 Peter 2:4).
>
> And the angels who did not keep their proper domain, but left their own abode, He has reserved in everlasting chains under darkness for the judgment of the great day (Jude 1:6).

And four of those angels will be released for a short while to kill mankind at the end time.

> Saying to the sixth angel who had the trumpet, "Release the four angels who are bound at the great river Euphrates." So the four angels, who had been prepared for the hour and day and month and year, were released to kill a third of mankind (Revelation 9:14-15).

The Bible never addresses demons or evil spirits as fallen angels. If the demons we cast out from people were angels, we would not be able to cast them out. We do not yet have power over angels, neither do we have authority to judge them right now, but we will in the future (1 Corinthians 6:3).

Angels are much more powerful than human beings. One angel of God killed 185,000 humans in one night (2 Kings 19:35). Jesus never mentioned angels when He was dealing with demon spirits. He always addressed them as demons or evil spirits. There are different kinds of spirit beings, and angels are one of them. Jesus addressed demons as evil spirits. Demon spirits are beings lesser in authority and power than angels and human spirits.

Demon spirits are the disembodied spirits of those fallen beings from the pre-Adamic world. God allowed those spirits to remain here for some reason. I believe it is because the earth was their original abode before the creation of Adam.

I believe this is the reason God gave this earth (stewardship) to them first to rule and to have dominion. God decided to restore the earth and create another spiritual being, called humans, to rule and to have dominion. This man had to subdue not only the planet, but also the spiritual rebellion that was already taking place on this earth. This is God's absolute will and purpose for every single human being: to have dominion and authority over the earth. Both groups will be on this earth until this present world is destroyed with fire.

What Lucifer wanted was the worship and the wealth that belongs to God; and now through unsaved and blinded human beings he receives that for a time. The devil and his kingdom (through unregenerate human beings) manage the majority of the wealth today.

Where Did the Evil Spirits Go?

Man had twofold responsibilities. One was to have dominion, which is to rule this planet for God and establish His kingdom. The second one was to keep the demonic forces from gaining a foothold on earth through any living creatures. If the demonic spirits had to gain access to the earth, they had to use something that had a living "body." They had to use one of the creatures God mentioned in Genesis 1:26. There were no other human bodies at that time for demons to enter other than Adam and Eve, and they were protected by God's glory. That is why He told them to subdue and take dominion over every creature God had made.

In the Bible, we see people worshiping fish as their god (1 Samuel 5:4). In Greek mythology, birds were objects of worship. In some Asian countries, people worship cattle and other animals as gods. It is interesting to see that the four categories of creatures God told Adam to subdue and take dominion over are the objects of worship in some part of the world. They are not actually worshiping these creatures themselves, but the spirits they represent. I have also personally seen that when demons manifest in people, they act like different creatures and animals. There is a reason for this.

Animals do not go to heaven when they die, as some might think. When I came to the West, I saw people treating their pets like they treated a person or even better. I have seen demon-possessed animals, including cats, dogs, cows, and others. Sometimes these spirits manifest through animals and bite and attack humans, and if they do not receive treatment, the person will eventually die.

Most animals do not have the concept of family or a moral conscience like humans do. They do not have morality or guilt like human beings either. In any culture in which animals are treated like people or gods, people do everything with them as they would with humans, and then those people also end up behaving like the animals.

Idol worship, incest, and bestiality are the result of animal love and the deception of the enemy through those animals. It is the intention of the enemy to bring humans down to the level of animals. In some countries, animals have more rights and privileges than humans! I have seen people who have soul ties with their pets and cannot go anywhere without them. I am not against having pets, but if the pets *have* you instead of you having the pet, then it is a problem.

Bestiality is a growing problem in different cultures of the world. Incest has destroyed millions of lives and continues to destroy many families. This happens when man loses his human sense of conscience and adopts an animal one instead, doing what is right in their own minds. When you spend time with something or someone, eventually you will become like that creature or person. The Bible says if you walk with the wise you will become wise (Proverbs 13:20), and if you walk with the foolish, you will act foolish.

It is sad to hear that people spend more money on their pets than they spend for preaching the gospel and caring for the poor around the world.

THE GOSPEL OF THE KINGDOM

It is time to take dominion over the things and creatures that God said to subdue in the beginning. Otherwise, they will take dominion over you. It is interesting to note that whenever evil people dress up for carnivals or parades, they always dress up like an animal or a bird. Please do not get offended, this is the truth, and truth is hard—sometimes it hurts.

Another reason people worship animals as gods is because of the relationship the demonic world has with them. The Bible describes Satan as a beast and a serpent in the books of Genesis and Revelation. The Bible also compares birds, animals, and creeping things to evil spirits.

When the devil came to tempt Eve, he entered a serpent and disguised himself as a creature that was familiar to Eve. She did not believe or recognize any danger because she might have talked to the serpent before that incident. I do not believe she knew it was Satan who was talking to her at the time. Scripture says Eve was deceived.

In the book of Revelation, we read about frogs coming out of the mouth of the dragon, which represents evil spirits.

> And I saw three unclean spirits like frogs coming out of the mouth of the dragon, out of the mouth of the beast, and out of the mouth of the false prophet. For they are spirits of demons, performing signs, which go out to the kings of the earth and of the whole world, to gather them to the battle of that great day of God Almighty (Revelation 16:13-14).

Daniel saw visions about what was going to happen in the future. He saw nations and rulers of those nations who looked like different animals. Those animals represented the character and the particular spirit that was going to control those kings and leaders of those nations (Daniel 7-8).

Based on the above scriptures, I believe that the reason God separated the clean and unclean animals is based on their relationship with the spirit world. Clean animals like the lamb and ox are pictured as Jesus and the dove as the Holy Spirit. Unclean animals and creatures are compared to evil spirits.

Jesus said in Luke 10:19 that He has given us authority to tread on serpents and scorpions and all the power of the enemy. Serpents and scorpions represent demons (evil spirits), and we have authority over them. Two unclean animals that are used in the Bible to represent evil people and spirits are dogs and pigs. (See Matthew 7:6; 8:31-32; Philippians 3:2; 2 Peter 2:22; and Revelation 22:15.)

Though the earth became without form, void, and full of darkness, the Spirit of God never forsook the earth. He hovered over the surface of the waters, protecting the earth from evil forces and further damage to it. This is because the Spirit of God knows what is in the heart of God. He searches the deep things of God (1 Corinthians 2:10). He knew that God was not yet done with this earth, and that one day He would restore and renew it again. He would create another type of spirit being, and this time they would be created in His image and likeness and would rule and reign here once again. Praise God!

Part III: The Present Earth

Chapter 11: The Diluvian Age

The word *diluvian* means "pertaining to or caused by a flood." The Great King called for another meeting in heaven of His close associates and His one and only Son. His Son came with much anticipation of what His Father had to say concerning the planet Earth. He had been watching all that was happening on the earth very closely until that day. He felt sorry for what had happened to Lucifer and the other spirit beings. The King was not willing to back down from His original plan concerning the earth. He said, "My kingdom will be established on the earth forever, and all the earth shall be filled with My glory. So have I decided, and so shall it be done."

"I will restore its beauty and glory, and create another spirit being better than Lucifer and his fallen creatures. This being will be created in Our own image and likeness, and with Our own Spirit I will give them life. Because they have come from Me and My Spirit gives them life, they will be My sons." Much later in time, Moses had a revelation about this meeting and wrote this in Genesis 1

> Let Us make man in Our image, according to Our likeness (Genesis 1:26).

"They will not only worship me as Lucifer did, but their primary job will be to make sure my kingdom is established on the earth as it was in the beginning. They will execute my will on the earth as it is in heaven, and I will give them power and authority over all that is on the earth." The King's words pleased everyone. His Son knew there might be difficulties ahead, but looked forward to having other members in His family.

The Son knew in His innermost being that this family was going to cause Him great pain and that He would have to be involved with this whole thing very closely. He said to the Father, "Father, why take all this trouble? What if these creatures also rebel like the other one?" The Father replied, "I know, My Son. I have provided a Lamb that was slain before the foundation of the world." The Son said, "Father, whatever You do, I am here to do Your will; and whenever You need any help in doing anything on the earth, You can call Me, and I will go to any extent to do anything to help You with these new beings, even if I have to go to the earth and live among them and lay down My own life."

> Behold, I have come—in the volume of the book it is written of Me—to do Your will, O God (Hebrews 10:7).

The Re-creation of the Earth

The Hebrew word used for "was" in Genesis 1:2 is *hayah*, which means the earth *became* void and empty.[18] That means God did not create the original earth empty and void; nothing God creates is empty, void, shapeless, or chaotic. Something happened to it and it became like that; the surface of the earth was flooded and covered with water.

If you go to some places on the earth, you can actually see that the formation of the earth is like the formations we see under the ocean. There is a place called the Garden of the Gods Park, a registered natural landmark, in Colorado Springs, Colorado in the USA. It is an amazing place made of red rocks which look like they have been under water for thousands of years.

We do not know how long the earth remained flooded. I believe it was for millions of years. The pre-Adamic world was buried under water. Some of its fossils and remains have been discovered that are thought to be millions of years old. Also, the oil and precious metals that we dig from the ground are from the debris of the world that existed before Adam.

---

18. Brown, Driver, and Briggs, "Hayah - Old Testament Hebrew Lexicon - New American Standard," Bible Study Tools, accessed June 17, 2019, https://www.biblestudytools.com/lexicons/hebrew/nas/hayah.html.

THE DILUVIAN AGE

The Great King looked at the Genesis 1:2 earth, and said, "Let there be light." As we know, whatever He declared, manifested immediately. Why did he have to create light first? He created the sun, moon, and stars only on the fourth day. As we know, the earth was filled with darkness. The Hebrew word for darkness is *choshek,* meaning the dark; hence (literally) darkness; figuratively, misery, destruction, death, ignorance, sorrow, wickedness.[19] Note that this also can refer to ignorance.

God created light and Hebrew word used is *'owr,* which also has more than one meaning.

a) the light of day

b) the light of heavenly luminaries (the moon, the sun, the stars)

c) daybreak, dawn, the morning light

d) daylight

e) lightning

f) the light of a lamp

g) the light of life

h) the light of prosperity

i) the light of instruction

j) the light of one's face (figuratively)

k) Yahweh as Israel's Light[20]

In the New Testament we read that God commanded the light to appear out of darkness.

---
19. James Strong, "H#2822. חֹשֶׁךְ (choshek)," Biblehub.com, accessed June 10, 2019, https://www.biblehub.com/hebrew/2822.htm.

20. James Strong, " H#216: 'owr," Definitions- Bible Tools, accessed June 10, 2019, https://www.bibletools.org/index.cfm/fuseaction/Lexicon.show/ID/H216/owr.htm.

> For it is the God who commanded light to shine out of darkness, who has shone in our hearts to give the light of the knowledge of the glory of God in the face of Jesus Christ (2 Corinthians 4:6).

We also read phrases like: We are the light of the world. Let your light shine. Your light has come. This also refers to wisdom, glory, knowledge, or brightness. The first light God created was *out of* darkness and not from the sun, moon, or stars. They were created on the fourth day. The new earth and new heaven will be lit by the brightness of Jesus, and not by terrestrial stars; there won't be any night either (Revelation 22:5). God separated night and day, dark and light, wisdom and ignorance.

In six days God re-created the whole earth and made it a beautiful place. God looked at what He had made and said it was good. Whatever God makes or creates is good.

Chapter 12: The Creation and Fall of Man

Why did God create Adam or the human species? If He wanted a species of beings worshiping Him in heaven, why would He create man and put him on earth? To be honest, He had already created plenty of beings that worshiped Him day and night in heaven. The Bible gives us plenty of references about those beings and their worship. Let's find out the real reason we were created.

God restored the earth once again and brought order to it. He put everything His people would ever need in the earth. All the treasure (precious stones and wealth) that were once handled by Lucifer and his kingdom were left on this earth. Instead of making the whole earth beautiful again as it was in the beginning, He made just one special spot (the garden of Eden) and put this new spirit being in that spot. Everything this being ever needed was included in the garden. Eden represented His kingdom on the earth and now it was this creature's job to replicate that spot throughout the earth and make the whole earth as beautiful as it was supposed to be, thus establishing the King's domain over all the earth once again.

The Bible says God created man in His own image and likeness. I am not going to take much time to explain the process of how God made man, since this is a book about the gospel of the kingdom. Please read my other volumes on the kingdom to learn more about man's purpose.

Man was created to represent the King on earth, so he was created in the same image and likeness of the King. The King knew there would be rebellion on earth in the future. He gave the man power to subdue and take dominion over any rebellion. He put all things under man's feet and crowned him with glory and honor. Mankind's job was to see the King's purpose done on the earth as it was in heaven. Satan did not like that idea. He wanted to take over the earth and bring chaos and disorder instead.

God created man to subdue and take dominion over the earth. He appointed man to rule the earth and cultivate and take care of it. God created a garden in the east called Eden and put the man in that garden. Everything man needed was provided for him by God. The garden of Eden was the most luxurious place on the earth.

He told man to take care of the garden and replenish the earth (Genesis 1:28 KJV). The word *replenish* means to "do it again." Whenever you see the prefix "re," it refers to doing something again, or repeating an action. That means the earth was "plenished" before, but was destroyed, so God told Adam to *re*plenish it.

Once again, the will of God was done on earth as it was in heaven. Earth and heaven were in perfect unity. There was no sickness, curse, death, poverty, or any evil on the earth. Everything was in plenty. There was perfect union between man and God. Every evening during the cool of the day, God came to the garden to commune with Adam and Eve. Adam and Eve did not have to worry about anything. Their food, accommodation, clothing, and whatever they needed was provided for them by God. They dwelt in the kingdom of God.

The Fall of Man

Satan noticed the new change that had taken place on the earth. The devil was not happy about the relationship God had with man. He got jealous and came up with a plan to break up that relationship. The only way he could do that was to get Adam and Eve to disobey God's commandment. Eve was deceived by the enemy and ate the fruit that she was not supposed to eat, and Adam ate with her.

The reason for the devil's jealousy was that this man whom God made, was made in God's own image and likeness. Satan felt like this man had taken his place and his kingdom. If he did not destroy them in the beginning,

THE CREATION AND FALL OF MAN

he could no longer exist. There was no possibility of peaceful coexistence between the devil and man.

He crafted a cunning plan to take over the earth. He knew he needed to regain his authority on the earth. To do that, he had to get it from this man, because the King had given the man all the authority, power, and dominion that he had once possessed (Psalm 8).

Satan and his demons could not enter into humans because the glory of God was protecting them. If the devil was to defeat the man, he had to make man willfully disobey God's Word first. The devil knew this very well, so he did not have a face-to-face confrontation with the man. Man could have easily defeated the devil. Instead, he disguised himself as the serpent to tempt and deceive the man to disobey God's Word. The devil did not defeat the man until man first disobeyed God's Word.

Satan's plot worked at that time, and he took legal authority over the earth from the man, and began to influence the sons and daughters of men to worship him instead of worshiping the Great King. He began to afflict human beings with all sorts of evil and drive them away from having any relationship with the Great King.

Once they disobeyed God, they lost the glory and dominion God had given them, and Satan and his demons legally received the authority to enter into humans. The nature and characteristics of demonic spirits manifest through that person when a spirit enters into a person. Those characteristics could include pride, rebellion, insubordination, sickness, perversion, disease, lust, and much more.

Through the help of the humans, the devil began to rebuild his kingdom here. Anyone who yields to the devil becomes his instrument in fulfilling his desire and intention, revealing his nature.

That is why the devil took Jesus to a high mountain and showed Him all the kingdoms and glory of the earth, telling Him that all of it had been delivered to him and he could give it to whomever he willed. Luke 4 says,

> Then the devil, taking Him up on a high mountain, showed Him all the kingdoms of the world in a moment of time. And the devil said to Him, "All this authority I will give You, and their glory; for this has been delivered to me, and I give it to whomever I wish. Therefore, if You will worship before me, all will be Yours" (Luke 4:5-7).

After man sinned, God came down and was walking in the garden. Meanwhile, man and woman were hiding in the garden from God. They committed sin against God and they could no longer stand in the presence of God. Fear, shame, and self-consciousness came upon them as the result of sin, and they lost the glory God had given them. God could no longer allow them to stay in the garden, which was His kingdom, and made them leave it. Mankind not only lost their relationship with God, but also the provision that went with that.

As we saw in the first chapter, sin affected seven levels of man's relationships. Now man was on his own and had to find things and work to meet his own needs. He was cast out of the kingdom of God and all the blessings that came with the kingdom were lost too. His food, shelter, glory, and all the material provision were lost with it.

Man lost the kingdom of God. He was put outside the garden of Eden, he lost almost everything God gave him. Now he had to trust in his own ability to provide and sustain his life. Sin entered the earth, and with sin came curses, sicknesses, poverty, and death. But God loved mankind so much that He was willing to give up His only Son to redeem them.

Since the fall of Adam, the kingdom of the Great King ceased to work directly on the earth, though He is its Owner. The devil became the ruler of the earth and the world systems. The King was not happy about it and He wanted His kingdom reestablished on the earth as it was in heaven. People began to multiply, and the enemy succeeded in influencing them to worship him instead of the King. However, the King also had His people who desired to accomplish His purposes until the time came for Him to reestablish His kingdom.

THE CREATION AND FALL OF MAN

Just like God used different individuals like Noah, Abraham, Moses, and others to accomplish His will, the devil also used some key individuals to accomplish his mission. Those names include Eve, Cain, Nimrod, Ishmael, Esau, and others.

At first, God chose to work through individuals like Seth, Enoch, and Noah. Then God chose Abraham, and through Abraham's children He established a nation called Israel. Israel did not remain faithful to God either, so God decided to create another nation made of whoever was willing and believing from every nation on earth.

This nation is called the church, or the *ekklesia* (1 Peter 2:9). As part of the church, it's our time to do the job God gave mankind to do in the first place, but the church has been hijacked by the religious spirit for a long time. They have been singing to escape from the planet where God put them to fulfill His will. They are focused away from the very purpose and inheritance God gave them. God is getting tired of our singing and shouting without much substance to back it up.

By partnering with humans, Satan began to build his kingdom on the earth. He helped man make things that would lead him astray, away from the things God gave to man. His intention was that man would trust in those things and be happy, and never have to depend on, or look for, God again. God, in His mercy, did not leave us in that state forever. He made a plan to restore His kingdom to us. We cannot enter His kingdom as sinners. We have to get rid of our sin before we can enter His kingdom.

God spoke the first prophetic word in Genesis 3:15. Because the devil deceived the woman first, He said the Seed of woman would one day crush the head of the serpent that deceived Eve. Since then, there have been many other prophetic words concerning the Seed of the woman, the Messiah that would come to crush the head of Satan and dethrone him from being a god of this world. Every prophet since Adam prophesied about the coming of Jesus Christ, who would restore the kingdom to mankind.

Before we explore the restoration process, I would like to give you a behind-the-scenes look at what is happening in the spirit world, and how Satan used humans to build his kingdom here.

Part IV: Kingdom of Darkness

Chapter 13: Origin of the Present World—Kingdom of Darkness

Have you expressed your frustration about how things are going in this world lately? At least once in our lives, each one of us has seen something happening and wished it were different or could be changed.

As we have seen earlier, it was always God's plan that man dwell in His kingdom here. When God created Adam, He put him in the garden of Eden, which was a visible form of the kingdom of God operating on the earth. Everything that pertains to the kingdom of God could be found in Eden.

There was a kingdom economy, agriculture, education, and family, as well as a kingdom culture and everything you can imagine. Man's duty was to expand that and fill the entire earth. That was the true world system that was created by Jesus Christ that we read about in John 1:10. Though the Father created everything, the Son was the One who brought everything into existence. All things were created and made through Him.

Man had everything he needed in the garden. He never lacked anything, and never became sick or poor. It was a place of plenty, peace, and joy. God's presence dwelt in the garden; He came down to commune with man every evening. We are created to live in communion with God. Only the joy that comes from His presence can satisfy our longings.

God needs man to establish His kingdom here. The devil also needs the help of man to establish his own kingdom on the earth. Originally, man was in God's kingdom, so the devil had to get man out of God's kingdom first so he could use him for his purpose. These two kingdoms cannot exist together at the same time and at the same place physically.

Man disobeyed God and sinned. As the result of disobedience and sin, man was removed from God's kingdom and began to live on his own. The enemy used that opportunity, and with man's cooperation, created a counterfeit of God's kingdom, which is called the current world system, or the kingdom of darkness. That is why Satan is known as the ruler and the god of this world. (See John 14:30 and 2 Corinthians 4:4.) Sometimes the Bible uses the word *world* as a synonym for the kingdom of darkness. The enemy is always striving to make counterfeits or copies of what God actually creates.

Jesus said there were two kingdoms operating on the earth.

> Jesus answered, "*My kingdom* is not of this world. If My kingdom were of this world, My servants would fight, so that I should not be delivered to the Jews; but now My kingdom is not from here" (John 18:36).

> "If Satan casts out Satan, he is divided against himself. How then will *his kingdom* stand?" (Matthew 12:26).

Jesus calls Satan the ruler of this world.

> Of judgment, because *the ruler of this world* is judged (John 16:11).

Satan said all the kingdoms of the world and their glory had been delivered to him.

> Then the devil took him up and revealed to him all the *kingdoms of the world* in a moment of time. "I will give you the glory of these kingdoms and authority over them," the devil said, "because they are mine to give to anyone I please" (Luke 4:5-6 NLT).

ORIGIN OF THE PRESENT WORLD—KINGDOM OF DARKNESS

In the following pages, I am going to explain how this present world system was formed. This system works directly opposite to the kingdom of God. When I use the word *world* I am talking about the system the devil created to deceive us as a substitute for everything God gave man in His kingdom. The Bible also uses the word *world* to represent this present age.

The Bible talks about two different worlds:

> For *God so loved the world* that He gave His only begotten Son, that whoever believes in Him should not perish but have everlasting life (John 3:16).
>
> *Do not love the world* or the things in the world. If anyone loves the world, the love of the Father is not in him (1 John 2:15).
>
> For Demas has forsaken me, having *loved this present world*, and has departed for Thessalonica (2 Timothy 4:10).
>
> By which *the world* that then existed *perished*, being flooded with water (2 Peter 3:6).

The above scripture talks about the destruction of the world during Noah's time. The world perished through the flood, but the earth did not.

Jesus said this of His disciples in John 17

> As You sent Me into the world, I also have sent them into the world (John 17:18).

The God of This World

The Bible talks about Satan as the god of this world.

> In whom the *god of this world* hath blinded the minds of them which believe not, lest the light of the glorious gospel of Christ, who is the image of God, should shine unto them (2 Corinthians 4:4 KJV).

Jesus calls him the ruler of this world.

John 16:11 says, "Of judgment, because the *ruler of this world* is judged." He is known as the prince of the power of the air.

> In which you once walked according to the course of this world, according to *the prince of the power of the air,* the spirit who now works in the sons of disobedience (Ephesians 2:2).

He is also known as the prince of this world.

> Now is the judgment of this world: now shall *the prince of this world* be cast out (John 12:31 KJV).

> Hereafter I will not talk much with you: for *the prince of this world* cometh, and hath nothing in me (John 14:30 KJV).

Jesus said in Matthew that Satan has a kingdom.

> If Satan casts out Satan, he is divided against himself. How then will *his kingdom* stand? (Matthew 12:26).

> The *whole world* around us is under the control of the evil one (1 John 5:19 NLT).

The world we see today will end.

> *And the world is passing away,* and the lust of it; but he who does the will of God abides forever (1 John 2:17).

> Teaching them to observe all things whatsoever I have commanded you: and, lo, I am with you always, even unto the *end of the world.* Amen (Matthew 28:20 KJV).

The Bible talks about two groups of people: the children of God and the children of the world.

> For the sons of this world are more shrewd in their generation than the sons of light (Luke 16:8).
>
> If the world hates you, you know that it hated Me before *it hated* you. If you were of the world, the world would love its own. Yet because you are not of the world, but I chose you out of the world, therefore the world hates you (John 15:18-19).
>
> You are of God, little children, and have overcome them, because He who is in you is greater than he who is in the world. They are of the world. Therefore they speak as of the world, and the world hears them. We are of God. He who knows God hears us; he who is not of God does not hear us. By this we know the spirit of truth and the spirit of error (1 John 4:4-6).

These verses show how the whole world is under the influence of the devil. Some people (nice Christians) think the devil is busy only in societies where there is idol worship, voodoo, and practicing witches. The devil has deceived them. He does not use the same tactics in the society they are living in that he uses elsewhere. He uses different names depending on which part of the world we live in, and different tools that appeal to our culture and flesh, so that people will not recognize the true force behind what they are being influenced by and attracted to. We will discuss this further, later.

We do not see either Adam or Eve asking God to forgive them. They never did. Instead, they blamed each other and everything else and hid their sin (Job 31:33). That's why God had to send them out of the garden. They disqualified themselves from living in His kingdom.

How Satan Used Humans to Establish a Counterfeit Kingdom

How did Satan become the god and ruler of this world, and earn the titles of prince of this world and prince of the power of the air? How did he gain influence over the whole world? What and where is his kingdom located, and how does it operate? We know that he took the earth from Adam, but how does he operate his kingdom today and how does it affect us? How does he manage to deceive people by making them believe that he doesn't exist? We will be exploring the answers to all these questions and more.

Some believe that Satan's kingdom is located somewhere in the heavenly realm or in hell, so they always *look up* or *down* to fight with the devil. But if his kingdom were located in the heavenly places, he would have been called the god of heaven, or prince of heaven, but he was not. He is called *the ruler and god of this world* and the *prince of the power of the air.*

The headquarters of his kingdom is located in the heavenly places, also called the second heaven, but his kingdom is vibrant and operating on your doorstep, sometimes even in your home and in your living room. I will explain that in detail. We are living in this world, and the devil is called the ruler of this world, and not the ruler of heaven.

Satan's desire was to be like God. He wanted to be worshiped and be the king like God Almighty. He still wants that. Unfortunately, he cannot create anything new. He can only distort and copy what God has already made and done. He does not want us to live in the garden (kingdom), enjoying the blessings and the presence of God. He wants to use us to create a counterfeit kingdom here and enthrone himself as the king and god of it. He wants people to worship and serve him instead of God and His kingdom. As in the beginning, the devil will not put his original name on any of it; instead he has made himself so many aliases that people do not recognize who is behind the evil that takes place on the earth. *The biggest deception the enemy has ever come up with is to convince people that he does not exist.*

Satan will only reveal himself toward the end. Once he deceives a person, and that person has reached a point of no return, then he will reveal his true nature. That is why there are open satanic churches established in many countries already.

The initial thing to do was to deceive us. After that, his plan was to defeat us and steal the stewardship of the earth from us. So he came to Eve in the

ORIGIN OF THE PRESENT WORLD—KINGDOM OF DARKNESS

form of a serpent; he deceived her and influenced her to disobey God. Man fell for the trap and was deprived of everything God had given him.

After that, man was left alone outside the garden with no food, no shelter, no peace, and no one to fellowship with like God. God loved them but he could not fellowship with them as He did before because of sin. Instead of asking God to help him, man fell deeper into the hands of the enemy. The enemy used that as an opportunity to establish his kingdom on the earth. He slowly began to introduce the things he had learned from God; the enemy had firsthand knowledge of how God's kingdom worked. The only difference between this one and the other was that the devil's version was only a substitute of what God had for man originally.

God told man to increase and multiply and replenish the earth. Once Adam came out of the garden, he did not do what he was supposed to do. Instead, the devil—with the help of man—created a counterfeit kingdom (or the world). After Adam and Eve were outside the garden (the kingdom of God), they had two sons named Cain and Abel. Cain was a farmer and Abel was a shepherd.

The Bible says Cain was from Satan.

> Not as Cain who was of the wicked one and murdered his brother. And why did he murder him? Because his works were evil and his brother's righteous (1 John 3:12).

The Living Bible puts it this way:

> We are not to be like Cain, who belonged to Satan and killed his brother. Why did he kill him? Because Cain had been doing wrong and he knew very well that his brother's life was better than his (1 John 3:12 TLB).

How did Cain come from the devil? There are all kinds of speculations and theories about this. The simple truth is that it happened in the same way it still occurs today. How do people become wicked in the world today? *The spiritual influence parents are under when they conceive a child determines the seed they will produce.* This also has to do with spiritual allegiance. If a person committed his soul to Satan, then the seed that person produces will be called the seed of the wicked. This can happen to any parent—both Christian or non-Christian alike. Just because you go to church doesn't mean you belong to God or serve Him. There are two kinds of seeds on the earth today: the seed of the righteous and the seed of the wicked.

In the course of time, these two sons brought sacrifices to God. God was pleased with Abel's and rejected Cain's sacrifice, which caused hatred and anger in Cain's heart toward his brother. One day Cain invited Abel to the field and killed him. That was the first murder that took place on the earth. It displeased God and He pronounced a curse on Cain. Cain was a farmer, but now God said the earth would not yield its strength anymore to him because of his sin, and he could not be a farmer any longer.

> So now you are cursed from the earth, which has opened its mouth to receive your brother's blood from your hand. When you till the ground, it shall no longer yield its strength to you. A fugitive and a vagabond you shall be on the earth (Genesis 4:11-12).

Cain was not willing to repent either because of his anger. He could not cultivate anything. He was estranged from the favor of God, so he began to wander around on this earth. He went out of the presence of the Lord and fled to a place called Nod, and there he built a city. It was the first city ever built by men on earth, and Cain named it after his son, Enoch. Once you are outside the favor of God, you are under the influence of the evil one. This means the devil took hold of Cain's fallen nature and began to use him to accomplish his purpose, using Cain and his sons. Since he could not receive any help from God, guess who came to offer him the help he needed? The devil did.

If the devil has to rule the earth through humankind, he has to occupy the key places of this earth and key positions in this world system. He had to come up with ideas and things which man would need the most to live here, so that people would depend on him, and not seek God again. Once people are dependent on the enemy, men and their children will not feel bad about using the devil's system and the things he provides for them, because without that stuff, human life will be difficult on this earth.

We are going to see how the devil used Cain and his children to establish a kingdom here now, called the world system.

> Then Cain went out from the presence of the Lord and dwelt in the land of Nod on the east of Eden. And Cain knew his wife, and she conceived and bore Enoch. And he built a city, and called the name of the city after the name of his son—Enoch (Genesis 4:16-17).

It was Cain who built the first city. Why a city, and not a village or a garden? Because the devil knew that cities controlled everything that happened in a country. Cities were the thriving centers of commerce in a region. To build something that never existed before, you need creativity and craftsmanship. How could a person cursed by God build something that had never existed before? The force that was working behind Cain's creativity was evil. No wonder the cities of this world are controlled by the spirit of Cain, filled with anger, hatred, murder, greed, and jealousy. These spirits were used to form the first demonic culture on earth.

The enemy brought a counterfeit economy, agriculture, educational system, culture, government, and everything else God's kingdom had. The only thing is that *they are not real*. He made a counterfeit world system and began to rule mankind and the earth through it. Let's go deeper and see how exactly the enemy did that.

The Spirit of Cain

Unfortunately, we see this spirit working in some believers. What are the spirits of Cain? The spirit of Cain is actually the spirit of this world. Through Cain, the following spirits and their fruit entered the earth and began to work in and through humankind: selfishness, ambition, murder, hatred, wrath, greed, jealousy, envy, self-centeredness, independence, self-seeking, self-prominence, arrogance, rude behaviors, pride, a devotion to pleasure, cheating, manipulation, stubbornness, unrepentant, wandering, poverty, barrenness, insecurity, fear, and discord within families.

All these evil spirits were working in Cain when he murdered his innocent brother. Whatever spirits started operating on earth from the time of Cain are still working here now. In fact, Cain is known as the "forgotten father" of the world in many of the secret cults and special orders in the world. If you do any research on the spirit of Cain, you will find some bizarre things. Many of those who worship Satan also worship Cain as their father.

Nod was in the east of Eden. Why did he choose the east and not any other direction? There is a spiritual connection to this too. If you study any heathen worship or even some churches, you will find that many worship while looking toward the east. Greek Orthodox, Catholic, and Eastern churches all look toward the east while they do their rituals. Now you know whom they worship. In India, the Hindus worship by looking toward the east. They are worshiping the sun god.

> So He brought me into the inner court of the Lord's house; and there, at the door of the temple of the Lord, between the porch and the altar, *were* about twenty-five men with their backs toward the temple of the Lord and their faces toward the east, and they were worshiping the sun toward the east (Ezekiel 8:16).

Cain found a wife (probably one of his sisters) and began to have children. Together they began to expand and explore to create a world without God and leave their mark on history. In Genesis 4, we find the genealogy of Cain and his children, and read about how they began to develop different businesses and technologies.

The Way of Cain

> Woe to them! For they have gone in *the way of Cain*, have run greedily in the error of Balaam for profit, and perished in the rebellion of Korah (Jude 11).

ORIGIN OF THE PRESENT WORLD—KINGDOM OF DARKNESS

From the beginning there were two paths available, two choices for mankind. The Tree of Life and the Tree of the Knowledge of Good and Evil: the way of life and the way of death—the way of blessing and the way of curse. The Bible says Cain chose a way that was not righteous and did not lead to life. The way of Cain is opposite to the way of life; those who follow his way run away from the presence of God, just as he did. He wanted to make a name for himself, and that was his number one goal. He did not care about his brother or anyone else. He built a city and named it after his son. Below are some manifestations of the way of Cain.

The Cain spirit's mission is to kill anointing and destinies. It is motivated by greed and its goal is to make a profit. Abel had a destiny, but Cain took his life and did not care about his brother. You need to overcome this spirit if you are going to fulfill your purpose on earth. Cain had no regard for God or men. He opposed anything that was godly. He sold himself to do wickedness to the point of no return. His sole intention was to make a name for himself. Those who walk in his way exhibit these characteristics too.

> And Adah bore Jabal. He was *the father* of those who dwell in tents and have livestock (Genesis 4:20).

Cain's grandson was the father of real estate and farming. They built the first house (tent). Again, we see the devil using these peoples' minds, making things so that God's children will depend on them instead of God.

> His brother's name was Jubal. He was *the father* of all those who play the harp and flute (Genesis 4:21).

They were the first ones to use and play music instruments, which are a major facet of the media and entertainment world.

> And as for Zillah, she also bore Tubal-Cain, *an instructor* of every craftsman in bronze and iron. And the sister of Tubal-Cain was Naamah (Genesis 4:22).

Tubal-Cain started the first technical school (an expression of the *chokmah* wisdom, which refers to creating things out of the imagination), for it says Tubal-Cain was an instructor of *every craftsman* using different metals. They began to use their imagination and come up with ideas and products that helped human life on earth.

It is interesting to note that the Bible uses the word *father* when it refers to these people and what they did. The word *father* means "source" or "sustainer," or refers to someone who initiates and sets up something in motion. Historically, we name particular people as the father of nations, father of medicine, father of impressionism (art), and many more. All these abilities were in the devil when God made him: creativity, business, music, and so on. Thus the devil began to unfold his age-old plan of ruling the earth through Cain and his descendants once again.

Cain's Stuff

Did you know that most of our time is spent on Cain's stuff? What is Cain's stuff? *Anything this world produces is Cain's stuff.* Most of our money is spent on buying or managing Cain's stuff. He is the father of this world system. Many think that having the best of everything this world has to offer is kingdom prosperity. That is far from the truth. What if those things the world considers best are actually vile before God?

> Now the Pharisees, who were lovers of money, also heard all these things, and they derided Him. And He said to them, "You are those who justify yourselves before men, but God knows your hearts. *For what is highly esteemed among men is an abomination in the sight of God*" (Luke 16:14-15).

Jesus said the life of man does not consist in the abundance of the things he possesses (Luke 12:15). That is another great lie the devil has used to deceive the church. They misunderstood abundant "life" with abundant "stuff."

Jesus said this about life:

ORIGIN OF THE PRESENT WORLD—KINGDOM OF DARKNESS

> I have come that they may have life, and that they may have it more abundantly (John 10:10).

He came to give us life, but many have interpreted that as goods. Neither Jesus nor the apostles had an abundance of goods. They never promoted the accumulation of goods. Their teaching was that we should be content if we had enough to eat and clothing to wear (1 Timothy 6:7-8).

Every one of them had abundant life. So what is life? In John 1:4, we read that in Him (Jesus) was life and the life was the light of men. If we want to know what life looks like, then we need to look at Jesus and how He lived. He was full of life. Though He did not own a mansion, He never lacked anything. When we discover the kingdom of God, we discover true life. Jesus is the door to that kingdom (John 10:9).

Do you realize that most of our time is spent working to get and maintain Cain's stuff? The majority of the money we make, we give back to the world so we can use their products and services. Most of the believers I have met across the globe are financially broke or in survival mode. Why? Because we give ten percent to God and the remaining ninety percent is given to make the people in the world rich. We are indirectly building the kingdom of darkness.

The children of the wicked began to excel in technology, the arts, agriculture, and music. This was the first known *world* or the *kingdom of darkness*. Meanwhile the children of God (the righteous) were waiting for God to send the Seed of the woman to crush the head of the serpent. All they did was to eat, sleep, and have children. They did not use the creativity and imagination God gave them to produce anything. They became *consumers* of all that Cain and his children *produced*. How did that happen, and where did that come from? It came from the corrupted *chokmah* wisdom and *mimshach* anointing of the devil.

If we are going to influence the world and its systems for Christ, we need to understand more about this anointing. Without that understanding, your influence will not grow outside the four walls of your own home. You will feel like you are stuck — with an invisible boundary around you which you cannot break through. This pattern will prevent you from being able to grow your life and dreams.

This is how the world we see today began. The devil took the opportunity and went with it, while Seth and his descendants waited around for God to show up. Music and technology does not come from the devil. God created music to praise Him; but the devil, who likes to be worshiped as god, stole what God created. As His church, we need to take back what was stolen from us. Part of my calling is to heal that which was made crooked, build that which was demolished, and take back that which was stolen.

After the death of Abel, God gave Adam and Eve another righteous seed. His name was Seth. In Genesis 5, we read the genealogy of Adam and his son Seth, but we do not read about anyone doing anything innovative or creative. They ate, slept, and gave birth to more children. That is all that is mentioned there. For hundreds and hundreds of years, that is all they did. When they needed to buy a tent or livestock, they went to Jabal and his children. When they needed to hear some music or buy musical instruments, they went to Jubal. When they needed to buy a tool or equipment made with metal, they went to Tubal-Cain.

Does that sound familiar to you? To whom do we go to purchase something? Seth and his children were waiting and hoping the Lord would do something (or everything) for them. Even today I see most believers and preachers running around telling people about an upcoming revival. They have been waiting for this coming revival for hundreds of years. They don't teach people about how to use what God has given them. They do not teach them what salvation is all about. They don't teach them about what happened to the cities and churches where revival took place in the recent history. They would rather roll on the floor and bark like a dog while the devil steals their children and their very inheritance.

There is nothing wrong with waiting and hoping the Lord will do something when it is the right time to do it, but remember that God created man to work and have dominion here. They totally ignored that. While we are spending time practicing our new song for the next Sunday service, the devil and his children are busy inventing new things, so that you and I will emerge from our music practice and spend money on all the amazing stuff produced by the children of Cain.

In America, chain restaurants are tremendously busy throughout the week, but especially on Sunday afternoons when many Christians eat out after Sunday services. Most of these establishments belong to the children of Cain, so we put in our time with God and then go give our money to the devil. What has any of this to do with accomplishing our purpose?

Seth and his children began to depend on Cain and his children for houses, livestock, music (entertainment), and technology. Who do we depend on for most of the products we use? Whose shops do we frequent when we need something? Who produces what we buy? Who consumes the most? Most producers are heathens, and most consumers are Christians.

Who does the children of the devil exploit the most to fill their pockets with money and fill the earth with the multitude of their violence and iniquity? The church! The church is the most consuming agency on this earth. In truth, as a whole, we do not produce much. This has to change and it will change, but *it will only change if the church receives and practices the gospel of the kingdom.*

Do you realize that the majority of the money you make through your hard work goes directly into the pockets of Cain's children? The clothes you wear, the mortgage you pay monthly, the phone and utility bills you pay: almost everything you buy and use at home has been made by the children of the devil. And the profit goes to build and expand his kingdom on earth. Why can't we come up with ideas, businesses, and products that help human life here too? God used the Jewish nation to bless the earth, and we will study that shortly, but right now, let's focus on the church.

Who are the most successful businessmen in your country? Who are the best musicians in your country? It is the same in every country on earth. Meanwhile the church waits around for God to do things for them as they watch their favorite TV programs or run to a football game after church. They are going to see the children of the devil making millions of dollars while they sit in their easy chairs, sipping soda, and shouting for their team. And so the children of the devil continue to excel in their works.

The Bible says that men began to multiply and their wickedness increased. God found only one family righteous out of all the people who were alive at that time. The devil and his kingdom were flourishing. The devil had filled the earth with violence once again.

They built cities and towns and named them. It grieved God and He decided to destroy the world and its inhabitants with another flood. The flood came, and Noah and his family were the only ones rescued. The Bible particularly says that only Noah found grace in the sight of the Lord, not all of his family or his three sons (Genesis 6:8). The flood destroyed the people and all living creatures except the ones in the ark, but as you and I know, a flood cannot kill demonic forces and spirits.

Once again, God wiped out the kingdom of darkness from the earth as He had before. The demonic forces waited for another opportunity to enter into humans and manifest their works and begin building Satan's kingdom again.

The demonic forces never gave up. They just bided their time, looking for an opportunity to enter into humans and establish the kingdom of darkness once again. Right after the flood, Noah planted a vineyard and drank of the wine and became drunk. He lost his senses and lay naked in his tent. The devil influenced one of Noah's sons, Ham, to go in and look at the nakedness of his father; afterward, he told his brothers outside (Genesis 9:20-23).

When Noah woke up from his drunkenness and realized what Ham had done to him, Noah spoke a curse over Ham. The first time we read of anyone being cursed, it was Cain. That gave the devil an open door to work through Cain. After the flood, the first person who was cursed was Ham, and the devil began to work through him as well—to create a world without God. (To be cursed means to be cut off from God's favor and presence). Through this, the kingdom of darkness began to operate on this earth again.

ORIGIN OF THE PRESENT WORLD—KINGDOM OF DARKNESS

We see the same pattern we saw before the flood. The sons of Ham began to multiply and expand on the earth in culture, government, technology, and other areas. The Bible says in Genesis 10:

> The sons of Ham were Cush, Mizraim, Put, and Canaan. The sons of Cush were Seba, Havilah, Sabtah, Raamah, and Sabtechah; and the sons of Raamah were Sheba and Dedan. Cush begot Nimrod; he began to be a mighty one on the earth. *He was a mighty hunter before the Lord; therefore it is said, "Like Nimrod the mighty hunter before the Lord." And the beginning of his kingdom was Babel,* Erech, Accad, and Calneh, in the land of Shinar. From that land he went to Assyria and built Nineveh, Rehoboth Ir, Calah, and Resen between Nineveh and Calah (that is the principal city). Mizraim begot Ludim, Anamim, Lehabim, Naphtuhim, Pathrusim, and Casluhim (from whom came the Philistines and Caphtorim). Canaan begot Sidon his firstborn, and Heth; the Jebusite, the Amorite, and the Girgashite; the Hivite, the Arkite, and the Sinite; the Arvadite, the Zemarite, and the Hamathite. Afterward the families of the Canaanites were dispersed. And the border of the Canaanites was from Sidon as you go toward Gerar, as far as Gaza; then as you go toward Sodom, Gomorrah, Admah, and Zeboiim, as far as Lasha. These were the sons of Ham, according to their families, according to their languages, in their lands and in their nations (Genesis 10:6-20).

One of Ham's grandsons was Cush, who had a son named Nimrod. He was the first king and built the first kingdom, which was called Babel. Out of Babel emerged the great empire Babylon, which is the mother of this modern world. Remember, Cain was the father of this world's system. The heavenly Jerusalem is our mother (Galatians 4:26). We will learn more about this later. The Bible says Nimrod was a mighty hunter before the

Lord. The word *mighty* in Hebrew is *gibbor,* and it means "a tyrant."[21] According to some commentators, the name *Nimrod* in Hebrew means "rebellion."[22]

> Cush begot Nimrod; he began to be a mighty one on the earth. He was a mighty hunter before the Lord; therefore it is said, "Like Nimrod the mighty hunter before the Lord." And the beginning of his kingdom was Babel, Erech, Accad, and Calneh, in the land of Shinar (Genesis 10:8-10).

Through Nimrod, the devil established his system once again. Nimrod was a mighty hunter. He was the first person whom people began to worship as a god. Through him, the enemy introduced the religious system and idol worship we still see today. He also established Babel, the first human kingdom under the rulership of the devil.

Personality or hero worship began with Nimrod, because he introduced idol worship. He demanded that his followers treat him like a god. This pattern continued in many kings throughout history who demanded that their people worship them.

How did all that come about? It says in Genesis 11,

> Now the whole earth had one language and one speech. And it came to pass, as they journeyed from the *east,* that they found a plain in the land of Shinar, and they dwelt there. Then they said to one another, "Come, let us make bricks and bake them thoroughly." They had brick for stone, and they had asphalt for mortar. And they said, *"Come, let us build ourselves a city, and a tower whose top is in the heavens; let us make a name for ourselves, lest we be scattered abroad over the face of the whole earth"* (Genesis 11:1-4).

---

21. James Strong, "1368. Gibbor גִּבּוֹר," Biblehub.com, accessed June 16, 2019, https://biblehub.com/hebrew/1368.htm.

22. M. G. Easton, M. A., D. D., "Nimrod Definition and Meaning - Bible Dictionary," Bible Study Tools, accessed June 16, 2019, https://www.biblestudytools.com/dictionary/nimrod/.

ORIGIN OF THE PRESENT WORLD—KINGDOM OF DARKNESS

We see the same pattern again: they want to build a city and make a name for themselves. This same spirit is very active in churches today as well. Leaders want to build huge churches and make a name for themselves. This is not an example of godly ambition, but of man's. We need to discern the source of our motivation. There are preachers who tried to build cities after their names, but did not succeed. Jesus did not call us to build cities and monuments named for us. He wants us to go to the whole world and preach the gospel of the kingdom instead.

Instead of the garden, the devil instigated man to build a tower to dwell in, the tower of Babel. God came down and confused their language to disperse them. Because of that confusion, multiple languages blossomed. Before that there was only one language. God gave believers one language: faith. Faith is the language of the kingdom of God.

All the Gentile nations and kingdoms came out of Ham and Japheth. Once again, which direction did they come from? They came from the *east*. God started His kingdom from the east in a place called Eden. The devil wants to duplicate whatever God does. Do you see the same pattern here? God came down and confused the people, multiplying their languages, and dispersed them throughout the earth. Once again, we see a repetition of what happened in the book of Genesis playing out in history.

Once again, we do not see Shem and his descendants doing much on the earth, except eating and making children. They did not obey the command of the Lord to subdue the earth and take dominion and multiply. They did not do the first part of the command at this time, only the latter. They multiplied.

This present world was formed by the enemy through the help of wicked men who had given themselves over to do his will. From then on, the world system evolved into a dominating force. Today, the same system is dominating man, instead of us dominating it and the earth like we are supposed to do. We are born into this upside-down system, so it feels normal, even though it is not. Many things that we feel are *normal* are things that God never intended.

Man is a slave to this world's system. The god of this world is spitting out his venom every way he can, and mankind is drinking it, oblivious to the fact that it is a deadly poison. Unfortunately, many Christians are lured away by the enemy, thinking that the world system is part of the kingdom of God. We were not created to become slaves to this evil and fallen world. Each believer in Christ needs to overcome this world if he or she wants to inherit the kingdom of God. We are supposed to overcome this world system through the kingdom of God.

Chapter 14: The Seven Mountains of this World

You might have heard of the teaching on the Seven Mountains. The current world system is made up of seven segments; the Bible calls them seven mountains in Revelation 17. They are culture, religion, government, educational system, economy, media and entertainment, and science and technology. Keep in mind that each of these that we see in the world system is a *substitute* for what God gave us in the garden or what He has in His kingdom.

The devil's agenda is to infiltrate and occupy the key positions in these seven segments of influence, and operate his kingdom to control the human race. I have written extensively about them in the *Power and Authority of the Church*. I highly recommend you read that book after this one, so you can gain a good understanding of each.

Each of those seven areas is ruled by a principality. The apostolic ministry needs to destroy the stronghold of these principalities from the minds of people before they can establish God's kingdom in any region.

As citizens of the kingdom of God, we are not supposed to be ruled or dominated by any of them. As long as we keep them subject to the kingdom of God, we will be fine. We need to make sure we are not blinded or controlled from experiencing the true life in the kingdom of God. Let's take a look at each one.

If you take the city or town where you live, you can divide it into these seven areas. Each of these is ruled by a principality. It is interesting to note that each continent, nation, city, and individual is influenced by one or more of these major principalities. In turn, these areas use one of the above to rule the people of that region. Each of these segments is a substitute for what God had given man initially in the garden. Their purpose is to blind men from seeing the glorious gospel of Jesus Christ.

For example, in the Far East, culture and religion are the major strongholds the devil uses to keep people in bondage and blinded to the gospel. For them the gospel is another religion, and Jesus is just another god. When they become a Christian, dos and don'ts are more important to them than their relationship with God because they have been trained to follow those. Following or performing rituals, wearing special clothing, and focusing on how they look are very important in their culture. If they do not destroy their religious strongholds, they attach the gospel to their existing (and ancient) mindset, and it becomes another religion in time.

In the Middle East, the controlling principality *is* religion. People are blinded by the spirit of religion, and they cannot see outside of it. If you say anything against their religion, they will kill you. If you want to get killed in Asia or the Middle East, just say something against religion or speak against one of the gods or the culture. You will go to heaven very quickly.

In Europe, the ruling principality is government. Kings, queens, and empires played major roles in shaping the history of Europe. Even today, the European Union is the new form of government that controls these nations. If you speak against a king or a queen, you will face some serious repercussions in Europe. Next to the government comes education, economy, and entertainment.

The Renaissance and Reformation periods in Europe were based on knowledge and personal enlightenment that resulted in philosophies and the establishment of now-famous universities. Eventually, the fruit of this was individualism (if it feels right, do it) and humanism (the worship of man in the place of God) which slowly became the foundation of Western civilization.

In these Western countries, the principalities that work are different. In these societies, they use the name of Jesus as a curse word and nobody cares about that. However, if you speak ill of their favorite sports team, pet, movie star, music group, singer, or TV program, you will get quite the reaction. People's faces will turn red over that, but if you speak against Jesus, their Lord, they do not care. Their TV programs, sports teams, and money are like the gods in the West. These are all different types of gods and idols. The Bible calls them *strange* gods; in the East they worship *false* gods.

A westerner will look at all the idols in the east and think it is horrible that people worship these things. An easterner will be appalled at the way a westerner idolizes a sport, star, music, pet or TV program. The principalities and powers that work in Western civilization are not the same as those of the East. It is like one blind man making fun of another blind man for being blind.

In America, people are controlled by the principality that rules the economy. The next would be entertainment, then government, and then science and technology. If the church is not entertaining, no one will go. If something is not fun, then people will not do it. Everything has to be *fun*. If school and church are not fun, then children do not want to go there. Whatever we do, we say it was fun. Whenever we begin a conversation, we often ask others if they had fun.

In the East, that is opposite. If you make your church a fun place, no one will come. Everything in the East will have a religious flavor. They are coming to church to *be religious*. That's the whole point there! If you make it more religious, the people will throng outside to get in. In the West, it is a little different. Whatever they do will have an economic and entertainment flavor instead.

Do you see how the enemy has used these tactics to keep people away from having the need for God? He wants to pacify that longing in us and make people callous about the things of God. If you tell an Asian to stop their religious rituals, they will oppose you. Everything they do while they are awake is oriented around doing something religious; from the time they rise to the time they go to bed at night, everything is religious. Their business, family life, travel, schools; everything is bathed in this religious bondage.

In India, religion and culture are like Siamese twins. You cannot separate one from the other. On the other hand, in the Western world, business, schools, churches and family are bathed in the economy and entertainment. In America, the economy comes first, then entertainment, then government, and then science and technology.

In Asia, it is culture, religion, education, government, and then economy, in that order.

If you study the history of some nations in Africa, you will find many instances in which kings or dictators rose in the government and killed their own people. The devil used them to commit genocide, butchering people like animals and tearing down the very foundations of their society repeatedly. This is still happening there today, and is the result of demonic principalities working through their government and religion.

The Fruit of the World Systems

You can see the predominant principality the enemy uses to rule any nation by its fruit. That area is the enemy that must be conquered to bring God's kingdom there. The church needs to war against those particular principalities if they want to see breakthrough in each nation.

In the West, when people read the Bible, they look for scriptures that bless and reassure them, give them more money, and promise fun. In the East, when people read the Bible, they look for ways to make them look more religious. They look for lists of dos and don'ts. They want to add another ritual to their list. The more religious it looks and feels, the more they feel satisfied and spiritual.

My God, we need to rip these things from their foundations if people are to be free to worship God and become everything God intended them to be! Whenever we look at life, or at any person or situation, we see it through the crooked lens implanted in us by the principalities that rule over our region (on top of our fallen human nature)! If those living in the West find that something is more fun than what they already have, or will make them more independent and free, they will want to do it. Those in the East or Middle East will be attracted to anything that looks like it will make them more religious than they already are.

Which is the most influential segment over your country or city? When you present the gospel to someone, he views God and the Bible through the perspective formed by his background. If the truth of the gospel needs to shine in his heart, he first must be freed from those fortresses that were formed in his mind by the principalities that control him or his nation.

God is tilting things around now: the westerners are becoming more religious and the easterners are being drawn more to entertainment and the economy. God will mix these things around in different nations and cultures so His kingdom will be established on this earth. It is coming. In fact, it is slowly happening right now as you are reading this book.

The Church Should Be Influencing World Systems

If you study the lives of people God used in the Bible (or in modern day), you will see that He used them to influence one or more of these areas of the world with the kingdom of God and its principles. Joseph was used by God to influence the government and economy of Egypt. He became the second most influential man in Egypt.

Abraham was used to birth a new culture and a nation, the Jewish nation. The power of God works through each of us in different ways to influence the world. God uses His people in two different ways. One is through the power of the Holy Spirit: healing sick bodies and doing signs and wonders, but there is a second way God uses His people that is ignored by the church today. That is to manifest His wisdom over the principalities and powers of darkness through influencing one of the seven segments through which the world operates.

What are we doing these days? In India there are ministries who claim to have five thousand and six thousand churches! How many of these churches are really influencing their communities or culture? They have two to five people gather in a hut somewhere in a village, and call that a church. Spiritually speaking, that is a church, because when two or more believers gather together, that forms a church. What is the purpose of the church? Does that kind of church fulfill God's purpose?

One of the purposes of the church is to make known the manifold wisdom of God to the principalities and powers (Ephesians 3:10). We need to demonstrate the wisdom of God in these seven segments of the world system. Believers throughout the world are running after the *power* of God. It is time for the church to show forth the *wisdom* of God.

The church is supposed to be training believers to live in the kingdom, and go out and influence the world with the wisdom of God. As I said before, Jesus did not start church so that a bunch of people would sing to Him for twenty minutes every Sunday morning. I was standing in a church during a song service and had a talk with the Lord about what we were doing. (There was no real worship going on because all the songs being sung were about the coming of the Lord or about "I, me, and mine"!) I asked the Lord what He got out of all of it. What would He miss if we did not do this? Sometimes I just sit down because it irritates me so much. Lord have mercy!

The first man who received the testimony of having the Spirit of God living in him was Joseph, and a heathen king declared that about him. How did a heathen king recognize that Joseph had the Spirit of God? Was it his mannerisms when he came into the court? Did Joseph say "praise the Lord" to the king? Was he wearing a white cloth? No, it was not the outward appearance that enabled the king to see this. It was the demonstration of the wisdom of God to save Egypt from a crisis that would have crippled and crumbled its glory forever. That is what we need these days too.

Many religious folk walk around saying "praise the Lord" and "glory to Jesus" all day long, when they are supposed to be working with their hands and showing the world their God through the products they make. Instead, these precious saints consume what the world produces all day long, and say their God is the Almighty. We need to show the world that our God is Almighty through our lives and actions. There are two groups of people: producers and consumers. To which group do you belong?

Is your church teaching the principalities and powers in your area the manifold wisdom of God? If not, that church is not functioning as God intended. Pastor David Cho started a church in South Korea that revolutionized the whole country with the kingdom of God. He was lying in bed, dying with TB, but the miraculous power of the gospel of Jesus Christ set him free and healed him from that sickness, Korean culture and religious bondage all at the same time. The wisdom of God entered into His heart. God used him to establish the largest church on earth, and hundreds of other churches came from it.

Thousands of businesses came out of the lives of the believers of that church, many of which are now known worldwide. Most of them were poor when they came to Christ. We need people and churches like that one in every nation—ones that do not simply attach the gospel to their culture and religion, but get totally delivered from it instead, and are immersed in the kingdom of God.

The Old Testament saints perished in the wilderness, not because God did not deliver them or they did not see the power of God. God totally set them free from Egypt, which represents the world and sin, and from the hold of Pharaoh, who represents the devil. We are not perishing today because God did not deliver us, but for this reason:

> He has delivered us from the power of darkness and conveyed us into the kingdom of the Son of His love, in whom we have redemption through His blood, the forgiveness of sins (Colossians 1:13-14).

God brought us into His kingdom. He redeemed us and forgave our sins. What are we waiting for? What else needs to happen? We need to *believe it.*

Believers need to not get attached to the things of this world. When we come into the kingdom of God, *we need to die to the things of the world* and be transformed by God's kingdom principles. The kingdom of God has its own operating system. It is not based on the things of this world.

It was not until God called Abraham and gave him a promise—that he would be a blessing to all the nations and families of the earth—that God began to influence these seven segments of society through His people. From Abraham onward, every person God used was supposed to influence one of these seven areas. David really influenced the music industry during his lifetime. He had four thousand people singing and playing instruments in the house of the Lord (1 Chronicles 23:5). Joseph was a prime minister of Egypt.

The church depends on the world for technology, methods, and expertise. That is not the way God intended. He wants His children in leadership positions. We borrow the world's technologies, methods, and tactics, and bring them into church to grow the church. Today there are church growth experts available. If you hire them, they will come and train the pastors and leaders, teaching them to follow particular techniques and tricks. If the leaders do as they are told for a certain time, these church growth gurus guarantee a certain increase in numbers in the church. Does this sound like a New Testament church or a club to you?

Everything the devil produces has to do with meeting the carnal needs of our flesh. His devices never meet the real needs we have for joy and peace. This is why some of the most successful business people and entertainment stars are also some of the most miserable people on earth. Many are on drugs, or addicted to sex or alcohol. The more successful they are, the further they go from anything called real life. Those who think they are entertaining you, do not follow their lifestyle—they are entertaining your senses at the expense of their own lives. The Bible says the joy of the Lord is our strength.

Everyone who is not born again is part of the kingdom of darkness or the world and Satan rules over them.

> We know that we are children of God and that the world around us is under the control of the evil one (1 John 5:19 NLT).

1 John 3 says:

> So don't be surprised, dear brothers and sisters, if the world hates you (1 John 3:13 NLT).

This world has a spirit of its own working in it.

> In which you once walked according to the course of this world, according to the prince of the power of the air, *the spirit* who now works in the sons of disobedience (Ephesians 2:2).
>
> Now we have received, not *the spirit of the world*, but the Spirit who is from God, that we might know the things that have been freely given to us by God (1 Corinthians 2:12).

What Must a Believer Do in This World?

Though we are in this world, we are not of this world. It is very important for us to know what we must do here. After all, we are here to *reach this world*. We cannot be part of this world and reach the world at the same time. We cannot leave this world and reach them either. We cannot look and act like the world to identify with them and reach them that way. None of that will work. First of all, we need to be separated from the world. We need to *come out* of it and be delivered from the spirit that is working in it before we can influence it.

> Do not be unequally yoked together with unbelievers. For what fellowship has righteousness with lawlessness? And what communion has light with darkness? And what accord has Christ with Belial? Or what part has a believer with an unbeliever? And what agreement has the temple of God with idols? For you are the temple of the living God. As God has said: "I will dwell in them and walk among them. I will be their God, and they shall be My people." Therefore *"Come out from among them and be separate, says the Lord. Do not touch what is unclean, and I will receive you." "I will be a Father to you, and you shall be My sons and daughters, says the Lord Almighty"* (2 Corinthians 6:14-18).

The above verses are in the New Testament and they are written for the church. Deliverance from this world is a spiritual deliverance. Otherwise, as Paul says, we need to leave this world. We need to die to this world and the lust of it. The things of the world should not have any hold on a believer. The spirit that works in this world is not from God.

> Now we have received, not the *spirit of the world*, but the Spirit who is from God, that we might know the things that have been freely given to us by God (1 Corinthians 2:12).

Only when a believer is freed from this spirit, can he see things from a kingdom perspective. It will be difficult for you to understand what I am writing if you are controlled by the spirit of the world. This message will only cause offense and anger. You will think that what I am saying is crazy stuff, but the Bible says we should not love the world or the things of this world.

> Do not love the world or the things in the world. If anyone loves the world, the love of the Father is not in him. For *all that is in the world*—the lust of the flesh, the lust of the eyes, and the pride of life—is not of the Father but is of the world. And the world is passing away, and the lust of it; but he who does the will of God abides forever (1 John 2:15-17).

The foundation of the kingdom of darkness is lust: lust of the eye, lust of the flesh, and the pride of life. That's all there is in the world.

> Ye are of your father the devil, and the lusts of your father ye will do. He was a murderer from the beginning (John 8:44a KJV).

The foundation of the kingdom of God is love and serving one another in love.

> But through love serve one another (Galatians 5:13).

> In which you once walked according to the course of this world, according to the prince of the power of the

air, *the spirit who now works in the sons of disobedience* (Ephesians 2:2).

As long as we live in the world, *we need to fight the spirit of the world.* Though it says "*the* spirit" in these verses, there is more than one spirit working under the leadership of Satan through the world system.

Chapter 15: The Mystery of Great Babylon—the Counterfeit Church

The book of Revelation talks about the mystery of the great Babylon. As we have seen earlier, Babylon was the first ungodly kingdom established on the earth in Genesis by Nimrod. He was the first ungodly king on the earth. After that, Babylon or the Babylonian system is mentioned throughout the Bible, and culminates in its judgment in the book of Revelation. In Isaiah 14, Lucifer is depicted as the king of Babylon.

Physical and Spiritual Babylon

Babylon was an actual place and a physical kingdom, but also has a spiritual meaning. There is a spiritual Babylon, the world system, and it rules over the kings and kingdoms of the earth. Satan is the king of that spiritual Babylon. In the Bible, Zion was a name of a real place, the city of David, but there is also spiritual Zion both in heaven and where God dwells, which is our spirit.

In our day, Babylon is not a physical place, but represents the devil and his kingdom that operates throughout the whole earth. In the Old Testament, Israel was God's chosen people and nation. Babylon represented Satan's chosen people and nation. In the New Testament, the church is comprised of God's chosen people. We are His nation, and the church is the bride of Christ. Babylon is depicted as a woman and is the bride of Satan. Jesus calls them the children of the world (Luke 16:8). Babylon is the devil's counterfeit of God's kingdom. He is not capable of coming up with anything original.

The church and believers in Christ needs to overcome the spirit of Babylon if we are going to inherit the kingdom of God. As long as the spirit of Babylon has blinded your heart, you will not even see the kingdom of God nor benefit from it. What is the spirit of Babylon? The spirit of Babylon represents *what man can achieve apart from God*. It is rooted in humanism, a belief system in which men and women and the systems of this world are worshiped as gods. We see an example of this in the book of Daniel, where the people came to the king and asked him to declare that he was a god, demanding that everyone should bow down and worship him.

The spirit of Babylon, or the spirit of this world, loves pleasure, luxury, and entertainment more than true spirituality. It loves material prosperity and wealth. In fact, the motive of people who are influenced by this spirit is to become materially wealthy and make more money. If you study the Babylonian kingdoms, we can see these traits very clearly. Roads and gardens and palaces were their specialties. They love to feast and show off their pomp. If they are not happy with one wife, they will get rid of her and find another one. When you read the books of Esther and Daniel, you can see all these parallels in them.

We are commanded to flee from this spirit as a believer.

In Revelation 17, we read that the Babylon is depicted as a harlot, a woman who has seven heads and ten horns.

> Then one of the seven angels who had the seven bowls came and talked with me, saying to me, "Come, I will show you the judgment of the great harlot *who sits on many waters, with whom the kings of the earth committed fornication, and the inhabitants of the earth were made drunk with the wine of her fornication*." So he carried me away in the Spirit into the wilderness. And I saw a woman sitting on a scarlet beast which was full of names of blasphemy, *having seven heads and ten horns* (Revelation 17:1-3).
>
> And on her forehead a name was written: MYSTERY, BABYLON THE GREAT, THE *MOTHER OF HARLOTS*

THE MYSTERY OF GREAT BABYLON—THE COUNTERFEIT CHURCH

AND OF THE ABOMINATIONS OF THE *EARTH* (Revelation 17:5).

Who is this woman, the great mystery Babylon? Why she is called the mother of harlots and abomination of the whole earth? What are the seven heads?

Parallels to Babylon and the Church

Just as the church, the bride of Christ, is depicted as a woman, so is Babylon. The church is made up of people from all nations and tongues. Babylon is similarly described as a woman, the bride of Satan made of people from every nation. As a counterfeit and a copycat, the devil called her his bride. Babylon is made up of the children of this world.

The church (the kingdom of God) and the world system (mystery Babylon) are operating parallel to one another on the earth. They are in enmity to each other, because they both belong to two different kings and represent two different kingdoms. The spiritual Babylonian kingdom, which is the world and the bride of Satan, has seven heads which represents seven kings. We have learned that this world system is made of seven segments (or mountains) and they are ruled by seven different principalities (the seven heads) under Satan. There were seven angels appointed to the seven churches. The church is waiting for her bridegroom, Jesus Christ, and Babylon (the world system) is waiting for her bridegroom, the Antichrist.

> Here is the mind which has wisdom: *The seven heads are seven mountains on which the woman sits.* There are also seven kings. Five have fallen, one is, and the other has not yet come. And when he comes, he must continue a short time (Revelation 17:9-10).

It is important to notice that the church, which is the bride of Christ, God's kingdom, also has seven churches and seven spirits.

> The mystery of the seven stars which you saw in My right hand, and the seven golden lampstands: The seven stars are

> the angels of the seven churches, and the seven lampstands which you saw are the seven churches (Revelation 1:20).

> And I looked, and behold, in the midst of the throne and of the four living creatures, and in the midst of the elders, stood a Lamb as though it had been slain, having seven horns and seven eyes, which are the seven Spirits of God sent out into all the earth (Revelation 5:6).

> Then he said to me, "The waters which you saw, where the harlot sits, are *peoples, multitudes, nations,* and *tongues*" (Revelation 17:15).

The Babylonian system is a global phenomenon, not limited to just one nation or city on the earth. The waters where the harlot sits are peoples, multitudes, nations, and tongues—which means people from all over the world are influenced by her. The reason the woman was called a harlot is because her purpose is to distract the body of Christ from their first love to Jesus and draw them to love the world and things in it instead. A harlot entices and lures people to commit adultery with her. When we leave our first love to Jesus and love other things, we are committing spiritual adultery and fornication.

The purpose of the Babylonian system is to blind people so they will never discover the kingdom of God. Through products, entertainment, money, luxury, fun, sex, and various addictions, this spirit seeks to enslave people. That way they will never have to think about God or trust Him for anything.

> The woman was arrayed in purple and scarlet, and adorned with gold and precious stones and pearls, having in her hand a golden cup full of abominations and the filthiness of her fornication (Revelation 17:4).

The Babylonian system is comprised of a religious, economic, and political system. This woman influences the religious, economic, and political systems of every nation. God will judge all three at the same time. In fact, it has already begun. Why was there an attack on the World Trade Center? It was the center for world commerce. God was sending a warning sign for His people to get ready.

The devil has used this world system to destroy more people, saints, and prophets of the Lord than any other weapon in his arsenal.

> I saw the woman, drunk with the blood of the saints and with the blood of the martyrs of Jesus. And when I saw her, I marveled with great amazement (Revelation 17:6).

This world system has deceived and killed more prophets, apostles, and ministers of the gospel than anything else. God will avenge the blood of those martyrs on this world system and its rulers.

> Rejoice over her, O heaven, and you holy apostles and prophets, for God has avenged you on her! (Revelation 18:20).

Babylon and Lucifer

God is going to destroy this world system. The world system that we see today had a beginning and has an end. If you read the description of Babylon the Great in Revelation, it has all the characteristics and qualities of Lucifer that we saw in his description in Ezekiel. Let us compare them and study that a little bit.

Lucifer was covered with precious stones and gold.

> The woman was arrayed in purple and scarlet, and adorned with gold and precious stones and pearls, having in her hand a golden cup full of abominations and the filthiness of her fornication (Revelation 17:4).

Lucifer was in charge of business and was covered with precious stones. Babylon is famous for her businesses and trade.

> For all the nations have drunk of the wine of the wrath of her fornication, the kings of the earth have committed fornication with her, and the merchants of the earth have become rich through the abundance of her luxury (Revelation 18:3).

We saw that Lucifer had innumerable merchandise and did trade, and so does Babylon.

> And the merchants of the earth will weep and mourn over her, for no one buys their merchandise anymore: merchandise of gold and silver, precious stones and pearls, fine linen and purple, silk and scarlet, every kind of citron wood, every kind of object of ivory, every kind of object of most precious wood, bronze, iron, and marble; and cinnamon and incense, fragrant oil and frankincense, wine and oil, fine flour and wheat, cattle and sheep, horses and chariots, and bodies and souls of men. The fruit that your soul longed for has gone from you, and all the things which are rich and splendid have gone from you, and you shall find them no more at all. The merchants of these things, who became rich by her, will stand at a distance for fear of her torment, weeping and wailing, and saying, "Alas, alas, that great city that was clothed in fine linen, purple, and scarlet, and adorned with gold and precious stones and pearls! For in one hour such great riches came to nothing." Every shipmaster, all who travel by ship, sailors, and as many as trade on the sea, stood at a distance and cried out when they saw the smoke of her burning, saying, "What is like this great city?" (Revelation 18:11-18).

Lucifer was built with music in him. Babylon too, is famous for her music and entertainment.

> The sound of harpists, musicians, flutists, and trumpeters shall not be heard in you anymore (Revelation 18:22a).

THE MYSTERY OF GREAT BABYLON—THE COUNTERFEIT CHURCH

Lucifer was a master craftsman; he was able to imagine and create, and so does Babylon.

> No craftsman of any craft shall be found in you anymore, and the sound of a millstone shall not be heard in you anymore (Revelation 18:22b).

Lucifer's world was filled with violence, wickedness, and iniquity. Babylon was filled with the same.

> Then a mighty angel took up a stone like a great millstone and threw it into the sea, saying, "Thus with violence the great city Babylon shall be thrown down, and shall not be found anymore" (Revelation 18:21).
>
> With whom the kings of the earth committed fornication, and the inhabitants of the earth were made drunk with the wine of her fornication (Revelation 17:2).

Fornication and filth refer to spiritual and sexual fornication. When we leave our first love with God and love the world or the things of the world, we commit fornication or adultery. There are numerous verses in the Old Testament that talk about when the Israelites left God and worshiped idols. Whenever that occurred, God sent prophets who prophesied against their fornication and adultery.

> Adulterers and adulteresses! Do you not know that friendship with the world is enmity with God? Whoever therefore wants to be a friend of the world makes himself an enemy of God (James 4:4).
>
> For her sins have reached to heaven, and God has remembered her iniquities (Revelation 18:5).

Babylon was a literal city on this earth, but this spiritual Babylon is the world. This world we see today will come to an end. There is a capital city (nation) where this spiritual Babylon resides on this earth today, which will be destroyed, and it is not a city in the Middle East as some think. I do not want to mention its name because of political reasons. You will hear about it in the news when it happens!

> And the woman whom you saw is that great city which reigns over the kings of the earth (Revelation 17:18).

There are other prophecies in the Bible that discuss what is going to happen to the wealth of the world.

They will throw their silver into the streets, and their gold will be like refuse; their silver and their gold will not be able to deliver them in the day of the wrath of the Lord; they will not satisfy their souls, nor fill their stomachs, because it became their stumbling block of iniquity (Ezekiel 7:19).

The Believer's Approach to Babylon

What is the solution? It is mentioned in Job 22:

> Then you will lay your gold in the dust, and the gold of Ophir among the stones of the brooks. Yes, the Almighty will be your gold and your precious silver; for then you will have your delight in the Almighty, and lift up your face to God. You will make your prayer to Him, He will hear you, and you will pay your vows. You will also declare a thing, and it will be established for you; so light will shine on your ways (Job 22:24-28).

Do not sell everything you have and buy gold just because you hear about it on TV. Even though its value is high now, there is a time coming when people will throw their gold on the street because it will be good for nothing. Before God judges the great Babylon, we as believers need to learn how to live in the kingdom of God. Those who live depending and trusting in the Babylonian system will fall with it. I believe that is why God had me write this book: to prepare believers worldwide for what is coming.

The best thing a believer can do now is turn to God's original plan. We depend on the earth for everything. Food prices are going to go up as never before. Many will not be able to afford even necessities. We should start farming communities, and go back into farming and raising our own food. If you can raise enough and sell it, you will be the richest man on earth. During the time of famine, those who have food to sell will be the kings.

There is a divine wisdom contained in this. When the famine hit Egypt, God forewarned the king through a dream. God is incredibly smart. If He had given that dream to Joseph, he could not have done anything with it, and no one would have believed him. God gave the dream to the king and the interpretation to Joseph. They collected food from the seven fat years to have a supply for the seven lean years. The whole known world came to Egypt to buy food. As a result, all this wealth came to Egypt. You can turn a famine into the biggest opportunity ever, turning our adversaries' plans to our advantage.

As I was writing this, I was listening and watching about the droughts, fires, and floods in America and other parts of the world. What do those three do? They affect food production. We need to sell everything we can and buy farmland. We need to move into desolate areas and start cultivating them now. Churches need to initiate this, encouraging their congregants. If we prepare now, then we will not have to worry when the hard times come. This is the word of the Lord.

You can compare a believer in the world to how a fish is in the ocean. It does not matter how long the fish stays and drinks the salty water, the salt never gets into the fish. When we cook the fish, we always need to add salt. We live in this world, but the world should not get inside of us. It is the same with a rock in a river. If you break the rock, it will be still dry inside, even though it's been lying in the water for hundreds of years.

God has delivered us from the power of darkness and translated us into the kingdom of His dear Son, Jesus Christ (Colossians 1:13). We are no longer in the kingdom of this world (darkness) but in the kingdom of God. Since that is the case, we need to learn how to think and function as God wants us to. Unfortunately, we think and function as the world does, and transformation has not taken place in our minds and hearts. That is the real work. That is referred to as "working out our salvation with fear and trembling" (Philippians 2:12). God saved our spirit from hell; that was free. Now we need to appropriate that salvation into our soul and body. As our soul prospers (and is renewed), our life will also prosper.

The church is depending on the system of this world for everything. Even so, God will use everything for His purpose and glory. What the devil intended for evil, God will turn for good. A believer is the light of this world. What type of *light* is God talking about? The light is the good work that we need to do. By seeing that, the world will know who our Father is (Matthew 5:16). We reveal our God through the works we do. Whatever we do must represent our God.

> You are the light of the world. A city that is set on a hill cannot be hidden. Nor do they light a lamp and put it under a basket, but on a lampstand, and it gives light to all who are in the house. Let your *light so shine before men*, that they may see *your good works* and glorify your Father in heaven (Matthew 5:14-17).

Am I saying that all science is of the devil? Is there not something good and useful in it? Of course there is. Science and technology made our life easier, but it also poses the biggest threat to human life on earth. Every religion contains something good along with a trace of truth. But they do not have the whole truth. Most religions teach about helping the poor. That does not mean they are doing it based on God's love. Most religion teach about life after death and heaven or hell. These are traces of truth, but not the whole truth.

Having an economy is good; we cannot live on this earth without money. At the time same time, the Bible says that the *love* of money is the root of *all* evil (1 Timothy 6:10). If there is any evil here, the love of money is the root of it. Amazing! We need to be careful when we accept something as though it is from God. The devil transforms himself as an angel of light. We only know he was not God's messenger after we have listened and done what he has bid us to do.

As long as we live on the earth, we need each segment of the world to function well. Paul wrote that we could use the world system (1 Corinthians 7:31), and not abuse it. When you go out to reach the world, you need to see who is ruling behind that particular segment. I am not saying all technology is an invention of the devil. But the devil is the one who is using it the most to propagate his lies and build his kingdom. *We need to take it back from him!*

Trapped in the World System

How does the devil trap us using this world system? He does it by using three primary weapons: the lust of the eye, the lust of the flesh, and the pride of life. The Bible says these are not of the Father, but of the world. These are the same weapons he used against Eve in the garden.

> Do not love the world or the things in the world. If anyone loves the world, the love of the Father is not in him. For all that is in the world—the lust of the flesh, the lust of the eyes, and the pride of life—is not of the Father but is of the world. And the world is passing away, and the lust of it; but he who does the will of God abides forever (1 John 2:15-17).

The devil uses these three weapons to lure a believer into his kingdom. The devil feeds on our sinful nature and traps us in the system of this world. We need to overcome it by faith. That is why Jesus said He would build His church and the gates of hell would not prevail against it. The word used for *gates* is plural. That means there are multiple gates of hell. The devil uses one of the segments by which this world is made to lure people to hell.

In 2 Corinthians 4, we read that the enemy blinds the heart of people from seeing the glorious light of the gospel of Jesus Christ. He uses one of the areas we have discussed to blind the hearts of people.

Repentance means to get free from these forces and reprogram our minds according to kingdom principles. We need to get a biblical perspective about the world around us and outside us. Many are blinded and do not see anything outside the world system. They do not see anything differently than they used to before they became Christians. This must change.

Daniel's Vision

Another individual who saw the coming of the kingdom of God to earth prophetically was Daniel in the Old Testament. Daniel interpreted the dream Nebuchadnezzar had about the image that represented different kingdoms that were to rule the earth from that time until the establishment of God's kingdom.

Daniel said that four earthly kingdoms would rise after Babylon. It was during the time of the fourth kingdom's rule that the God of heaven would establish His kingdom on earth. The legs of that image was made of iron, which represented Rome. The feet of the image was made of iron and clay, representing the government systems we have on the earth right now.

> And in the days of these kings the God of heaven will set up a kingdom which shall never be destroyed; and the kingdom shall not be left to other people; it shall break in pieces and consume all these kingdoms, and it shall stand forever. Inasmuch as you saw that the stone was cut out of the mountain without hands, and that it broke in pieces the iron, the bronze, the clay, the silver, and the gold—the great God has made known to the king what will come to pass after this. The dream is certain, and its interpretation is sure (Daniel 2:44-45).

In his dream, Nebuchadnezzar saw a stone that was cut without hands. It struck the image on its feet, breaking them into pieces and grinding them to powder. That stone became a great mountain and filled the whole earth (Daniel 2:31-35). That stone represented the kingdom of God. In Matthew 21:44, Jesus talked about His kingdom being a stone that crushes everything that it falls on into powder.

Part V: Restoration of the Kingdom

Chapter 16: The Restoration of Man

Mankind waited for more than four thousand years. When the fullness of the time came, God sent His one and only Son to the planet Earth. That is where we began this book. The Seed of the woman was born through the Virgin Mary. They called Him Jesus. Jesus waited thirty years to begin His work; in the first chapter, we read about His first day of ministry and the message He had to communicate to mankind.

The message was simple and straightforward: repent because the kingdom of heaven is near (or about to come back to earth once again). That was the greatest news ever, and Jesus wanted to share that with mankind. How did the Seed of the woman crush the head of the serpent and take back everything he stole from Adam? Jesus restored the same authority and kingship back to mankind that God had given Adam in the beginning.

We have not yet come to the full realization of what Jesus accomplished on the cross. We have heard bits and pieces. We have heard about the cross, the blood, gifts, the nails and the resurrection — but nobody told us the whole story. Now you know the whole story. Let's learn about everything Jesus accomplished for us.

Another Heavenly Meeting

God sent His only Son to the earth to die for our sin. Whoever would believe in Him would become a child of God and be qualified to enter the kingdom of God and become part of His *ekklesia*. This is why Jesus said that if we sought first His kingdom and His righteousness, all the other things that we needed in our lives would be added to us. Now let's go back to another meeting that took place in heaven.

The Great King called another important meeting in heaven. He was not willing to give up that easily and give away His sons and daughters on earth. Now He was dealing with His own family. He wanted to redeem the man and restore man's relationship with Him. He knew this job would be tough, but it had to be done. He knew He could not violate His own principles. He had said that the soul who sinned must die. Either He had to kill this new race, or Someone had to die in their place.

He could not go to the earth because the earth was a physical world, and He is a Spirit. Only a person who has a physical body can live on the earth. He could not die because He was an everlasting King. It had to be a human being just like Adam who went to the earth and died on behalf of the humans. Before he died, that person had to teach and demonstrate the kingdom to the people of the earth, and show them what it meant to be living in His kingdom.

He said, "Whom shall I send and who shall go for Me?" (Isaiah 6:8). There was a moment of silence and His Son spoke up, "Father, remember what I said before. If you ever needed any help with the earth, I will do anything." He continued by saying, "I will go. Send Me." The King looked at His Son and whispered, "I knew that, My Son. I knew one day I had to let You go for a special mission like this. I also knew that for one agonizing moment I would have to hide my face from You and forsake You. I will be with You all the way." In one way, the King was happy because He was getting His family back; but in another way, He felt overwhelmed at the thought of letting His Son go through the pain and suffering ahead of Him.

The King knew there needed to be a great price paid to restore man to his original position. He told His Son, "You must die in their place so that I can have fellowship with them again. I want to fellowship with them, but they cannot see Me or understand Me because they are so blinded by the darkness in them. Son, I am sending you to earth to become a man like them and pay the price for their freedom. Judge Satan and dethrone him from his position, and give the keys of My kingdom to My *ekklesia*."

The King continued, "I want my kingdom restored on the earth. As you go, My Son, tell the people to prepare to enter My kingdom once again. Show them what it is like to live in My kingdom. Teach them what they must know and do to inherit My kingdom. After You come back from accomplishing Your part, I will send the Comforter (the Governor-General of the kingdom) to be with them and to be *in* them, enabling them to live in and manifest My kingdom.

"This time My kingdom is going to be invisible, and only those who believe in You, My Son, will be able to see, enter, and inherit our kingdom. For those who believe in You and Your death on the cross and resurrection, I will forgive of their sins, and qualify them to enter My kingdom. Wherever two or three are gathered in Your name, I will go and dwell in their midst. I will pour out My Spirit upon those who believe in You and enable them to live victoriously. They will come together to worship and praise me and administer my kingdom. They will be called the *ekklesia*." (*Ekklesia* is a group of people who are called out to represent the kingdom and execute the will of the Great King here on earth.)

"Through this *ekklesia*, I will accomplish my purpose on the earth. It will be the only visible form of my kingdom on the earth for a while. It will be the embassy and the governing body of My kingdom, and I will give them My power and authority over all the power of the enemy. Nothing shall by any means hurt them. Those who are trained by the *ekklesia* will go forth and preach the gospel of My kingdom and bring more people into the fold.

"The *ekklesia* will be the only force on earth that can thwart and destroy the power of the enemy and keep him where he belongs. They will go forward in My power and take new territories for Me until the whole earth is filled with My glory, as it was in the beginning. Then, at the end, I will destroy the enemy forever and cast him into the lake of fire. After You finish the works I have given You to do, You, My Son, shall sit at My right hand until I make Your enemies Your footstool through the *ekklesia*." (This particular Old Testament scripture is the most repeated scripture in the New Testament. It is mentioned seven times.)

"It all depends on how My *ekklesia* will train the people to live in My kingdom. The more they speak the language of My kingdom and understand its culture and how it functions, the more victorious and successful they will be. My kingdom will be a spiritual kingdom; natural people will not be able to see, enter, or understand it.

"This time, I am going to keep Satan on the earth for a time, but I will rule and reign My kingdom in the midst of My enemies. No matter what Satan tries, he will not be able to thwart My purpose. I will build My kingdom, and the gates of hell shall not prevail against it. The Comforter will come to dwell in anyone who believes in You, My Son. He will help them establish My kingdom and empower them to execute My original plan for the earth. That way My original intent for the earth will come to pass, and My kingdom shall be established on the earth forever."

Saved to Live in the Kingdom

When a person believes in Jesus, God forgives their sin and they are entitled to go to heaven when they die. But that does not necessarily mean they will inherit the kingdom and its blessings while they live on earth. Most believers do not inherit the kingdom and its benefits while they are alive. There is an earthly perspective of the kingdom, and God wants His children to enjoy all the blessings He has promised in His Word.

Most people believe God saved them simply to take them to heaven. That is only half of the truth. God saved us from our sin and restored everything that was lost because of the fall. When God brought the Israelites out of Egypt, He promised them a land flowing with milk and honey. God told them it was theirs, but most of them did not inherit the Promised Land. Instead, they perished in the wilderness. This Old Testament incident was a shadow of what we also experience in the New Testament.

Jesus spoke specifically about how to enter His kingdom. He laid out those principles in the gospels. Whoever practices them will inherit the kingdom of God. With the fall, man lost his dominion over the earth and was spiritually dead. God planned to restore and redeem him, allowing him to regain his original position. He sent His Son to die on our behalf; and through His blood, Jesus reconciled us to the Father. Through Jesus, we receive power and authority over the earth once again, but that power and authority will be limited until the redemption of our bodies.

Jesus defeated Satan and his kingdom. There are two key verses that I would like you to pay attention to from the gospel of John.

> Now is the judgment of this world; now the *ruler* of this world will be cast out (John 12:31).

> And when He has come, He will convict the world of sin, and of righteousness, and of judgment: of sin, because they do not believe in Me; of righteousness, because I go to My Father and you see Me no more; of judgment, because the ruler of this world is judged (John 16:8-11).

These two verses say Jesus judged and cast out the ruler of this world, Satan. Everything the enemy does today, he does *illegally*, meaning he no longer has any right to do what he is doing. The only reason he does what he does is because the people of God, who should be enforcing the victory of Jesus, have been blindfolded by the devil, and are not doing that. Though he has power, he has no authority to exercise his power any longer.

That does not mean they do not have any power, as some think. If one kingdom defeats another kingdom, that does not mean all their power has vanished. They only lost the authority to rule. After the resurrection, Jesus said, "All authority has been given to Me in heaven and on earth" (Matthew 28:18). He did not say *all power*.

Satan Has Power, But it Is Limited

Jesus told Paul that He was sending him to deliver people out of the power of Satan (Acts 26:18). Jesus gave us power and authority over all the power of the enemy (Luke 10:19). The enemy still has power, but the kingdom that defeated him has authority over him and his kingdom, and keeps them in a defeated position. The Bible acknowledges the power of Satan, and we need to recognize it but not be afraid of him. Instead, we need to walk in that knowledge.

In Acts 22, Paul testified about his encounter with Jesus. Let us read it.

> So I said, "Who are You, Lord?" And He said, "I am Jesus, whom you are persecuting. But rise and stand on your feet; for I have appeared to you for this purpose, to make you a minister and a witness both of the things which you have seen and of the things which I will yet reveal to you. I will deliver you from the Jewish people, as well as from the Gentiles, to whom I now send you, to open their eyes, in order to turn them from darkness to light, and from *the power of Satan* to God, that they may receive forgiveness of sins and an inheritance among those who are sanctified by faith in Me" (Acts 26:15-18).

This is the resurrected Jesus who is saying Satan has power. The Greek word used for power is *exousia*, which means authority or delegated power. His power is limited; and through Jesus, we have power and authority over all of Satan's power and authority. We do not need to be afraid of him, but stay close to Jesus and do His will.

Paul wrote this in Colossians:

> He has delivered us from the power of darkness and conveyed us into the kingdom of the Son of His love (Colossians 1:13).

When we were saved, we were transferred from one kingdom to the other. An unsaved person is in the kingdom of darkness, or the world. When we were saved, God transported us (or conveyed) us to the kingdom of His Son. Unfortunately, many continue to live in the world and do not enjoy the benefits of salvation. Their mind and thinking is programmed by the world.

Satan has access to God's presence, as we read in the books of Job and Revelation. In Revelation, we see that he is accusing the brethren before God. (See Job 1:6 and Revelation 12:10.) This does not mean he has access to heaven. God can have meeting places with His angels anywhere in the universe (Isaiah 14:13).

Though Satan has power, if he needs to do anything on this earth, mankind has to give him permission and authority. What does that mean? Satan and demons are spiritual beings and the earth is a physical planet. For any spirit being to operate on the earth requires a physical body. The spirit world and natural worlds operate under laws that were created by God. They cannot violate those laws.

Although we are spirit beings, we live in a physical body (our earth-suits), and that gives us access to the physical world, so we can live and operate here on earth. That is why Jesus had to take on a human form (or body) to come and redeem us. He had to be able to come and live among us, and it was the only way.

What Satan does now, as in the beginning, is to tempt men and women. If we yield to this temptation, then he has power over us and the realm around us. If we resist the devil, as the Bible tells us, he will flee (James 4:7).

The Bible calls him the god of this world. As we discussed before, the world refers to the system by which the earth operates. It was created by Jesus and for Him; but through deception, Satan took over the world system and now controls what happens on the earth. Most people on earth are not born again and do not believe Jesus is the Son of God. These people unknowingly have given themselves to do Satan's will, and he operates the system of this world through them.

The devil is not the true god of the earth. Earth is the physical planet created by God. The Bible says the Earth and its fullness belongs to the Lord. (See Psalm 24:1 and 89:11.) The world was also created by Jesus. Every dominion, principality, and kingdom, and all that is on the earth was created by Jesus and for Him (Colossians 1:16). Nevertheless, the devil has influence over the world system because of unbelievers. The devil perverted the world system and corrupted it through his evil devices.

God did not change his mind about man. His absolute will for us is to rule and reign on the earth in partnership with Him. The process we are going through now is to regain our original position, the one God gave to Adam in the beginning. There is a time appointed by God for the redemption of all creation (Romans 8:19-20). Then there will be a new earth and a new heaven, and we will rule and reign with Jesus on this earth forever. Amen.

Before we understand God's specific will for each of us, we need to understand the Big Picture. Each individual purpose is connected to what God is doing overall here. We are co-laborers (partners) with Him in accomplishing His purpose on the earth. Whether you are in ministry, business, politics, or working a regular job, your purpose is to fulfill God's purpose in that particular area.

God's purpose is to accomplish His will on the earth as it is in heaven. He accomplishes His will on this earth through us. God is Spirit (John 4:24) and He cannot operate in the physical world without a physical body. *Our body is His temple* (1 Corinthians 6:19), His spiritual house (1 Peter 2:5). Whatever He does, He does it through us.

Chapter 17: Arrival of the Kingdom

The time finally came when God decided to restore the kingdom to us. He sent His Son Jesus to reveal and teach us about it, and show us how to live in it too. That is why Jesus preached more on the kingdom of God than any other subject. It was the first and last message He preached.

> Now after John was put in prison, Jesus came to Galilee, preaching the gospel of the kingdom of God, and saying, "The time is fulfilled, and the kingdom of God is at hand. Repent, and believe in the gospel" (Mark 1:14-15).

Jesus was saying that the time was fulfilled for the kingdom of God to be restored to man. Jesus came to announce the *imminent arrival* of the kingdom of God to the earth. That is why He said, "The kingdom is at hand." "At hand" means *near*.

The reason the phrase *kingdom of heaven* appears only in the gospel of Matthew is because it is the first book of the New Testament and it is announcing the reentry of this heavenly country to planet Earth. (See Matthew 4:17 and Mark 1:14-15.) *Jesus came with a kingdom, or a country; His pivotal message was not that He was taking us to heaven, but that He was bringing heaven to us.*

That is why He said in Luke 12:

> Do not fear, little flock, for it is your Father's good pleasure to give you the kingdom (Luke 12:32).

He did not come to give us a church or a particular denomination, but the very kingdom itself (Luke 22:29).

That is why Jesus began His preaching by announcing, "Repent, for the kingdom of heaven is at hand" (Matthew 4:17b). What He meant by this was that everything the people on earth, especially the Old Testament saints, had been longing to see was finally at hand. It was almost here. Wow! What good news! The gospel is called good news, and sadly we have turned it into a religion.

The Time of the Arrival

Jesus was announcing the imminent arrival of the kingdom of God on earth. Then He told them exactly when it was going to arrive.

> And He said to them, "Assuredly, I say to you that there are some standing here who will not taste death till they see the kingdom of God present with power" (Mark 9:1).

We read similar verses in two other gospels.

> Assuredly, I say to you, there are some standing here who shall not taste death till they see the Son of Man coming in His kingdom (Matthew 16:28).

> But I tell you truly, there are some standing here who shall not taste death till they see the kingdom of God (Luke 9:27).

What did He mean here?

This is a key verse in all of the Gospels, and a turning point in the New Testament. What was Jesus talking about? If He was referring to His second coming, it would not be true. It would not be possible for some people who were alive then to continue to remain alive until His second coming. That would be impossible because humans do not live that long.

He was talking about the day of Pentecost, when the Holy Spirit came with power. Since that day, the kingdom of God began to operate on earth once again. That is what He meant when He said, "The kingdom of heaven is at hand." Many who had heard Jesus were alive to see Pentecost come with their own eyes.

As I mentioned before, nowhere in the book of Acts do we hear any of the apostles preaching a kingdom-at-hand message. With the coming of the Holy Spirit in Acts 2, the kingdom of God had arrived on earth, and it has been operating here ever since. Does everyone see and experience it? No. Why? Because it does not come with observation. A born-again believer can see it with his or her spiritual eyes. That is why Jesus said, "Most assuredly, I say to you, unless one is born again, he cannot *see* the kingdom of God" (John 3:3). The first result of the born-again experience is the ability to see the kingdom of God with the eyes of our spirit.

The Kingdom Came in Power

The kingdom of God came in power on the day of Pentecost. They heard a sound of a mighty rushing wind and tongues of fire came and sat on the heads of those 120 believers. The word for "mighty" in Greek is *biaios*, which means "violent" or "forcefully."[23] The word for rushing is *pheró*, which means "to carry on a shoulder" or "bear."[24] The mighty rushing wind was like the sound of an army entering an enemy's territory.

The kingdom of God forcefully entered the earth realm on the day of Pentecost and has been functioning on earth ever since. Why tongues of fire, and not swords of fire? The present kingdom of God is ruled and governed by *the tongues* of men and women, by what they say. God saves people by what we preach (the foolishness of preaching). Jesus said we shall have whatever we say (Mark 11:23). Only a few receive the benefits of the kingdom, because only a few know how to *speak the language* of the kingdom. Jesus said, "My kingdom is not of this world." One of the reasons people are not receiving it is because they cannot see it with their natural eyes.

---

23. James Strong, "972. Biaios, βίαιος," Biblehub.com, accessed June 16, 2019, https://biblehub.com/greek/972.htm.

24. James Strong, "5342. φέρω (pheró)," Biblehub.com, accessed June 16, 2019, https://biblehub.com/str/greek/5342.htm.

He also said in Matthew 12:

> But if I cast out demons by the Spirit of God, surely the kingdom of God has come upon you (Matthew 12:28).

The Holy Spirit Came with the Kingdom

The Holy Spirit came with the kingdom of God. He still comes to make it real to us and manifest it in the natural. That means that wherever the activities of the Holy Spirit are manifest, the kingdom of God is there. At present, without the Holy Spirit, no operation of the kingdom of God will ever be made manifest. We need to make sure we do not limit the Holy Spirit only to casting out demons. He can do so much more! Many people limit God, and know Him only for His gifts. He is much bigger than that.

Why don't we see the outpouring and the manifestation of the Holy Spirit today as we saw in the first century? Many are asking and waiting for an outpouring of the Holy Spirit. He will be poured out only over a people who are ready to establish and execute God's kingdom purpose on the earth.

That is why Jesus had to preach and teach on the kingdom of God for three years before the Father poured out the Holy Spirit. He was not given so we could feel good or have an emotional experience. He is the Governor of the kingdom. He comes to accomplish the will of the King who sent Him. If we want to see Him operate as we see in the book of Acts, then we need to preach what they preached and prepare the people. Otherwise, it does not matter what program we have or how long we cry or shout, He will not manifest.

Do a study on the work of the Holy Spirit from Genesis to Revelation. He does everything God Himself does, because He is God. When a person or a place becomes fully yielded to the Spirit of God, the kingdom of God will manifest and be in full operation there.

Grace Follows after the Kingdom

When you discover the kingdom of God, the longing of your spirit will cease; for the very first time you will feel in your spirit that you are finally *home*. Until you discover this, nothing else will satisfy you—no matter how rich or poor you are or how long you have been Spirit-filled or in ministry. Instead of first seeking God's kingdom, which Jesus told us to do, believers today keep going from one revival meeting to another and one conference to the next, being robbed and taken advantage of by so-called ministers. *We must seek His kingdom with everything we have until we discover it.* In Hebrews 12, the author concludes by saying,

> Therefore, since we are receiving a kingdom which cannot be shaken, let us have grace (Hebrews 12:28).

Many go after the teaching of grace these days too. The trouble is that before we can gain it, we must first have a revelation of the kingdom of God. This verse says we will have grace *after* we receive a kingdom that cannot be shaken, because grace is the operating system of the kingdom of God. In His kingdom, God deals with us through His grace. In computer terms, the kingdom is the *hardware* and grace is the *software*. What good is having the most powerful software in the world with no hardware to operate it? How does that benefit anyone?

Every nation has a political or governing system. India is democratic and China is communist in its government. The kingdom of God is a nation ruled by a King, who is God, and He uses grace as His governing system. Before we go after grace, we need to discover His kingdom. That is why Jesus commanded, "Seek *first* the kingdom" (Matthew 6:33).

Though the kingdom of God is now in operation on earth, not everyone will find it because it is like a treasure hidden in a field. Treasure is not easy to find, and only those who are very serious and willing to risk their life will find it.

> Again, the kingdom of heaven is like treasure hidden in a field, which a man found and hid; and for joy over it he goes and sells all that he has and buys that field (Matthew 13:44).

In the above parable, the *field* is the world, and the *treasure* is the kingdom of heaven (Matthew 13:38). It is hidden, and God wants us to seek it. In another parable, Jesus compared the kingdom of heaven to a pearl of great price.

> Again, the kingdom of heaven is like a merchant seeking beautiful pearls, who, when he had found one pearl of great price, went and sold all that he had and bought it (Matthew 13:45-46).

The Present Kingdom

Everything we need is in the kingdom of God. Once we know how to seek and discover how it operates, we will have everything we need. In the Gospels, we see that John the Baptist, Jesus, and the disciples went around and preached about the coming of the kingdom of God to earth. They said, "Repent for the kingdom of God is at hand."

With the coming of the Holy Spirit on the day of Pentecost, the kingdom of God began to operate on the earth again. Jesus lived in the kingdom because He lived by the power of the Holy Spirit and was led by the Holy Spirit.

The reason the apostles did not preach about the kingdom coming in the book of Acts was because it had already come, so they demonstrated and taught about that kingdom that was already in operation on the earth.

God extended the invitation to enter His kingdom to whoever believed in the name of Jesus and what Jesus did on the cross. Unfortunately, many believers do not know how to benefit from the kingdom they are in. Their struggle and worries in life did not end, even though they became Christians. They live like the ordinary people in this world.

"Cashing In" on the Kingdom

They do not know how to seek the kingdom and His righteousness, so everything they need will be added to them. They live like they have received the million dollar check, but it not benefiting them one bit because they do not how to turn that check into cash. They carry the check around and tell everybody they got the check, but they live like orphans.

Most are trying to just *survive* as Christians. They are in debt, sick, depressed, and anxious, and have broken relationships—just like the ungodly people on the earth. That is not God's plan for His children who are living in His kingdom. Jesus said,

> The thief does not come except to steal, and to kill, and to destroy. I have come that they may have life, and that they may have it more abundantly (John 10:10).

God wants you to know how to turn that check into cash. His promises in the Bible are like signed checks from Him. Whatever we need is promised in His Word. We need to know how to receive it. Once we learn about the kingdom and how it operates, we can turn those promises into reality.

He Is a Good Father and King

In the early days, one kingdom would declare war against another, and subdue them and plunder their goods. In the Spirit, we do not wage war against flesh and blood but against dark forces. We do not fight against God for our stuff or for miracles, because He is always good and there is no evil in Him. The Bible says that if our son ask for bread, we will not give him a stone, and if he ask for a fish, we will not give him a serpent. If we know how to give good gifts to our children how much more will our heavenly Father give good things to those who ask Him (Matthew 7:9-11).

Before we set out to do any spiritual warfare, we need to be established and convinced about the goodness of God. He is after you to bless you and not do you harm. The thoughts He thinks toward you are for your peace. One of the biggest deceptions of the devil is to portray God as evil, and attribute the evil that happens in people's lives to God. Jesus said He came that people might have life, and life more abundantly.

Jesus brought the kingdom of God here. With the kingdom, came all the blessings, both material and spiritual. Everything you need is in the kingdom, and God has already blessed you with all you require. When Jesus taught us to pray, He said, "Let Your kingdom come and Your will be done."

God's will is in His kingdom, and when the kingdom comes, His will comes too. Many hunger to know His will, but they do not know how to enter His kingdom. Before the will of God can be done, His kingdom needs to come. When we receive the kingdom, everything we need in our lives will follow. Seek first the kingdom of God and His righteousness, and all these things shall be added to you!

There are two primary reasons people do not receive what they need or request. Either they do not seek first the kingdom, or they depend on their own righteousness instead of God's righteousness. The Bible calls those people Gentiles. Unfortunately, I have heard many believers say that they want to work and earn enough money for themselves and for their families first; and when they reach a level of comfort, then they want to seek the kingdom. Those precious souls do not understand the principles of the kingdom. What they are trying to do is to function the opposite to what Jesus said. You do not seek things first and get everything you need, and then start to seek the kingdom. You seek the kingdom first, and all things follow.

Take It by Force

> And from the days of John the Baptist until now the kingdom of heaven suffers violence, and the violent take it by force (Matthew 11:12).

Most of us are familiar with this verse. I have ministered in conferences where that verse was the theme. In the early days, I thought I had to take the kingdom of God by force, until I understood what that verse really said. The key phrase in the verse is not taking it by force but "until now."

That means it was happening *until* Jesus said that verse. It is no longer applicable today. What does that mean? The kingdom of God was not made available to mankind until Jesus came to give us His kingdom. If people wanted it before He came, they had to fight to get it. Once something is given to you, you don't need to fight or become violent to grab it anymore. All you have to do is to receive it and say "Thank You."

John the Baptist came announcing the coming of the Lord. When Jesus came, He came with the kingdom, announcing its imminent arrival. During Jesus' time, the kingdom manifested wherever He was. It was still limited. When the kingdom of God arrived on the day of Pentecost with the coming of the Holy Spirit, it could now be made manifest anywhere, anytime because the Holy Spirit is everywhere.

Jesus came to give us the kingdom. (See Luke 12:32 and 22:29.)

Chapter 18: Understanding Salvation

The Bible says in everything we set out to get, most of all, we should get understanding (Proverbs 4:7). There is only one reason we perish, and that is because of a lack of knowledge (Hosea 4:6). *Ignorance is deadly.* If a person is ignorant and doesn't recognize it, that is even more deadly.

If we do not understand and lay our foundation correctly, we cannot build anything on it that will stand. The reason believers remain ineffective in most places is because they have been misinformed about their purpose. We inherited a gloom-and-despair eschatology. We have been living on a shaky and unsure foundation.

Another sad scenario with the majority of Christians is that they do not understand what salvation is all about. The doctrine of salvation is the most misunderstood doctrine in the Bible, next to our purpose. We believe the purpose of salvation is to get us to heaven when we die or when Jesus comes back—whichever comes first. Most are taught that we lost *heaven* when Adam fell. They received a religious concept that said God created man to live in heaven, or that we fell from heaven and lost it, and for some reason we are stuck on earth now. Did God make a mistake, so He sent Jesus to take us all back to heaven to make it right?

Jesus talked about the born-again experience only once to a Jewish religious leader in a private meeting during the middle of the night. He never preached it in public or told any Gentile about being born again. That really shocked me when I first realized it. Think about it and research it in the Bible for yourself.

Restored to Adam's Place

Why and how did this salvation program of God come about? The whole program came because of the fall of Adam, right? Everyone universally accepts that fact. But some have forgotten from whence Adam fell, and what he lost because of that fall. Through salvation, God's intent was to restore man to the position and place Adam had before the fall. If that is not your understanding of salvation, then you were influenced by the religious spirit somewhere along the way.

Where did Adam fall from? What did he lose because of the fall? What kind of relationship did he have with God before the fall, and what was he required to do before he met with God every day? What would Adam and his children be doing now if he hadn't fallen? The Bible does not mention any particular requirement Adam was expected to perform, other than to show up when God came down and called him. They had a father/son relationship. The Bible says Adam was the son of God (Luke 3:38).

Adam did not have to sing three fast songs and then two slow songs before he met with God or to feel His presence in the garden. Eden and heaven were united in every aspect. When we are saved, the first thing God does for us is restore our position as His children. *We became part of His family.*

> But as many as received Him, to them He gave the right to become children of God, to those who believe in His name (John 1:12).

After we become God's children, we are supposed to relate to Him as our Father—just like Adam and Jesus did. All the singing and worship came because of the fall. For more on this topic, please read my book Purpose, Calling, and Gifts. We are supposed to go to Him as a child goes to His Father, and talk and commune with Him anytime we choose.

True Worship

After we are saved, everything we do in life has to flow from that foundation of our relationship with God as our Father. Our worship has nothing to do with singing songs. If what we are actually doing is not flowing from our Father/child relationship with God, things will not work the way they should. That is why most Christians are struggling in life. *They are waiting to escape from the assignment God gave them.*

God gave us another example to show how a son or daughter is supposed to connect with their heavenly Father. That is none other than Jesus, the Son of the Living God. The Bible calls Jesus the last Adam. How did Jesus connect with His Father while He was here on earth? Or how did the disciples connect with Jesus? They were not required to sing four songs each morning before they came into His presence. He was with them all the time. He is with us all the time now too.

Our theology has been twisted and manipulated by ignorance and the religious spirit. Because we have traditionally done some things for a long time, we think that these actions are normal, or that the present state of things is the way it always has been or should be. It was not like this for all of time. Naturally, we teach others the things we "know" with great passion—but it is not helping them, nor is it helping us. We have been hiding behind a religious mask. We know in our hearts that something has been missing or out of place all along.

We do need to praise and magnify God. When we do it, we have to do it the best we can and give Him the maximum glory that is due His name. We need to do this for the right reasons too. In the New Testament, we praise Him for what He does. In Acts 2, we read that they praised God—not to feel His presence, but as an act of gratitude.

> So continuing daily with one accord in the temple, and breaking bread from house to house, they ate their food with gladness and simplicity of heart, praising God and having favor with all the people. And the Lord added to the church daily those who were being saved (Acts 2:46-47).

In another place in Acts 3, we read of the lame man who was healed. He walked, leaped, and praised God for the miracle. He was thanking and praising God for healing him. That is what we should be doing. When God does an amazing act, we should all come together to praise and thank Him. We should not do this as some sort of religious duty every time we meet so we can feel the presence of God. Either God is in you, or you are not saved. It's that simple.

When you are born again, Jesus comes to dwell within you. You become the temple of God and His Holy Spirit. *You become His residence.* If He is in you, and you are not feeling Him, then there is something blocking that feeling. We need to find out what it is and why.

I used to be devoted to praise and worship. Because I was raised in a religious circle, I did what I was taught. I did not understand the truth. I bought all types of cassette tapes and CDs of praise and worship music. I played them and felt good; I had my favorites that gave me special emotional goosebumps. Then I received the revelation of sonship and the New Testament teaching on the temple of God and threw them away. My focus changed completely.

What to Do When You Don't "Feel" God

I had a rough childhood, and my relationship with my father was not healthy. I had a hard time relating to my heavenly Father too, because our concept of our heavenly Father is formed by our relationship with our earthly father. I had to go through a healing process to understand God's love for me. When that occurred, I began to relate to God as my Father on a moment-by-moment basis like Adam and Jesus did, not on a weekend basis or when I heard a particular type of music. Now I sense Him all the time. He is faithful to show me if there is anything in my life that is not pleasing to Him.

If you do not feel or sense God's (Holy Spirit) presence on a continual basis, it means there is something blocking Him. You need to find out what that is and deal with it. It is not God's problem that you are not feeling

Him. You need to deal with the blockage or wound in your soul that is causing this.

> But he who is joined to the Lord is one spirit with *Him* (1 Corinthians 6:17).

You have been made one with God. There is no separation between you and God. If you feel a separation, then it is on your side that the problem exists.

> The Spirit of truth, whom the world cannot receive, because it neither sees Him nor knows Him; but you know Him, for He dwells with you and will be in you (John 14:17).

> Jesus answered and said to him, "If anyone loves Me, he will keep My word; and My Father will love him, and We will come to him and make Our home with him" (John 14:23).

Everything on earth and in heaven has been reconciled (or brought together) in Christ Jesus as it was in Eden. There is no broken relationship between heaven and earth, or man and God anymore. Everything has been reconciled in Christ Jesus and brought to peace. Do you see that manifest in the natural? No. Because not very many people believe it and play their part to restore it. They keep cursing the earth and what God has created. They are all waiting to fly away instead!

> That in the dispensation of the fullness of the times He might gather together in one all things in Christ, both which are in heaven and which are on earth—in Him (Ephesians 1:10).

> For it pleased the Father that in Him all the fullness should dwell, and by Him to reconcile all things to Himself, by Him, whether things on earth or things in heaven, having made peace through the blood of His cross (Colossians 1:19-20).

THE GOSPEL OF THE KINGDOM

The New Generation of Believers

God is raising up a new generation of sons and daughters who will fully understand and walk in the revelation Adam had in God before the fall. I dedicate this book to that group of people. This book is not about rapture and revival. If you are looking for that, then you are wasting your time. This book is intended to restore the foundation that has been broken down for generations.

When you read it, some things might sound strange, shocking, or just plain new; but if the Holy Spirit is in you, He will bear witness with your spirit that this is the word of the Lord for you right now. This message will resonate within you. Open up your heart and allow Him to transform your thinking, because now is the time for that. If there is a religious spirit or the spirit of this world in you, they will fight with everything they have against what you are reading. God talks about this generation of people in Isaiah:

> Thus says the Lord: "In an acceptable time I have heard You, and in the day of salvation I have helped You; I will preserve You and give You as a covenant to the people, to restore the earth, to cause them to inherit the desolate heritages" (Isaiah 49:8).

> Those from among you shall build the old waste places; you shall raise up the foundations of many generations; and you shall be called the Repairer of the Breach, the Restorer of Streets to Dwell In (Isaiah 58:12).

> And they shall rebuild the old ruins, they shall raise up the former desolations, and they shall repair the ruined cities, the desolations of many generations (Isaiah 61:4).

If the earth is waiting to be burned or destroyed, when do you think these verses will be fulfilled? I believe this is happening now. If those verses were only meant for the people of Israel and their land, then they would not also speak of restoring the whole earth. This book was written to equip the body of Christ to become part of that restoration process.

UNDERSTANDING SALVATION

If you are saved, you need to return from where you have fallen. If you are to be restored, you need to know what you lost. I remember hearing the story of a drunkard. One night he was coming home, and when he reached his house he couldn't find his keys. He retraced his steps, looking for a streetlight. When he found one, he began to search for his keys under that light. He kept looking and looking for hours and could not find the keys.

One of his friends came by and asked him what he was searching for. He told him he had lost his keys and was looking for them. His friend asked if he knew where he lost them, and the drunkard replied that he didn't know, but he saw the light and thought he would find them there if he looked there.

That story is similar to many people's lives. We don't know what we have lost or where to find it, but have been searching and searching all of our lives in the light we have found. I pray that God will use this book to end that search. If you need to know what we lost when Adam fell and how God restored everything to us through Jesus Christ, please read my book *ReDiscovering the Lost Kingdom*. You can download it free at www.thekingdomnetwork.org

In order to understand the doctrine of salvation, God included a five-step process in His Word. That is what we are going to study in the next chapter.

Chapter 19: The Process of Salvation, Part I

Be still, and know that I am God; I will be exalted among the nations, I will be exalted in the earth!" (Psalm 46:10).

In order to restore us to His original intent, God introduced a process called salvation. Through listening to a religious spirit, we have focused salvation on going to heaven when people die, as if that is what we lost when Adam fell. Salvation is much more than that, though. Most of us have prayed a prayer or gone to the altar in a meeting and accepted Jesus as our Lord, but only a few understand what really happened to them. Our salvation experience is only an inch deep, and we miss the mile God wants to restore to us. Once we are saved we should begin to think and act like Adam did *before* he fell. Let us find out what that truly means.

Five Steps to Salvation

God uses five different words in the Bible to help us understand what salvation is all about and reveal His plan. He divided the process of salvation into five steps. *Only when you receive the benefits of all five steps will you receive everything God has in store for you.* Only then will everything we lost because of sin be restored. Each individual is at some level of this five-step process. The five steps are:

1) Salvation (or becoming born again)

2) Deliverance

3) Redemption

4) Restoration

5) Transformation

Step One: Becoming Born Again

The first step is the born-again experience. The majority of believers stop at this first experience. They are born again and then wait for the rest of their life to go to heaven because the only gospel they heard was the gospel of salvation with its focus on going to heaven and escaping hell. They have never heard and understood the gospel of the kingdom that Jesus and the disciples preached.

I came to the faith through the Pentecostal movement. The ultimate goal of the Pentecostal movement is to rescue people out of hell, get them born again, and then filled with the Holy Spirit and speaking in tongues. Once they arrive at this point, they stop growing. Because of spiritual pride, for the rest of their life they behave as though they are spiritually superior to everyone else because they speak in tongues. They don't realize that speaking in tongues is only the beginning of our life with the Holy Spirit, not the end. A majority of these people don't have a clue about what they are saved from.

In order to show us what God meant through salvation, God put a shadow of it in the Old Testament, as seen through the lives of the people of Israel. They were slaves in Egypt for hundreds of years before God moved to save (or deliver) them from their slavery. When we study the process and the results of their freedom from Egypt, we get an idea of what our salvation experience through Jesus Christ should be like too.

They were not saved to go to heaven. When they were freed from Egypt, which represented the kingdom of darkness, everything they lost was restored to them: their health, freedom, wealth, and their purpose were all restored to them. God promised them a land that flowed with milk and honey, which was their place of destiny.

THE PROCESS OF SALVATION, PART I

Why do we need to be born again? When we were born the first time, we were created in the likeness of the first Adam who sinned and disobeyed God. There is a big difference between the first and Last Adam.

When we were naturally born, we inherited the image and frailties of the first Adam. All of our weaknesses, sins, and failures came from him and through him. But God gave us another chance—to be born again through another Adam: Jesus. The Bible calls Him the Last Adam (1 Corinthians 15:45).

When you are born again, you inherit the image, qualities, and blessings of the Last Adam. We receive a new DNA for our spirit; we are adopted into a royal bloodline. That is why being born again is a very important principle. It is the beginning point, but we don't become born again just to go to heaven.

> For whom He foreknew, He also predestined to be conformed to the image of His Son, that He might be the firstborn among many brethren (Romans 8:29)

> The Spirit Himself bears witness with our spirit that we are children of God, and if children, then heirs—heirs of God and joint heirs with Christ, if indeed we suffer with *Him*, that we may also be glorified together (Romans 8:16-17).

We become born again to get rid of the things we inherited from the first Adam. It's our choice to remain in the first Adam or the Last Adam. Every form of evil, sin, sickness, curses, poverty, failure, pain, and brokenness came from the first Adam through our parents. You don't have to allow these problems to dictate your future; you have a choice.

This is what the Bible says about it:

> Therefore, if anyone is in Christ, he is a new creation; old things have passed away; behold, all things have become new (2 Corinthians 5:17).

We need to be conformed into the image of Jesus Christ. This happens through our confession. We are bone of His bone and flesh of His flesh (Ephesians 5:30).

When we were first born, we became a citizen of our country. When we are born again, we become a citizen of the kingdom of God. After we were born, we began to learn the language of our country, calling our parents Mamma and Daddy. After we are born again, we need to learn the language of the kingdom. Everything in the kingdom works by faith and by speaking the right words. It is important that we learn to speak and live by faith, and not by sight and feeling. We have been programmed by the language, culture, economy, and environment we grew up in to live according to the first Adam. Once we are in the kingdom, it is our responsibility to learn kingdom culture, economy, family, education, government, and so on, following the ways of the Last Adam.

Step Two: Deliverance

> He has delivered us from the power of darkness and conveyed us into the kingdom of the Son of His love, in whom we have redemption through His blood, the forgiveness of sins (Colossians 1:13-14).

The second step of salvation is deliverance. After we are born again, we all need to go through some form of deliverance. None of us are exempt from any of these five steps, regardless of which country, family, or culture we grew up in. You could be born into a royal family, but you still need to go through these five steps. We all come with different strongholds and forms of oppression, dysfunction, and deception, and sometimes even possession of the enemy operating in different areas of our lives.

According to the verse we just read, when we were born again we were delivered from the power of darkness, which is the kingdom of darkness and transferred to the kingdom of the Son of God. This new kingdom does not work the same as the nation we grew up in. Just like any other

THE PROCESS OF SALVATION, PART I

kingdom, it has its own culture, economy, government, education, and so on. The culture we grew up in taught us that we should hate our enemies; the culture of the kingdom of God says we need to love our enemies. In the kingdom of God, most things work opposite to the culture we grew up in.

It is not easy for us to change our mindset from our old culture to the kingdom culture. God incorporated a deliverance process into our journey to help us get rid of those old ways and mindsets. Either we can yield to this process willingly, or we will be initiated into it by various forms of trials and temptations and delivered slowly from one thing at a time. That process will continue until we die.

When God called Abraham in Genesis 12, He told him to get out of his country, and away from his family and his father's house. He wanted him to go to a land He was going to show him.

> Now the Lord had said to Abram: "Get out of your country, from your family and from your father's house, to a land that I will show you" (Genesis 12:1).

Why did God ask Abraham to get away from those three areas before He could take him to the land He was going to show him? Those were the areas Abraham needed to be *delivered* from before he could receive what God had for him. Each area represents something specific, and we need to go through that process of deliverance too.

The country represents the culture that we live in. Family represents our reputation or other people's opinions of us. And the father's house represents the traditions and experiences with which we grew up. We all need to be delivered from these three areas if we are going to see God's kingdom and receive what He has for us. Otherwise, you can be a good "worldly" Christian and go to heaven when you die—*and miss everything God has for you right here in this life.* What a waste of energy and resources that would be!

This agrees with what Jesus told Nicodemus: unless he was born again, he would not *see* the kingdom of God (John 3:3). God did not promise

Abraham that he was going to give him the land. First He said He was only going to show it to him.

These three areas create a "box" in which we live our lives. Normally, we do not think outside of that box. In fact, we do not even recognize that there *is* anything outside that box. Often enough, because of deception, we do not even acknowledge that we are in a box in the first place. When you are delivered, you come out of that box and into a life that flows with milk and honey. It is not easy to come out of that box though. Everything around you will try and fight to keep you in it for as long as possible. It takes revelation knowledge and deliberate action to get free.

Many precious believers hide behind their religious, cultural, or racial pride, and never go through the deliverance process. As a result, we have all kinds of problems in the church like racism, the caste system, malice, hatred, envy, sickness, poverty, and curses, in addition to other works of the flesh.

If there is any area in your life where you falter and you are not able to live based on what God says in His Word, you need deliverance in that area. There are nine major areas from which every believer needs to be delivered.

We are what is written in our DNA. We look, think, and function the way our DNA is programmed. It's the *software* by which we operate in our system called *life*. Originally, our DNA was coded by the Word. We thought, spoke, and functioned like God on earth. It has been scientifically proven that we can decode and reprogram our DNA. That's good news. Most of us carry defective DNA, which lets us think and function to less than our potential and purpose for which God created us. We carry the roots of many sinful default settings (malfunctions, curses, habits, and sicknesses) in that faulty DNA. Our deliverance needs to start with our DNA.

Cleanse your DNA with the blood of Jesus by speaking, and commanding your DNA to align with the DNA of Jesus Christ, the Last Adam, through whom you are born again. Deliverance starts from the very atom from which you were created and flows into every other area of life. We do not start the deliverance process from the outside; it starts from within.

THE PROCESS OF SALVATION, PART I

Deliverance has to begin from Genesis 1.

> Then God said, "Let Us make man in Our image, according to Our likeness; let them have dominion over the fish of the sea, over the birds of the air, and over the cattle, over all the earth and over every creeping thing that creeps on the earth" (Genesis 1:26).

There are four areas God mentioned through which the demonic forces could operate to deceive and destroy humans. They were through the fish of the sea, the birds of the air, cattle, and the produce of the earth and every creature that creeps on the face of the earth.

There is a specific reason that God mentioned those four categories. There are demonic forces that work through these four mediums. Each of these are gateways for spirits to receive a legal right to operate on the earth. They provide "bodies" to these demonic forces. First we need to be delivered from every force that is operating through bodies of water. That includes oceans, seas, rivers, lakes, streams, and so on. In many cultures, water spirits or marine spirits and their operation is very dominant.

The Bible mentions different sea creatures, which represent demonic forces. Leviathan and Rahab are a couple of examples. (See Job 41:1-4; Psalm 74:14; Psalm 89:9-10; Isaiah 27:1; and Isaiah 51:9.) In the Old Testament, one of the gods the Philistines worshiped was a half-fish, half-human god called Dagon (1 Samuel 5:4).

Modern-day Buddhism, Hinduism, and many other religions use fish as a symbol of their faith. There is a reason for this. I do not even recommend Christians using the fish as symbol of our faith. There are many people who put a fish on the back of their cars and in their houses, thinking it is a pure symbol of our faith, but nobody checks to find out where that symbol sprang from.

Jesus did not make necklaces or bracelets with a fish symbol and give them to His disciples. He only said He would make them fishers of men. We do not need to carry the symbol of fish to show that we are Christians or that we believe in creation instead of the theory of evolution. I highly recommend removing such things from your home and possessions if you have them.

There are powerful demonic creatures and fallen angels that are bound under the oceans. The Bible proves this by saying in Revelation that fallen angels were bound in the river Euphrates and will later be released to kill people on earth (Revelation 9:14-15).

You need to be free from the influence of these demonic spirits. You might have seen a doll that looks like a mermaid and you might have bought one for your child when they were little. That mermaid represents a demonic entity.

The fashion and makeup industries are under the influence of these spirits. People are not happy the way they look because they believe a lie from the pit of hell. Either they compare themselves to someone else or they believe the old lie of the devil that says God didn't do a good job when He made them, so they need to do something to make themselves more attractive. This is the same lie he told Eve in the garden. Mankind was created in the image and likeness of God already, but the devil brought doubt to that truth, telling them they could only be like God if they ate the fruit of the tree.

Many mythologies and religions around the world worship creatures that are connected to the water. You can search this out on the Internet if you like. You will be surprised what you find there. Unfortunately, many false prophets and pastors operate under the influence of these demons. There are sea serpents or dragons that are part of many religions.

There are angels of God that are in charge of water, fire, and the winds of the earth. (See Revelation 7:1; 14:18; and 16:5.) Remember, the enemy tries to copy everything God does. He has also appointed demonic forces as though they are in charge of these things, and continues to manipulate and deceive people with his lies. People in different cultures worship these natural phenomena as gods. Actually they are worshipping the demonic forces that are attached to them.

Water

Water is essential to our existence, so the enemy uses that to destroy us too. Floods, tsunamis, drownings, and any addiction related to drinking are works of the enemy. As God's children, we need to have power and authority over every power of darkness that operates through water. We need to take authority and receive deliverance from these demons intentionally.

Birds of the Air

The second area we need to be delivered from are the forces that operate through air. Satan uses air or atmosphere to attack humans. He is called the prince of the power of the air in the New Testament (Ephesians 2:2). There is a reason for this. Air is essential for our existence and communication. There is demonic communication going on all the time. There are demons that Satan appointed to gather news about you and spread false rumors and slander about you. He always uses other humans to accomplish that task.

That is why God forbids gossiping and spreading false news (Exodus 23:1). These were considered punishable sins in the Bible. In our day and time, we are familiar with the term "fake news." Demons are in control of most of the media and news outlets that spread false news.

We need to be delivered from demonic forces that operate through air. There are witches, wizards, and satanic agents that operate through air. You must speak and break the influences of these forces from your life and renounce and cast them out.

We can't live without air for too long. The enemy uses air to destroy us too. Through winds, cyclones, and tornadoes every year, hundreds of people die by the destructive power of the air.

In the book of Ecclesiastes, Solomon exhorts us by saying not to revile a king in our thoughts, nor curse a rich man even in our bedroom. Why? Because a bird on the wing may report what you say. He is talking about demonic spirits that are acting as news reporters here. They collect information about you and me and give it to Satan's headquarters.

> Do not revile the king even in your thoughts, or curse the rich in your bedroom, because a bird in the sky may carry your words, and a bird on the wing may report what you say (Ecclesiastes 10:20 NIV).

Cattle

Cattles are worshiped as gods in many religions. For example, they worship cows and many other animals as gods in India. It is interesting to note that while some cultures worship them, other cultures eat them. Just examine your life. What animals do you love and adore? In some other culture, they eat them. The forces that work behind all these customs and practices are completely demonic.

Produce of the Earth

God cursed the land in Genesis 3:17-18, and curses give demons a legal ability to operate and afflict people. Everything we take or produce out of the earth needs to be blessed before we eat or use it. Otherwise you won't know where it is coming from and what spiritual influence is behind it. Whether you buy it from a store, eat it in a restaurant: everything needs to be blessed in Jesus' name.

That is why God specifically said He will bless our going out, our coming in, and the food we cook and the produce of the land. If you read Deuteronomy 28, you will read the long list of things God said He will bless. We need to believe and receive those blessings and operate in them. Just because it is in the Bible, doesn't make it ours automatically. We need to believe and appropriate these blessings one by one.

Every product we use: electronics, vegetables, drugs, alcohol, clothing, are all produce of the earth. The enemy uses products to entice, infiltrate, deceive, and destroy people. We need to be careful when we see a product. Don't be influenced or tempted by them. The devil tempted Eve with the fruit, which was a product. He uses the same method now.

THE PROCESS OF SALVATION, PART I

Every Creature That Creeps on the Earth

There are demons that look like each creature God has created. Satan is called a snake or serpent for a reason. False ministers are called wolves. That is true on the other side as well. We are called sheep, and Jesus is the Lion of the Tribe of Judah. There are other demonic forces that are compared to frogs, locusts, bears, and leopards in the Bible. (See Revelation 9:3; 13:2; and 16:13.)

The next area that we need to be delivered from is the Babylonian system and its ways. Every person born into this world is raised in that system. Since we are born into it, we must receive deliverance intentionally. Otherwise, we will never realize we are even under its influence in the first place.

The Bible calls this system the mother of harlots, Babylon the Great (Revelation 17:5). There are seven mountains on which this harlot sits and deceives the whole world. (Revelation 17:9). A child of God needs to be free from each of these seven mountains. The majority of people are controlled by this system and don't even recognize it. They are born into it and they die in it. We will learn more about the Mystery Babylon in a different chapter.

Pride

The first and maybe the hardest thing for us to be delivered from is pride. Pride is the biggest hindrance to us in entering the kingdom of God. When Jesus announced the culture of His kingdom in Matthew 5 (the Sermon on the Mount or the Beatitudes), the first thing He said was, "Blessed are the poor in spirit, for theirs is the kingdom of heaven" (Matthew 5:3). *Poor in spirit* means being willing to admit that we need help and willing to receive that help. It describes someone who is hungry for God.

In my ministry life, one of the things I found is how hard it is for people to admit that they need help, that they are broken in some ways, and that they are willing to show their real self and be authentic with themselves and others. That is the first step toward receiving deliverance.

It is common for us to say, "I am proud of this or that" or "I am jealous." We need to put that language away and learn to speak the language of the kingdom. In the kingdom, we say, "I am pleased with you," or "I am happy for you." Imagine the Father, looking at the Son, and saying, "I am proud of You!" Or Jesus telling Peter, "I am so proud of you; you walked on water!" Ridiculous! Pride and jealousy originated in the heart of Lucifer, and we should not give an inch in our heart to them. They will destroy us.

Why do so many wonderful Christians die without ever entering or knowing about the kingdom? The number one reason is pride. Once we are born again, the pride of our nationality, color, culture, race, and whatever else, needs to be cleansed from our heart. We need to humble ourselves as Jesus did, as the Bible says in 1 Peter 5:6. Otherwise in the end, we will be humbled by force.

Culture

Once we are born again, we become a citizen of the kingdom of heaven. Thus, we need to be delivered from the culture of the country we grew up in, with all its malfunctions and the mindset that it formed in us, and learn about the culture of heaven. We each have past experiences, abuses, pride, prejudices, and sins that left a scar or a wound on our soul. We must be healed or delivered from those.

People everywhere think their particular culture and language are better than every other culture and language. It is the pride of man that makes us feel like that, and we need to be delivered from it. Once you are free from the pride of your culture, nationality, race, and language, you will have the heart to completely accept people from other cultures.

Once you are freed from your culture, you will still speak your language and eat that food, but you will not feel prejudiced or prideful over others. A culture is made of eight ingredients: manners, traditions, customs, food, laws, language, race, and superstitions.

Evil spirits take control of those areas in our lives and work through them, causing us to feel as if there is nothing wrong or nothing missing. The opposite is also true. Some people believe there is nothing good in them and that they are irreparable. That is also a deception. Its purpose is to keep us trapped in a lie, so we will never experience the fullness of what God has promised us.

There are demonic influences in every culture on earth. What we think is normal and good, many times is not normal and good in the kingdom of God. On many occasions, the culture we grew up in has imposed and ingrained limitations on us and twisted our view of life, the world, and God. We are created to live in the culture of heaven, which manifested in Eden in the beginning.

When the Israelites came out of Egypt, God had to create a new culture for them by giving them His Law. The Law He gave them covered every aspect of life, including diet, feasts, and festivals. He was training them to have a new mindset and a new way of thinking. He wanted them to completely cut ties with Egypt. It took forty years to get rid of the culture and influence of Egypt over them. That's the power of culture.

I am not saying we should go back to Old Testament Laws and its regulations. If you are a believer, God already wrote His laws in your heart. Jesus revealed the culture of His kingdom in the Sermon on the Mount. Matthew 5-7 are the foundation of kingdom culture.

Traditions

Culture forms within us our *way of thinking*, and traditions form our *way of doing* things. Many of us struggle with traditions we received from our parents, and most of us don't realize it because they are normal for us. When we hear or see something outside of those traditions, we tend to fight it. Once we start to live in God's kingdom, we need to learn to live above all the traditions of men, and be flexible and adaptable like Jesus was when He lived on earth (1 Peter 1:18).

The Opinions of Others

We all like to hear people say good things about us. Unfortunately, there will be people speaking negative things about us too, regardless of what we do. Jesus did everything perfectly and people spoke against Him. We may not do anything perfectly on this side of heaven, plus we all have the "junk" we went through. The enemy will use people to speak badly about us. His intention is to discourage us.

Religious Spirit

Even if we do not get free from other spirits, there is one spirit that we all need to be free from, and that is the religious spirit. This spirit works like an umbrella over many others. If we tackle this one, many others that torment us will manifest as well. Any time you stand up and live for the kingdom of God, this spirit will oppose you. Below are symptoms of the religious spirit in operation.

1. The religious spirit will always prompt us to look for miracles. A kingdom mindset will prompt us to use God's wisdom first, which when applied, will bring forth miracles.

2. The religious spirit will tell you that revival is the solution to all our problems. The Holy Spirit tells us the kingdom of God is the solution to our problems.

3. The religious spirit will convince you that the earth and its resources do not belong to us, but to the devil and his children.

4. The religious spirit will teach you that God created man to worship Him. The Holy Spirit will tell you that God our Father created us to have dominion over the earth.

5. The religious spirit will always require a sign from heaven in order to believe and prove God's credibility. The Holy Spirit will tell us that Jesus Christ is the Sign and the Wonder.

6. The religious spirit will make you passionate about a religion called Christianity. The Holy Spirit will make you passionate about Jesus and His kingdom.

7. The religious spirit will always look for an emotional experience. The Holy Spirit will help us to walk and live by faith, moment by moment.

THE PROCESS OF SALVATION, PART I

8. The religious spirit will always oppose the kingdom of God and its teachings. The Holy Spirit was sent as the Governor of the kingdom of God.

9. The religious spirit loves the past and the future. It has nothing to offer you for the present. It is stuck in the past. Its plan is to make you a *someday* Christian and to steal from you what God has *right now*.

10. The religious spirit is the meanest spirit and the worst enemy to the love of God. It will cause us to be judgmental and critical of ourselves and others, and will not allow us to show any compassion, mercy, or kindness.

11. The religious spirit will create zeal in us for the Lord, but it will blind us from gaining any kind of real knowledge. It will keep us ineffective, but full of a false sense of zeal. The religious spirit thrives on ignorance.

12. Religion is always heaven-focused. The kingdom is always earth-focused: desiring to see God's kingdom come and His will be done on earth as it is in heaven.

13. Religion is focused on escaping earth and reaching heaven. The kingdom is focused on transforming the earth.

14. Religion is about populating heaven. The kingdom is about being fruitful and having dominion on earth.

15. The religious spirit will always keep you in condemnation, regret, and guilt. The Holy Spirit will always give you boldness and confidence in and toward God.

16. The religious spirit will deceive and steal every inheritance your heavenly Father has given you as His child, so that you will not be a blessing to anyone. Or it will keep you deprived from having any resources with which you can impact the earth.

17. The religious spirit will try to imitate almost everything the Holy Spirit does to make people feel it is the right spirit, but it is

only spiritualism or emotionalism. It has nothing to do with the kingdom of God.

18. The religious spirit will either make you too spiritual and no earthly good, or too worldly with no revelation about the kingdom of God. You would be surprised to find how many believers know very little or nothing about the kingdom of God, even though they have been in church for decades. It is the most important subject in the Bible. God brings real balance.

19. The religious spirit will make you feel that you are a good Christian and doing God and yourself a great favor, just because you go to church on a Sunday morning, and maybe two other meetings (probably a mid-week service and Bible study during the week days). Life with the Holy Spirit is a moment-by-moment communion with Him.

20. The religious spirit will deceive you and limit your salvation experience, so you think it's only about reaching heaven when you die. The Holy Spirit will guide you into all the works He has prepared for you beforehand (Ephesians 2:10).

21. The religious spirit will always oppose the anointing, and is the strong defender and protector of human and religious traditions. The Holy Spirit is creative and free.

22. The religious spirit will keep you doing the same religious rituals over and over again, while expecting different results. The Holy Spirit is a Spirit of innovation and creativity, which means He seldom does the same thing twice.

23. The religious spirit thrives on fear, pride, and ignorance. The Holy Spirit brings joy, peace, and righteousness (Romans 14:17).

24. The religious spirit will cause you to hate the earth and its resources. The Holy Spirit will make you a wise steward of everything God created.

25. The religious spirit will cause you to have a passion to help the poor and make you feel that this is the number one priority in

THE PROCESS OF SALVATION, PART I

life, but you won't have much to give. The Holy Spirit will tell you that helping the poor is only one of the ministries every church should have, and supply and direct our giving.

26. The religious spirit will try to limit our experiences with God by attaching our spirituality to buildings, particular places, or locations on earth. The Holy Spirit is omnipresent and the whole earth belongs to Him.

27. The religious spirit is the stingiest spirit in the whole world. The Holy Spirit will always lead us to be generous.

28. The religious spirit will not let us discover our purpose, but let us waste our time on religious rituals instead. The Holy Spirit was sent to help us discover and fulfill God's purpose.

29. The religious spirit will cause us to hate true wisdom, knowledge, and understanding. The Holy Spirit *is* the Spirit of wisdom, knowledge, and understanding.

30. The religious spirit focuses on the outward appearance and false holiness and humility. The Holy Spirit is the Spirit of truth and will always lead us into truth.

31. The religious spirit will cause you to believe that being poor is a sign of being humble, being stupid is wisdom, being clean is holiness, being insecure is polite, and doing the right thing will make you righteous. The Holy Spirit leads us in the paths of righteousness, and into true humility, wisdom, holiness, and kindness.

32. The religious spirit will cause people to be too heavenly-minded and not earthly good. They won't have a healthy balance between the spiritual and the natural. The Holy Spirit will teach you that God created the heavens and the earth.

33. The religious spirit will cause you to depend on and trust in your personal achievements, merits, abilities, and works to please God. As a result, we become self-reliant and take pride in our accomplishments. The Bible calls this self-righteousness. The

Holy Spirit teaches us to find our righteousness in God. Through Him, we rely on Jesus and not ourselves.

34. The religious spirit will cause us to be self-focused and self-conscious instead of God-conscious. This produces an unnatural fear of God in us, so that we become afraid of God instead of having a relationship with Him. The Holy Spirit immerses us in the love of God and helps us walk in His holiness so our lives are balanced and free.

35. The religious spirit will cause you to feel prideful about your religious background and traditions. The Holy Spirit wants to unveil and teach us something new every day.

36. The religious spirit will limit God to a mere temporary emotional experience or ecstasy. The Holy Spirit is the Spirit of faith; He wants us to live and walk by faith and not by what we feel.

Believe it or not, the religious spirit affects every single human being, unless they deliberately become free from it. It will not leave you alone. Take this list and use it to do a self-evaluation, and see if you are affected by the religious spirit in one way or another.

When the church becomes free from this religious spirit, we will go back to our original intent again, and the church will be restored to its original glory and power. As a result, nations will be restored to God. We need to get busy with kingdom evangelism once again. May the Lord open our eyes to see the world as He does.

The Spirit of This World

> Now we have received, not the spirit of the world, but the Spirit who is from God, that we might know the things that have been freely given to us by God (1 Corinthians 2:12).

This spirit causes us to love the things of this world. It loves to fight for position, prominence, personal success, pleasure, and material things. It

THE PROCESS OF SALVATION, PART I

will create a passion in your heart for the things of this world and blind you from receiving the true life that is in Christ Jesus.

Those who are deceived by this spirit will not receive the message of the kingdom. Their life has been stolen from them to make the god of this world richer. This spirit will let people have so much wealth, money, and connections that they think they are being successful, but none of that wealth or influence benefits the kingdom of God.

Notice the phrase "spirit of *the world*." It's all about this world, and not at all about the kingdom of God. There are many believers who think they are good Christians because they go to a church on a Sunday morning. The enemy is using them as pawns.

Anything you do or possess that does not benefit the expansion of God's kingdom on earth, is being used by the devil to fulfill his will on earth. The sooner you understand this and make a choice, the better for your life and future. Don't be a pawn in the hands of the devil, thinking you are living a good life and giving God and His kingdom a tip here and there. Do you remember what happened to the rich young ruler, and the story of the rich man and Lazarus? Don't let that happen to you.

> And when His disciples James and John saw this, they said, "Lord, do You want us to command fire to come down from heaven and consume them, just as Elijah did?" But He turned and rebuked them, and said, "You do not know what manner of spirit you are of" (Luke 9:54-55).

When Jesus told the disciples that He was going to go to Jerusalem to die on the cross, one of His closest disciples, Peter, began to rebuke Him. Peter did not want Jesus to die, and was willing to fight for Him with his own life. Jesus turned and rebuked him, calling him Satan (Matthew 16:21-23).

Demas was one of Paul's ministry companions. He traveled with him for a while, but when he saw an opportunity that benefitted him personally, he left the ministry team and followed that opportunity. Paul wrote that Demas loved the present world and went to Thessalonica (2 Timothy 4:10).

There are different spirits that work under the spirit of this world, and below are some of them.

The Spirit of Mammon

There are only two masters in this world: God and the spirit of mammon, which uses money to control people. You either serve God or money, depending on whose voice you obey. Money has a voice and it speaks to you. Who decides what you do or do not do? What you buy or do not buy? Is your money making that choice for you, or are you making that choice as led by the Holy Spirit?

Every believer needs to be delivered from the spirit of mammon. It won't leave you alone just because you are born again or Spirit filled. There is a process to be set free from this spirit. One of the main ways God uses to set His people free from this spirit is to tell them to give away something that is precious to them. That's the way He circumcises a heart—through sacrificial obedience. If your obedience did not require any sacrifice, then it did not cost you anything. If it did not cost you anything, it won't get registered in heaven.

The Spirit of Lust

If you have been alive for any period of time, you already understand that lust is connected to our body and flesh.

> Having escaped the corruption that is in the world through *lust* (2 Peter 1:4).

There are two kinds of lust the Bible talks about: the lust of the eye and the lust of the flesh (1 John 2:16). Both are part of this world. Every temptation and sin comes through one of these. One of the reasons destruction came upon the children of Israel in the wilderness was because of lust. They lusted for meat, which was the lust of the flesh. We can lust for various things: food, sex, independence, and much more. The spirit of lust is also

THE PROCESS OF SALVATION, PART I

the root of all sexual sins: fornication, adultery, homosexuality, lesbianism, and so on.

The Spirit of Individualism

Individualism is a term for extreme selfishness. We have been brought up to be selfish. When selfishness matures, it gives birth to individualism, and when individualism matures, it gives birth to humanism.

Imagine what the results would have been if people like Joseph, Moses, Esther, Jesus, and Paul cared only about their personal success. Esther would never have gone before the king if she cared only about her success. All these people had something bigger in their mind than themselves. They risked their lives for the betterment of their society and nations. People like Gandhi, Martin Luther King, Jr. and Mother Teresa cared more for others than themselves. Their lives are written in the pages of history.

One of the reasons for the epidemic of divorce in our society is individualism, or selfishness. Individualism is the attitude that believes, "I can do whatever I want, whenever I want, and however I want, regardless of how it might affect or hurt me or someone else." The focus is self-gratification. That opens the door to evil.

The Spirit of Pleasure

Have you noticed that our culture is all about having fun? I was talking with a life coach and she said, "God is all about fun, right?" I asked, "Which God?" Which verse in the Bible says God is all about having fun? That certainly does not describe the God of the Bible. That describes the god of this world. He wants to keep you busy having fun, so you will never discover your purpose or do anything meaningful with your life.

Paul warned that in the last days people would become lovers of pleasure rather than lovers of God.

> But know this, that in the last days perilous times will come: For men will be lovers of themselves, lovers of money,

boasters, proud, blasphemers, disobedient to parents, unthankful, unholy, unloving, unforgiving, slanderers, without self-control, brutal, despisers of good, traitors, headstrong, haughty, lovers of pleasure rather than lovers of God, having a form of godliness but denying its power. And from such people turn away! (2 Timothy 3:1-5).

There are spirits that are working behind that nature. People need to be delivered from those spirits.

Past Mistakes and Failures

The most unfortunate thing you can do to yourself is quit what God has called you to do because you made some mistakes. One thing I have heard from people who accomplished great things on earth is "never quit." Regardless of what has happened to you or what you did, know that there is life after that. The enemy *loves* our past mistakes. Though God *forgets* them, the devil will keep reminding us of our failures. He will never remind us of anything good we did, or that God did through us.

I once was feeling very discouraged. I began to make a list of all the mistakes and failures that happened in my life. I forgot all the wonderful things God had done for me. The only thing I could focus on was my mistakes, so I actually took a paper and wrote them all down on both sides. As I did, I felt even worse about myself. I thought I would never accomplish anything great in my life because of all the stupid things I had done. I fell into a black hole of despair. I did not realize at that time that it was a trap of the enemy.

After a couple of days, I went to look for that list and could not find it. I searched and searched but had no idea what happened to it. (I believe an angel came and took it away from me.) If I had kept that and kept looking at it, I never would have made any progress. Thank God that I never found that worthless list. The blood of Jesus washed every mistake and failure away. As the Bible says, the righteous will fall seven times but he will rise up and walk again (Proverbs 24:16).

THE PROCESS OF SALVATION, PART I

Fears and Insecurities

If there is one spirit that will try to stop you from stepping into what God has for you, it is the spirit of fear. It will remind you of all your inadequacies and insecurities and steal everything you have in Christ Jesus. If allowed, it will eventually steal your destiny. We need to keep reminding ourselves that God has not given us a spirit of fear, but of power, love, and a sound mind (2 Timothy 1:7).

David said he sought the Lord, and He delivered him from all his fears (Psalm 34:4). Different people struggle with different types of fear. There are all kinds of phobias and apprehensions. Three of the primary fears are fear of death, fear of failure, and fear of man. If you can be delivered from these three, there won't be room for any of the others to have a hold on your life.

We don't deliver ourselves. By faith, we appropriate the deliverance Christ accomplished for us on the cross in each area of our lives. This is done through various ways and methods. Some of these are prayer, fasting, counseling, love, knowledge, and many more. (See Matthew 17:21; Isaiah 9:6; and Proverbs 11:9.) There is no one-size-fits-all method in the kingdom. There are many innocent believers who have been saved, *but have never been delivered.* As a result, they go through life from problem to problem, from one emergency to another, wondering what is wrong with them. What is wrong? The enemy has a hold on some area(s) of their lives and he trips them up whenever they try to move forward. They never seem to get ahead in life, no matter how hard they try.

The Spirit of Poverty

The spirit of poverty affects every human being. If you think a lack of money is the reason you are not doing what God has called you to do, this spirit is affecting you. If you work for the purpose of making money instead of fulfilling your purpose, this spirit controls you. If you think money is your number one problem, you are a slave to the spirit of mammon. The spirit of poverty works in different ways in different cultures. We usually think of the person begging on the street as poor or afflicted by this spirit.

In the West, people think they are rich because they have more and better conveniences than people in developing countries.

What I have seen, percentage-wise, is that there are more poor people in the West than in the developing nations. In developing nations, whatever a poor person has, he or she owns. It might be a shack or a tent, but they own it. In developed countries, the banks own almost everything people use. If people do not make their payments to the bank every month, they can end up on the street and not owning anything. Many work almost their whole life to pay off the money they borrowed from banks.

There are two ways to live. We have just enough time to fulfill our purpose here, so we need to do that from the beginning instead of getting entangled in the other system. Once we discover our calling, we must establish that as our business to support ourselves to get out from under the spirit of poverty rampant in the world system.

Until you are free from the spirit of poverty, you will not be able to tap into the resources God has made available to you in His kingdom. You won't be able to see them or know them. We need to be able to draw from our kingdom inheritance.

Healing from Emotional Wounds

When you think of God, the emotions that come to your heart and spirit are very important. Remember, sin distorted our view of God. When you come to Him after you are saved, if you are feeling any emotions other than the love of your heavenly Father, it means there is some form of demonic intrusion or foothold in you that needs to be dealt with.

Just like we need deliverance from different spiritual strongholds, we need healing and restoration from emotional wounds. A majority of us have experienced different forms of abuse while we were growing up. Many of us did not receive the emotional and spiritual nurturing that we needed, so we grew up deprived of love, and as a result, we became defective in different areas.

THE PROCESS OF SALVATION, PART I

When you come to God, if you feel unworthy it means you need restoration of your identity. If you do not feel safe, it means fear is operating in your mind. If you do not feel accepted, then rejection is in operation. If you feel unclean, then shame is involved. If you feel guilty and condemned you need to be delivered from the law. If you are afraid of your future, then you have an issue with trust and trusting God. If you do not feel as though you belong, then abandonment is in operation.

If you sense any other emotions, then write them down one by one in your journal and deal with them; do not ignore them. Everything that your heavenly Father did not plant in you must be uprooted.

Others have experienced emotional, verbal, physical, or sexual abuse. We need to be healed from the wounds and scars they left in our soul. Others experienced trauma. The reason we are not able to function the way we should is because those wounds must be healed. Most of the time, this will require the help of others. The more you open up and seek the right help, the easier it will become to get healed. It will be a journey to wholeness and not a one-day retreat.

Emotional wounds might carry demonic strongholds. You need to cast those demons out of you. Don't come up with any excuses or negotiate with the demons. They have to go.

I have not met a single human being yet who does not have some kind of emotional wounds or deformities in their soul. Some don't admit it because of pride. The earlier you admit to it and seek healing for them, the better your life will be as you get older.

After you go through the above-mentioned process, you will be able to see yourself as God sees you and think about yourself according to how God thinks of you, and also understand His purpose for your life and for this planet for the FIRST TIME. You will have the right perspective toward this world and mankind for the first time as well.

Chapter 20: The Process of Salvation, Part II

Step Three: Redemption

After we experience deliverance, we need to move into the next step of redemption. *Without experiencing deliverance, you cannot appropriate redemption.* Without deliverance, you cannot even see what God has in store for you or what you lost because of sin. You could be saved, but all your inheritance as a child of God, your health, wealth, and emotional well-being might all be bound up by the enemy and you will not enjoy any of it now in this life.

Redemption is the process of buying, or taking back, what we lost when Adam fell. This is a vast subject. My book, *Overcoming the Spirit of Poverty*, can help you in understanding all God gave us through Adam. Jesus paid the price with His blood to redeem everything the enemy has stolen from us. We were taken captive by the enemy (through sin) and Jesus paid the price for our freedom. He bought us back and made us His own.

> For you were bought at a price; therefore glorify God in your body and in your spirit, which are God's (1 Corinthians 6:20; 7:23; 2 Peter 2:1).
>
> In Him we have redemption through His blood, the forgiveness of sins, according to the riches of His grace (Ephesians 1:7).

> But of Him you are in Christ Jesus, who became for us wisdom from God—and righteousness and sanctification and redemption (1 Corinthians 1:30).

Sanctification is part of the deliverance process. One by one, you reclaim everything the enemy has stolen from you: your land, blessings, and every other benefit you are supposed to receive from the Lord as His child. Our body will be redeemed only after we die or at the rapture. (See Romans 8:23 and Ephesians 1:14 and 4:30.) One of the names of our God is Redeemer. (See Job 19:25; Isaiah 54:8; and 59:20.)

Areas of Our Lives That God Redeems

He Redeems Us from the House of Bondage

> The Lord did not set His love on you nor choose you because you were more in number than any other people, for you were the least of all peoples; but because the Lord loves you, and because He would keep the oath which He swore to your fathers, the Lord has brought you out with a mighty hand, and redeemed you from the house of bondage, from the hand of Pharaoh king of Egypt (Deuteronomy 7:7-8).

We were all sold under sin, kept captive by the enemy, and without hope in this world. God redeemed Israel from their house of bondage, which was Egypt. "House of bondage" represents our past. Jesus paid the price and redeemed our lives from bondage, sin, and the devil, and brought us out to freedom. Once we are made free, we need to stay free, trusting in His grace.

He Redeems Our Lives from Adversity

> But David answered Rechab and Baanah his brother, the sons of Rimmon the Beerothite, and said to them,

THE PROCESS OF SALVATION, PART II

> "As the Lord lives, who has redeemed my life from all adversity" (2 Samuel 4:9).

As you begin your walk with the Lord to fulfill His purpose for your life, you will realize that many difficulties will come against you. It was David who wrote the above verse, and he was a man chosen by God to be king of Israel. On his way to fulfilling that call, he encountered an enormous amount of adversity, much of it life-threatening, but the Lord redeemed him out of it all. If you are going through any trouble right now, know that with God there is redemption available for you from that situation.

He Redeems Our Lives from Distress

> And the king took an oath and said, "As the Lord lives, who has redeemed my life from every distress" (1 Kings 1:29).

Adversity causes distress. God is able to redeem us from all distress.

He Redeems Our Soul

> But God will redeem my soul from the power of the grave, for He shall receive me (Psalm 49:15).

Though everyone's price for freedom was paid by Jesus, not everyone will receive or enjoy that freedom. It depends on the level of freedom they enjoy in their soul. As it says in 3 John 2, we will prosper and be in health as our soul prospers. Our soul needs to be redeemed and restored as it says in Psalm 23.

He Redeems Our Lives from Oppression and Violence

> He will redeem their life from oppression and violence; and precious shall be their blood in His sight (Psalm 72:14).

The enemy will try to destroy us any way he can. He looks for opportunities to cause havoc in our lives, but the Lord will not let him destroy us. He redeems us from the oppressor and violence.

He Redeems Our Lives from Destruction

> Who redeems your life from destruction, who crowns you with lovingkindness and tender mercies (Psalm 103:4).

Whatever the enemy brings to destroy us, the Lord will turn that around and use it to destroy our enemies. As the Bible says, those who bless us will be blessed and those who curse us will be cursed.

He Redeems Us from the Hand of the Enemy

> Let the redeemed of the Lord say so, whom He has redeemed from the hand of the enemy (Psalm 107:2).

We were held captive by the enemy of our soul. Jesus came to rescue and redeem us from our captors.

He Redeems Us from the Curse of the Law

> Christ has redeemed us from the curse of the law, having become a curse for us (for it is written, "Cursed is everyone who hangs on a tree") (Galatians 3:13).

Many believers in Christ operate under the curse of the law. They go back to the law and pick and choose what they want to believe, then obey without knowing they are bringing a curse upon their own life. Curse is the opposite of blessing. The reason we are not able to receive the blessings of the Lord is because of the curses that are operating in our lives.

THE PROCESS OF SALVATION, PART II

Step Four: Restoration

After we appropriate the redemption we received through Jesus, we move on to the next step: restoration. Restoration is the process of restoring something to its original intent, state, and position. If someone steals your television set and you find the thief, you redeem your television and bring it back into your home. If you leave it in your garage, it is redeemed, but it is not restored. When it is restored, it is returned to the place in which it was originally kept.

There are many things that have been redeemed, but are not restored yet. There is a lot of restoration that needs to be done in our land and in the body of Christ. God is in the process of restoration.

> Jesus answered and said to them, "Indeed, Elijah is coming first and will restore all things" (Matthew 17:11).

> And that He may send Jesus Christ, who was preached to you before, whom heaven must receive until the times of restoration of all things, which God has spoken by the mouth of all His holy prophets since the world began (Acts 3:20-21).

> But this is a people robbed and plundered; all of them are snared in holes, and they are hidden in prison houses; they are for prey, and no one delivers; for plunder, and no one says, "Restore!" (Isaiah 42:22).

Acts 3:21 says there will be a time for the restoration of *all things* that have been damaged by the fall of man, but we have been waiting for the destruction of all things for too long instead. God does not want to *destroy* but to *restore* mankind to their original *position* and the rest of creation to its original *state*. This verse also says that God has spoken this by the mouth of *all of His holy prophets* since the world began. Note the phrase *all of His holy prophets*, meaning not even one spoke anything different.

What about so-called modern day prophets who have been speaking destruction and not restoration? Do you think God sent them? I do not believe so. If God had sent them, they would speak the same thing that *all of His holy prophets* have been speaking since the beginning of the world. It is time for us to realign with God's plan and purpose and not waste any more of our precious time.

Here are some areas that need to be restored.

The Earth Needs to Be Restored

> Thus says the Lord: "In an acceptable time I have heard You, and in the day of salvation I have helped You; I will preserve You and give You as a covenant to the people, to restore the earth, to cause them to inherit the desolate heritages'" (Isaiah 49:8).

I do not believe we will restore the entire earth, but at least some areas of this planet will be restored to their original state and intent. God will do this through the body of Christ. The church has been waiting for God to show up in one of their services and begin the restoration and transformation process for too long. That is not the way He does things. He already showed up on the earth in person, gave us the keys, and told us what to do with them. He will not do this *in* the church; He wants to do it *through* the church. We are supposed to use what He has given us for the benefit of the planet.

Another utopian idea we have about the restoration of the earth is that when it is restored, it will look like some kind of magical world. There are some spots on earth that already look like a magical world. When the earth is restored, it will be in the same state as the Promised Land was when the Israelites lived in it. When they lived in obedience to God's Word, the earth produced its full strength, and no sickness or disease of any kind came upon anyone. It is absolutely possible in our day and time to have the same blessing upon the land we own. We need to redeem it and restore it back to God.

THE PROCESS OF SALVATION, PART II

The Leaders of the Nations Need to Be Restored

> I will restore your judges as at the first, and your counselors as at the beginning. Afterward you shall be called the city of righteousness, the faithful city (Isaiah 1:26).

It is sad when people who lack common sense are elected as heads of state. They have tried to redefine marriage, the first institution God established on earth. Lawmakers and leaders do not seem to understand the basic difference between male and female, or even animals and humans. They claim to be wise, but lack a healthy human conscience that can differentiate right from wrong.

Our Productivity and Years Need to Be Restored

> So I will restore to you the years that the swarming locust has eaten, the crawling locust, the consuming locust, and the chewing locust, My great army which I sent among you (Joel 2:25).

Many of us are behind on our purpose and the timing of its fulfillment. We have been derailed and distracted. Our years and our harvest have been eaten and stolen by the enemy. Through salvation, God wants to restore them to us, so we can catch up and be in line with His timing and purpose.

Our Soul Needs to Be Restored

> He restores my soul; He leads me in the paths of righteousness for His name's sake (Psalm 23:3).

Everyone's soul needs to be restored. When we fall or scrape ourselves, our body is wounded. When we go through abuse or any kind of trauma, our soul gets wounded and it needs to be healed. Time doesn't heal all emotional wounds, just like time doesn't heal all physical wounds. Wounds require healing. The wounds that we carry that no one can see, especially require the touch of the Great Physician.

Our Language Needs to Be Restored

> For then I will restore to the peoples a pure language, that they all may call on the name of the Lord, to serve Him with one accord (Zephaniah 3:9).

If there is one thing that needs to be restored, it is the unity of the body of Christ. The devil knows what our potential would be if we were united, so he brings all kinds of schisms to divide us. Jesus specifically prayed for us to be one, as He is one with the Father. He prayed this way so we would enjoy unity in the family and in the body of Christ.

There was a confusion of language at the tower of Babel. Once again, we need to enjoy clarity in our speech and language so we can maintain unity. Language does not necessarily refer to a particular earthly language, but an understanding in our communication that produces unity of heart instead. There is much confusion and chaos around us. When the Lord restores our language, we will all speak the same thing and think the same thing, as Paul explained to the church in Corinth.

> Now I plead with you, brethren, by the name of our Lord Jesus Christ, that you all speak the same thing, and that there be no divisions among you, but that you be perfectly joined together in the same mind and in the same judgment (1 Corinthians 1:10).

In Acts, we read the phrase *one accord* several times. It means they all had the same mind, goal, and priority. The Holy Spirit worked through the early church powerfully because of that. Today, we struggle to get even two people to agree on something because our language is not restored.

THE PROCESS OF SALVATION, PART II

Step Five: Transformation

After restoration, the final step is transformation, or glorification. Transformation begins with our mind:

> And do not be conformed to this world, but be transformed by the renewing of your mind, that you may prove what is that good and acceptable and perfect will of God (Romans 12:2).

Then it moves to our body. The more our mind is renewed, the more the life that is in our spirit will manifest in other areas of our lives.

> But we all, with unveiled face, beholding as in a mirror the glory of the Lord, are being transformed into the same image from glory to glory, just as by the Spirit of the Lord (2 Corinthians 3:18).

> Moreover whom He predestined, these He also called; whom He called, these He also justified; and whom He justified, these He also glorified (Romans 8:30).

The third stage of transformation is the renewal of our body. For most of us, it will happen either at the rapture or the resurrection. There were only two people who reached that level while they were alive: Enoch and Elijah.

Each of us is somewhere in this five-step process. When we have gone through all these steps, then we can say we are really saved. That is what Jesus meant by salvation. I want to encourage you not to get frustrated about where you are in that process. We will not all reach perfection in this life, though some may; but as long as we make progress daily, we are on the right track and we have reason to rejoice. Don't get stuck or give up in frustration.

That is why Paul encouraged the believers in Philippi to work out their own salvation, instead of just saying they were saved. We have to work it out to receive its benefits. It is interesting how he says, "work out *your own* salvation," not someone else's.

> Therefore, my beloved, as you have always obeyed, not as in my presence only, but now much more in my absence, work out your own salvation with fear and trembling (Philippians 2:12).

Jesus put the fivefold ministry gifts (apostles, prophets, evangelists, pastors, and teachers) in the church to help us appropriate everything God had made available through Christ. Once we are trained or equipped, each of us will become a perfect man.

Till we all come to the unity of the faith and of the knowledge of the Son of God, to a perfect man, to the measure of the stature of the fullness of Christ (Ephesians 4:13).

This verse says *we all* come to the unity of faith. It is talking about the entire body of Christ receiving the knowledge of the Son of God, to be a perfect man. The five-fold ministry gifts are supposed to bring the knowledge of the Son of God that produces the unity of faith in the church, so that we become a perfect man. So far, what most of the five-fold ministry gifts have been trying to do is create revival.

Who is a perfect man? There were only two perfect men that ever lived on earth: Adam before the fall and Jesus. Adam was perfect to an extent before he committed sin, but we do not have any history of how he lived or what he did before the fall, so we do not have an example to follow. To give us a model of how we should live once we were saved, God sent another Adam to this earth, Jesus Christ, who is called the Last Adam (1 Corinthians 15:45).

When we become perfect, we live up to the measure of the stature of the fullness of Christ. What is the measure of the stature of the fullness of Christ? Who is Christ in His fullness or in His originality? Christ is the Creator and He is the King. Once we are restored, we are supposed to live like the original Adam, or Jesus Christ, the Last Adam, as kings and creators. The above verse is talking about something that needs to happen here on earth and not in heaven.

Manifestation

The more we are transformed into the image and likeness of God, the more His glory and kingdom will begin to manifest through us. All of creation is waiting for the manifestation of the sons of God. Adam's fall affected the rest of creation, so our salvation or restoration should affect the rest of creation as well. Otherwise it is not salvation, but "fire insurance" or escape from hell.

The reason creation remains the same is because not very many believers are walking in their true identity as sons and daughters of God. Most are waiting to escape and go to heaven. They did not hear the gospel of the kingdom yet. God is raising up a new generation of sons and daughters who are willing to go all the way for God and His kingdom.

Chapter 21: Discipling Nations with the Gospel of the Kingdom

The gospel of the kingdom means that our God is a King and has a kingdom, and He wants to see it established on the earth. Now that we understand what the gospel of the kingdom is, let's see how to practically preach and apply it in every nation. That is God's heart and will. According to Jesus, only after we do this the end will come (Matthew 24:14).

The process of practically applying the gospel of the kingdom in a nation is called *discipling* a nation. We have preached the gospel of salvation, and millions of people are saved and waiting to go to heaven. Most of them have no idea what they were saved from and why they are here. It is time to preach the gospel of the kingdom, activating each believer and releasing them to fulfill their destiny.

Though there are churches in every nation, most nations are in a crisis mode. They are looking for solutions. Unfortunately, the group of people who are supposed to be the salt of the earth and light of the world have no clue how to solve the problems we are facing.

Only the gospel of the kingdom has the power to disciple a nation. How do we disciple a nation with the gospel of the kingdom? First of all, we need to understand how kingdoms operate.

The earth is now under the sway of the kingdom of darkness. Our politics, educational system, economy, and culture are infected and infiltrated, and most times controlled by Satan and his cohorts. We are trying to invade his kingdom with another kingdom, which is the kingdom of God.

We do not see Muslims, Mormons, and Jews preaching much about their faith, but they infiltrate every aspect of society in nearly every culture. I was in London a couple of weeks ago and realized that in many British cities, the mayors are Muslims. How did that happen? Muslims have a better kingdom mindset than most Christians I know.

They are working for the kingdom of darkness. We are supposed to be working for the kingdom of God, but we have a poverty and religious mindset, thinking we are only supposed to be helping the people on the streets. We always focus on helping the poor and needy first. As a result, we lost our nations. We should take care of the poor and the needy, but we should do it after we have reached a city or nation with the gospel of the kingdom.

Remember how Paul and his team did ministry when they reached a new city or nation? They did not go and start an orphanage or a food distribution center first. Neither did they conduct a concert. They occupied the gates or reached the people who had influence, but they always encouraged believers to help and take care of the poor, widows, and the needy once a church was established.

Do you remember what I said before? While we are practicing for our next musical production or raising funds to build another megachurch, the enemy came in through the back door and stole everything. Then we complain about it and blame the devil for every evil that is happening in our society. Who is letting him do what he does? The church!

We should begin with preaching, but never end there. Sadly we end with our preaching and an altar call. And we are done—but that should only be the beginning. After that, we should teach our people what they lost because of the fall and equip them with the process of taking it all back, as I shared in the previous chapter. Next, we should help them discover their purpose, calling, and gifts, and release them to fulfill their God-given destiny. Let's take a look at how we should disciple a nation with the gospel of the kingdom.

DISCIPLING NATIONS WITH THE GOSPEL OF THE KINGDOM

After the resurrection, Jesus spent forty days with the disciples, teaching them about the kingdom of God (Acts 1:3). Even after the resurrection, Jesus had only one subject to talk about. Before His ascension, He told them what He expected them to do next.

In Matthew 28 we read the Great Commission. Let us read it in His own words and find out what He said:

> Go therefore and make disciples of all the nations, baptizing them in the name of the Father and of the Son and of the Holy Spirit (Matthew 28:19).

Jesus' heart is to disciple nations. We have been discipling *individuals* instead. We have not been discipling individuals with the intention of them discipling their towns, cities, and nations for God either. That is the one thing which has been missing greatly in our ministry endeavors. We have only been committed to evangelizing, doing crusades, and getting people saved. We stop our operation right there. Getting people saved is only the first step and not the last.

The Great Commission will not be completed until every nation on earth is *discipled*. That process has only just begun. To understand more about discipling nations, let's find out what it is and how to do it.

Discipling a nation means they are brought under the kingship of Jesus, and are seeing God's will accomplished in that nation as it is in heaven. That is why Jesus told us we must teach them everything He had commanded, and baptize them in the name of the Father, Son, and the Holy Spirit. How do we baptize a city or a nation? When we baptize people in an entire town, we are baptizing that town. Everything in that town will come under the rule of the Father, Son, and the Holy Spirit.

For a long time I understood this as if Jesus was saying, "Go therefore, and make disciples *from* all nations." I always focused on an individual mandate. Jesus did not give an individual mandate; He gave a *national* mandate: *discipling nations*. He did not say *from* all nations, but *of* all nations. We are supposed to disciple nations. How do we do that? Is that even possible in our day and age?

To answer that question, we need to understand what discipleship is and how to do it. I could write a whole book on that subject alone!

What Is True Discipleship?

How did the early church disciple nations like Syria, Turkey, and many present-day western countries that were once Christian? When the church lost its purpose and became a mere building and a religious entity instead of *functioning* as a kingdom embassy, we lost nations and cities.

Though there are thousands of religious entities (more churches exist today than at any other time in the history of Christianity) functioning on almost every corner, they have no influence on what is happening around them, either in the spiritual or natural realm. We have left our *first love* (Jesus), our *first mandate* (to rule and reign on earth), and the *Great Commission* (to disciple nations).

When we talk about discipling nations and cities, it may seem like an impossible dream to many, but let me tell you that nothing is impossible with our God. The problem is that we lack the capacity to believe Him to do something. God is looking for a group of people to believe for something that only He can do; but we are so programmed in our religious and rapture mindset that when we hear anything contrary, we have a tendency to oppose it.

How did the early church disciple cities like Ephesus, Corinth, and Rome? I will answer that in the next pages. Idol worshippers, temples, and government institutions were brought under the feet of Jesus. We are not talking about something new here. What I am sharing has happened before in history; and if it happened once, there is the possibility of it happening again.

If we do not disciple our nations, someone else will do it. The devil will use his children to disciple our cities and nations, and our children. There is no point in blaming anyone for how things are going in our nations either—because we let it happen.

DISCIPLING NATIONS WITH THE GOSPEL OF THE KINGDOM

Everywhere I go, I meet people who are unhappy with the direction their cities and nations are headed. They are not happy about what is happening in their schools and neighborhoods. They feel helpless, and all they do is complain and murmur. This book is intended to train you to act, not just gain information, and then run and find another book without doing anything about what you just learned. If you keep doing that, you will become spiritually barren and a religious junkie.

I use an example of an airplane to show people what is happening in our nations and why our culture is going from bad to worse. It is easy to blame the devil, but he is doing what he is supposed to do. The problem is that we are not doing what we are supposed to do. I hope and pray this book will inspire you to *do* something.

Imagine traveling in an intercontinental airplane and the passengers in the cabin are the church. Suppose there are five hundred passengers and they are all seated comfortably. They all have the same destination; spiritually speaking, it is heaven. No one can jump off that plane in the middle of the trip. Once you get in and it takes off, you are stuck until it lands.

These believers are singing and having revivals. They shout, "Praise the Lord" and "Hallelujah" every time they meet a new believer. They sing songs with lyrics, like "We are going to meet the King!" Good food and entertainment are available every now and then. They are meeting new people, creating friendships, and everything is going smoothly.

What they do not realize is that their lives depend on the two people in the cockpit. Those two people decide almost everything for them—what they eat, when they eat, how much air they can breathe, when they sit down, when they can stand up, how often they can move around in the cabin, what kind of entertainment they can watch, when they can watch it, and what news they can hear. Everything is controlled from that cockpit. Their fate depends on those two people.

The sad thing is that the passengers pay those two guys to make all of the decisions for them. That is what is happening in our lives and nations. Though we have had many revivals, rallies, and crusades, nothing changes for the better because all the major decisions are made by the people who are in the *cockpits* of our nations, cities, and government buildings. The reason the situation is going from bad to worse, is because most of these people who make decisions for us are the embodiment of Satan himself.

We pay them to make those decisions for us; and unless we replace them with those who will make good and right decisions, nothing will change for the better. That is what we need to do right now. We should have done it years ago, but we let it go this long.

Who is discipling our nations and children? Corrupt politicians, media moguls, business tycoons, celebrities, and others who are in the cockpits of our nations. Every aspect of our society has a cockpit—those people who make decisions for the rest of society. Just because we gather in a building on Sunday morning for an hour and-a-half and shout, doesn't necessarily cause things to change for the better.

There are various ways to disciple a nation. How many people do you think someone like Michael Jackson discipled through his musical skills? Millions of people all over the world. How many people has Steve Jobs discipled through his products? How many children have been discipled by J.K. Rowling? Or the McDonalds chain? How many people and nations are discipled by communism or socialism?

For too long, we have limited our methods of discipling to preaching and teaching; these days, people are not very interested in that. Not everyone will listen to our preaching, but everybody needs and is interested in something. Seeing and meeting those needs is very critical in the process of discipling a nation.

Keep in mind that any time we leave a gap empty in our society, the enemy will bring something from his storehouse to fill it. That is what has happened. We neglected our gates and left the doors open for the enemy to bring anything he wanted through them to influence our culture.

There is a lot of talk and training on discipleship. When I was a young Christian, I was told that reading the Bible, witnessing, praying, being a good Christian, and going to church on Sunday morning was discipleship. If I practiced those habits, I was considered a good Christian or a disciple of Jesus Christ. Based on those qualifications, any religious person would be considered a good disciple of Jesus, but that is not accurate. I don't know how people came up with that idea. When we study the lives of those discipled, or mentored, by others in the Bible, we see a totally different picture.

How did Jesus disciple His twelve disciples? Did He give them a Bible (Torah) reading plan? Did He ask them to pray for a certain amount of time each day? Were they instructed to go to the temple on every Sabbath? No.

Why did Jesus select twelve disciples? Was the intent to turn them into "good Christians"? What benefit would He get if there were a bunch of good Christians walking around the streets of Jerusalem? In fact, there are millions of them in our day and time.

According to the Bible, we see that discipleship was practiced for an entirely different reason. It was not for any religious reason. It was not intended for taking people to heaven. From the discipleship program of Jesus Christ, we understand the following purposes.

We are going to look at discipleship from a kingdom perspective. The reason Jesus selected the Twelve was because the number twelve is the number of government in the Bible. He could have selected any number of people, but He specifically chose only twelve. He needed a governing body, and whatever God does has a kingdom flavor because He is King. From the biblical pattern of discipleship, we see the following principles evident.

Releasing People into Their Destiny

The first thing Jesus did for the disciples was release them into their destiny. That is the initiation process of discipleship. If there is no destiny, there is no discipleship. Discipleship must be geared toward releasing people into their destiny; otherwise, it is not true discipleship.

The devil stole our destinies through Adam. Ever since Adam lost the battle, the majority of people on earth go down into eternity without fulfilling their purpose. Cemeteries are filled with potentials and dreams that were never realized. Through the coming of the Last Adam, we got the opportunity to be restored and walk out our destiny.

Peter, Andrew, James, and John were fishermen, and they were stuck with that job. They were at the mercy of nature and their learned skill, or even luck, if they were to catch any fish. If they did not make a catch, they went hungry.

That's the situation with many of us too. We are at the mercy of other people and circumstances. That's not the way to live our lives. We should function only at the mercy of God. We have to be accountable and responsible to others.

Jesus set them free from the tyranny of luck and fate and released these men into their destiny. They became the founding apostles of the *ekklesia* of Jesus Christ on earth. They received the revelation of the kingdom of God in the form of a seed. We are supposed to be enjoying the fruit of it, but we have a lot of catching up to do. Unfortunately, we have to build on the foundation again because of the destruction caused by the religious spirit.

Millions of people in our society are stuck in jobs and circumstances they do not enjoy. They feel trapped with no way out. Their hearts are crying out for freedom, and they are looking for a Deliverer, just like the Israelites looked for a deliverer when they were in bondage in Egypt. Many are under the yokes of addiction, abuse, and debt. They know they need freedom, but they do not know how or where to get it. Setting those people free from their bondages and releasing them into the destiny God has for them is the first step in discipleship.

Their destinies have been taken captive: some to the survival system (jobs), religious system, habits, sin, their past, or any other tool the enemy can use. That is why Jesus said He came to set the captives free. Once they are released into their destiny, we need to train them to navigate life and fulfill their destiny; that is the process of discipleship.

Discipleship is not always preparing people to be in ministry, but releasing them to do whatever God created them to do. Often we have limited discipleship to religious purposes, and we need to remove those limitations before we go any further. Everything we do and every way, we, as believers, function is rooted and founded on those twelve men that Jesus chose and discipled and their teachings.

There is no particular length of time needed to disciple another person. Sometimes it takes just one meeting and an impartation to change someone's life for the better. Many times throughout my life I have had the experience of meeting someone, and grace was imparted to him or her, and their life was changed for the better. Each case is unique and will vary.

Below are some examples of people who were discipled by others and released into their destiny; God, in turn, used them to disciple nations. After Paul's conversion, Jesus appeared to a man called Ananias and told him to go and meet Paul. Actually, this command was to disciple Paul. Ananias was hesitant at first because of the news he had heard about Paul persecuting the church. Nevertheless, in obedience to the vision, Ananias went to Paul and released him into his destiny. He laid hands on him and Paul received the Holy Spirit. The rest is history. Paul went around establishing churches that discipled cities and nations. That is the power of true discipleship. *It doesn't take a lifetime to release someone into his or her destiny.*

Joshua was discipled by Moses, and it was done with one intention. Once Moses was done with his job, Joshua was to pick up where he left off and continue in his footsteps. Joshua was released into his destiny; he discipled the people of Israel to possess the Promised Land.

Elijah discipled Elisha, and he was released into his destiny. Then Elisha discipled the nation of Israel and other kings. In every example in the Bible, the disciple was released into his or her destiny.

Esther was discipled by her cousin, Mordecai; and when the time and opportunity came, he released her into her destiny. She was instrumental in discipling the kingdom of Persia and the Jewish nation.

If you study other examples in the Bible, you will see the same pattern. John the Baptist discipled Jesus by releasing Him into His destiny at the baptism in the Jordan.

In today's system of discipleship, people have been abused and misused by the personal agenda of the one discipling them. They have them polish their shoes and carry their bags and give massages to their master or their mistress, and they never get released into their destiny. That is not biblical discipleship; it is slavery or servanthood, and a form of bondage.

Every time people had an encounter with God, they were released into their destiny as well. Abraham, Moses, Gideon, Paul, and many others were propelled into their calling. That is what should happen to us at salvation. At the moment of salvation, people should have an encounter with their Savior that should release them into their destiny.

We have inherited a wrong understanding about salvation. We have limited salvation to a ticket to reach heaven, like buying fire insurance. Then we live the rest of our lives in fear of losing that insurance by doing something wrong. Nobody can live effectively for God with that kind of belief system. Salvation is not a reward for good merits or for religious works. It's a gift. We know what we need to do to receive a gift from someone: Just have a heart to receive, and be thankful for it.

How Do We Do This on a Practical Level?

Let's take Peter as an example. How did Jesus release Him to his God-given destiny? Before he had an encounter with Jesus, he was working as a fisherman. He was disappointed and not fulfilled, especially the night before he met Jesus. He admitted that he had not caught any fish though they toiled all night.

Fishing was his profession, his business. When he met Jesus, he had a miraculous catch and he was convicted, saved, and left his business all at once. Jesus told him to do something very important when he left his business. That is the key to releasing people into their divine destiny.

Jesus told His disciples this:

> Follow Me, and I will make you fishers of men (Matthew 4:19).

Jesus wanted to use the same gift He had given Peter in a new way. He would use it now for building His kingdom, instead of using it for survival or to build a personal empire.

That is what we should be doing when we release people to fulfill their destiny. Whatever gift, profession, or skills they have should be used for the benefit of God's kingdom instead of the enemy's kingdom.

We see this pattern throughout the Bible. Moses was a shepherd until he was called by God to lead His people. The skills and gifts he used to lead the sheep were now used for leading people. David was taken from the same profession to be a king.

Jesus was a carpenter until He was released to fulfill His destiny. Led by the Holy Spirit, He used the same gifts and skills to build, heal, restore, and shape people's lives. If you have a business, profession, or any other skills given by God, you will be released to fulfill your destiny, using them to build His kingdom. Too often our gifts and potential are being used by companies and businesses that the enemy is using to expand his kingdom. That should never happen.

It is important to notice that Jesus never asked Peter to leave his profession or skills. He asked him to follow Him. The same thing happened when Zacchaeus, the tax collector, met Jesus. He did not ask him to leave his profession, but because of his encounter with Jesus, Zacchaeus was transformed and began to use his profession for building God's kingdom. He returned everything he earned illegally fourfold to the people from whom he had taken it.

Paul is another example. The Bible says he was a tentmaker; I believe he used that business throughout his ministry season to make money and build relationships. Aquila and Priscilla were friends whom he met through his business. They were of the same trade (Acts 18:1-3).

Daniel and Joseph are the best examples. They were working in the most ungodly environment imaginable, but they did not let that defile or pollute them. They stayed true to their calling. There will be times you might need to leave your place of employment, but continue to use the gifts God gave you to build His kingdom.

There is misunderstanding about this among some circles of Christians. They think that when someone gets saved, they are not supposed to continue their profession, jobs, or businesses. That is not true according to the Bible. If God asks someone to leave a job behind, that is another situation, but usually God uses people where they are, transforming their job to support His kingdom purpose.

Once you are saved, you belong to God and His kingdom. Nobody teaches us that. We only heard the gospel of going to heaven when we die. We are told to continue to do what we were doing, bring the tithe into the storehouse, and wait for the rapture to take place.

God needs people in every sphere of society, in every profession, in every service sector and business, He wants His witnesses everywhere, doing what they are fitted to accomplish. They do not need to walk around and say hallelujah and praise the Lord, but witness through excelling in what they do, showing forth the excellence and glory of our God. We have to be better in every way than the people in the world, just as Daniel and his friends were in the Babylonian kingdom.

Releasing People to Disciple Cities and Nations

Why do we need to release people into their destinies? Nations are made of people. Each nation and city also has a divine destiny. Most nations are not fulfilling their destinies because the people in those nations are not fulfilling their personal destinies. When the people of a nation are released into their destinies, they in turn will disciple their nation by releasing its destiny.

Anything and everything we do, whether it's evangelism, missions, government, business, charity work, or anything at all, must be geared toward discipling our cities and nations. Western civilization became so busy building mega churches and cathedrals that they neglected to disciple their cities and nations. As a result, we lost them.

DISCIPLING NATIONS WITH THE GOSPEL OF THE KINGDOM

Western countries sent missionaries throughout the world with a passion to save souls and take them to heaven. Unfortunately, they neglected their own nations and didn't even teach the souls they'd won about their responsibilities and how to disciple their cities and nations.

Why do nations go through financial ruin and other chaos? It is because the citizens become selfish and self-centered and have no vision for their nation. They steal the resources from their own nation and sell them to multinational companies. They rob their own people and abuse them.

As disciples are released into their destinies, they must focus on releasing the destinies of their cities and nations. Most Christians have no vision for their own country. They only have a vision for heaven and are longing to walk on streets of gold and live in their heavenly mansions. They are looking for something for free.

Every discipleship program needs to be geared toward one purpose, which is eventually to disciple nations. For too long, our discipleship programs have been focused on producing *good* Christians who were mostly useless to their countries. *There was no such discipleship in the Bible.* Many believers are waiting to go to heaven and are more concerned about what is happening in heaven than on earth.

Now the question is: How do we disciple nations?

When we release people into their destiny, we are helping to fulfill the destiny of that nation. How do we release people into their destiny?

- By helping them discover their purpose
- By helping them realize their calling
- By helping them identify their gifts or imparting gifts

In the same way every individual has a divine destiny, each town, city, and nation also has its own destiny. Believers need to receive a blueprint from heaven for their towns and cities, then manifest or build according to the blueprint God has for them, making each aspect of those cities as it is in heaven.

THE GOSPEL OF THE KINGDOM

How do we disciple a town, a city, or a nation? Before I answer that question, my question to you is, "Who is discipling our cities and nations right now?" We can use a variety of methods and tools to disciple a city or nation. For example, the town I live in is discipled by a private Christian school. It is one of the best schools I have ever seen, and their motto is "Influence through Excellence."

We could use businesses, products, media, skills, or even government to disciple a nation or town. When I was in Bulgaria, the local leader took the ministry team to visit a nearby slum. It was a heartbreaking experience. We saw hundreds of families with children, just trying to survive. I saw more children per family than I have ever seen anywhere else.

Every slum has the same culture: dirt, disorder, chaos, hopelessness, and loud music. We had a medical doctor from France with us who had been involved in community development in many parts of Africa. After our visit, there was a time to debrief on our experience and come up with any possible solutions to solve the problems for that slum. Different people expressed different ideas on what could be done to help the people.

When the time came for this doctor to share her ideas, she came up with six needs this slum (or any other slum) has. The first thing she spoke of was the need for basic hygiene. I was surprised she didn't say they needed the gospel, or Jesus, or another church in that community. She spoke of their actual needs first because she had a kingdom mindset.

That struck me, and I began to think about why she said hygiene. I don't think that if we had gone there with the religious gospel that very many people would have showed any interest or received it, but if we did something to help them with any of their existing needs, that would open the door to share the gospel.

When Jesus called the disciples, He didn't ask if they wanted to go to heaven when they died. Instead, He met their immediate need. Their need was to catch some fish to survive another day. He gave them what they needed, and it opened their hearts to receive Him. As a result, they left everything and followed Him.

We read and studied about the price and size of discipleship. I remember reading different books on the price of discipleship when I was starting in the ministry. They were all good books, but none of them mentioned releasing people into their destinies. They were all focused on the religious experience, daily habits, and becoming a "gooder" Christian. Say three "Praise the Lords!" a day, and after discipleship, they were trained to say it five times a day and a little louder.

I heard about an interesting incident that took place in India. Christians in this particular community faced horrible persecution from Hindu fanatics. Their houses and church buildings were burned to the ground. Many of them were beaten and killed. When this persecution began to subside, the ministers and ministries began to think about how to continue ministry in that particular place again. People were not open to hearing the normal preaching. Additionally, they had warnings from the militia that no religious conversion or evangelistic meetings would be permitted.

God gave an idea to one of the ministers. Most of the people in that community were illiterate. The idea was to share the gospel through storytelling. They chose different stories and parables of Jesus and began to share them with the people on their level. They didn't need to attend a particular church meeting.

They shared these stories as part of normal everyday life. When people went to work, they shared these stories with those who were working with them. Ladies began to share stories with their neighbors. Farmers and quarry workers shared stories with their coworkers. The momentum began to build, and people wanted to know more stories and the source of those stories. They shared Jesus with them, and many came to the Lord because of that. The only problem was that all these discipleship programs were geared toward taking people to heaven.

Releasing the Destiny of the Nations

Why do people in a nation need to be released into their destinies? As a corporate body, they can then release the destiny of their nation. Each nation is unique and has a divine destiny, just like each individual has a unique destiny.

We talk about the American dream, Chinese food, French wine, German cars, Japanese technology, Canadian bacon, and Columbian coffee. Each nation is known for something. However, these items are not necessarily God's destinies for those nations. As believers, we have to recognize what each nation is known for in heaven and accomplish that will on earth.

Why did nations in the Western Hemisphere become godless societies? They were so focused on building big church buildings, cathedrals, and worldwide organizations that they forgot to disciple their nations. While they proceeded to "evangelize" the rest of the world, they left their own countries open to the enemies. The enemy came in and took over key places.

When you disciple a nation, that nation will fulfill its God-given destiny, just as an individual who is a disciple will fulfill their destiny. How do we disciple a nation? We need to receive a blueprint from heaven concerning the destiny of that nation. Everything we do has to be according to the blueprint in heaven.

As it is in heaven, so be it on earth. Jesus said He would only do what He saw His Father doing (John 5:19). That should be our motto as well. That is true ministry. Many are caught up doing many things and thinking they are in ministry or ministering and helping God, but that's not ministry. Anyone who was called into ministry was called to do something specific. God gave them a specific assignment.

Why Nations?

God is interested in nations, not just people. He is the One who started all nations. He wants nations to serve Him. Nations are Jesus' inheritance.

> I will declare the decree: the Lord has said to Me, "You are My Son, today I have begotten You. Ask of Me, and I will give You the nations for *Your inheritance*, and the ends of the earth for Your possession" (Psalm 2:7-8).

This is a promise to Jesus from His Father. We are part of fulfilling that promise for Jesus. Many have taken those verses personally and claimed nations for their own inheritance. That is not what those verses mean. When we ask for nations, we are asking for them *for Jesus*. For example, if we are asking for the Unites States of America, we should say something like this: "Father, I ask for the United States of America as an inheritance for Jesus Christ my King." All things are through Him and for Him and by Him.

Hebrews 11 really surprised me. It is about the people of faith and what they did. In verse 33, it says:

> Who through faith subdued kingdoms, worked righteousness, obtained promises, stopped the mouth of lions (Hebrews 11:33).

The first thing these disciples did was to subdue kingdoms or nations! Your calling and gifts are connected to discipling a particular nation.

I was surprised that it said the first thing they did as a result of exercising their faith was to subdue kingdoms or nations. Why did it not say how many souls they won for God or how many worship concerts they conducted? God's priority is nations and their destinies, both now and in the past. His heart is longing for the restoration of nations back to Him. He wants to be their King and rule over them. He is the King of all nations. That is why Jesus told us to go and disciple nations, not make converts that are waiting go to heaven.

Restoring the Creation

We have inherited a doom, gloom, and despair eschatology for the nations. I do not believe that is what Jesus taught. The Bible speaks of restoration, not destruction. Our God is a God of restoration and redemption. What joy would He receive if He destroyed all nations? That would be the ultimate loss. I believe God will extend every chance He can to restore a person or nation back to Him. That is what we are talking about here.

The Bible says God will hold back Jesus until the time for the restoration of all things, which every holy prophet has spoken of since the world began.

> Whom heaven must receive until the times of restoration of all things, which God has spoken by the mouth of all His holy prophets since the world began (Acts 3:21).

This verse says every holy prophet prophesied about restoration. That verse makes what God is thinking about creation very clear. He is planning to restore all things, not destroy all things. Discipling nations is part of that process. We are just beginning the process now.

God will restore this earth to its original state. Anytime you renew something, the old has to be there. The new comes out of the old. Scripture says if anyone is in Christ, he is a new creation, old things have passed away (2 Corinthians 5:17). As you know, when you were born again, you were made a new creation, but we are still dealing with the old.

Since we messed up the creation, I believe we have a part to play in its restoration. That is why the Bible says all creation is groaning for the manifestation of the sons of God. Some parts of the earth will be destroyed by fire, especially those regions that are occupied by the wicked. Whatever we possess and do for the Lord and His kingdom will remain forever.

Discipling the Nations by Sending Them into the World

In Matthew, we read that Jesus sent them to make disciples "of" all nations. Why nations? Nations are Jesus' inheritance. He is the King of Kings, King of all nations. He wants nations serving Him.

As previously mentioned, Jesus revealed how to disciple the nations in the gospel of Mark.

> He said to them, "Go into all the world and preach the gospel to every creature" (Mark 16:15).

Why would Jesus say "disciple nations" in Matthew and "go into all the world" in Mark? I thought He said, "Go around the world" and preach the gospel to every human. That is not what He told us to do. He told us to go "into" all the world.

God never sent anyone *around* the world. He always sent them *into* the world. Most of them were sent into government because God knew government was the key component that controlled every other aspect of society. If we lose our governments, eventually we will lose everything else.

We have translated this verse into going *around* the world and conducting crusades and collecting decision cards to show some people in the West how many people were "saved" because of our personal ambitions. God prepares His people and sends them into one of the components of which this world is made. I'm hoping you have already read the other volumes of the *Kingdom Series* and that you will find your calling and gifts.

Equipping Us to Fulfill Our Destiny and Call

Once we release people into their destiny, we need to equip them with the skill and everything else they need to fulfill that destiny. The only things Jesus did not give the disciples were material things. He did not promise them any money or other material things. Today, that's all we give people. We bless them with material things, so they do not have to trust God for anything. We do things opposite from the way Jesus did.

Almost everyone who has ever come to do ministry with me was primarily concerned with how much I was going to pay them each month. None of them remained long in the field. Jesus taught His disciples that their blessings were in the harvest they were going to bring in, not in money. Those who look for their reward before they reap any harvest will not succeed in the field. Always know that your blessing is in the harvest that will come to the kingdom through you.

The reason Jesus gave His disciples power and authority to cast out demons and heal sickness was because they needed that to fulfill the destiny He had for them. You may not need that to fulfill your destiny. You might need an education from a college or to develop a skill. In fact, this area is greatly differentiated among God's people. We are each uniquely created to do something for the Lord in a particular area. This is precisely why we must be free of the religious spirit and the other influences of the enemy in our lives. Only when we are free to hear the voice of the Lord directing us, do we know which way to go and what to develop. Where the spirit of the Lord is, there is freedom.

Methods of Discipling Nations

Through the Church

It is the original plan of God to disciple nations through local churches. The church should have the vision and the heart of Jesus for the nations and their cities. The reason Jesus establishes an *ekklesia* in a city or nation is to disciple them and bring them under His Lordship. As we read in the Word, He has been waiting until all His enemies are brought to His footstool.

When we study the early church, we find that they were not having revival services every Sunday, and they were not waiting to fly away. They turned the world upside-down and then turned it back right-side-up the way it was supposed to be. If we look at our society, we will notice things are functioning upside-down again. We are supposed to turn it back the way it's supposed to be.

The church is supposed to be equipping the saints to do the work of the ministry. Ministry is not preaching and helping the poor. *Everything and anything a person is called by God to do is their ministry.* All the methods of discipleship that are listed below should be done through the church, but today's church is limited in their vision, so God also uses parachurch organizations to do the job He always wanted done.

Through Governments

Church and government should never be separated. They're supposed to work in partnership. They are the two wings of the kingdom of God. One deals with the spiritual and the other deals with the natural. They're supposed to work hand-in-hand to solve problems and fix what is broken.

In the Old Testament, the kings and priests worked in partnership. They were not separated and doing their own thing. They were both instrumental in discipling the nation of Israel.

One example from the early church can be found in the life of the evangelist, Philip, when he met the eunuch from Ethiopia. Holy Spirit told him to go to the desert of Gaza where this eunuch was traveling back to his country after visiting Jerusalem. This was not an ordinary person. He was a man of great authority and in charge of all the treasury of the queen.

It's important to notice what the Bible says about him: "A eunuch of great authority under Candace the queen of the Ethiopians, who had charge of all her treasury" (Acts 8:27b). Philip shared the gospel with him, and he was saved and baptized right then and there. He went back to Ethiopia and shared what happened to him and discipled the whole nation as a result. Ethiopia was one of the first Christian nations, and "the only region of Africa to survive the expansion of Islam as a Christian state."[25]

Through Agriculture

Joseph used agriculture to disciple Egypt. It was the vehicle through which He reached the entire nation. There are many countries on earth that are struggling to produce enough food for their people. As a church, we are supposed to tap into the department of agriculture in heaven, and release ideas and plans to produce quality food that can feed the hungry. When a church trains its people to produce enough food for a village or a town, they are discipling that area and the people.

Through Education

Another method is through education. The majority of the world's political and business leaders were graduates of universities like Oxford, Yale, and Harvard. What an opportunity to shape leaders who in turn will shape the future of nations! As I mentioned earlier, the city where we are located is

---

25. "Religion in Ethiopia," Wikipedia, June 08, 2019, accessed June 16, 2019, https://en.wikipedia.org/wiki/Religion_in_Ethiopia.

being discipled by a Christian school. I don't mean that they do it with that intention, but it's the result of their influence.

Through Media

I don't need to explain much about the influence of media on our society. People wake and turn on their TVs or smartphones to see what is happening in the world. For the most part, people believe what the media says. Maybe that is changing nowadays because they have been called on the carpet for propagating "fake news." If one outlet of media is not trustworthy, people will tune into the next one. Either way, most of the media is controlled by the kingdom of darkness.

Through Science and Technology

Another way to disciple a city or nation is through science and technology. We cannot emphasize the importance of this in our lives. We are very dependent on technology. Today, we can't imagine a life without it.

Through Business (the Marketplace)

Another effective way to disciple nations is through businesses. In many countries, there are huge businesses which even the governments depend on for income. Taxes are what brings income to the government, and the more taxes citizens and companies pay, the richer the governments become. These multi-national companies literally disciple the nations in which they exist. People buy and depend on their products for survival. Believers need to start such companies with the intention of discipling nations.

When Joseph began to prepare Egypt for the drought, he ordered storehouses built in every town. Later, when the famine started, people came to him or to those storehouses to buy food. When they ran out of money, they sold their land for food. He not only used agriculture to disciple Egypt, but He used real estate and construction ventures as well. Imagine having to build storehouses through the entire land of Egypt, and how much land, materials, people, and money it took to do that. He became the wealthiest man in the whole nation, next to Pharaoh.

For example, there is a business in India that is run by a man that has had deep-rooted influence in the country for decades. They produce everything from software to salt. I don't think there is a sector they are not involved in. They are also the largest auto manufacturer in the whole country.

The power of business can be instrumental to win souls. Here's the testimony of a friend pertaining to this area:

"I'd like you to help us develop our marketing program beginning in January," said the CEO of a sports product company. This offer came at a time in which my friend, a consultant, was delighted to have an opportunity to use his talents again. It was the first new business opportunity he'd had in some time, and he had just come out of some very difficult business and personal circumstances. A few months into the position, the CEO asked this consultant to manage the entire marketing department, placing him over all the current marketing staff. It appeared that God was blessing his efforts with several successful initiatives. He began to build relationships with a few of the executives. One day, the sales manager came into his office and asked for help with a personal crisis. One thing led to another, and two months later the consultant found himself leading the sales manager in the sinner's prayer in the sales manager's office.

There is not a nation that is closed to the gospel of the kingdom. We need to find out the *key* we need to use to open the door for the gospel in each particular country. As Jesus said, He has given us the keys of His kingdom. Notice the word *key* is plural: there are many keys in a kingdom.

One of the above-mentioned methods would work in every country. The problem is we have not prepared or equipped our people and released them to do this work. I have heard of medical evangelism where Christian doctors dedicate their time to visit a country to donate their service and share the gospel with their patients. In the city of Philippi, Paul met a businesswoman whose heart the Lord opened to receive the gospel.

Through Miracles

I don't need to write more on this. We are all familiar with the influence miracles have on people. Though every other method mentioned above requires the power and the wisdom of God, there are particular cases in which this manifests to surpass natural laws. We call these miracles or signs and wonders.

When we apply all the methods of discipleship mentioned above, we can reach any nation on earth within the next ten to fifteen years. No nation is closed to the gospel of the kingdom. They are only closed to a religious gospel. May the Lord help and grant us wisdom on how to practice discipleship and on how to bring nations back to God.

Through Fasting and Prayer

When Jonah went to Nineveh to preach and announced what God was planning to do in that nation, the entire nation from the king to the livestock declared a three day fast. They didn't even drink water for those three days. When they humbled themselves before God, He relented from His wrath and forgave the whole nation.

Esther and Daniel are two other examples of God using fasting and prayer to change the course of nations. We need to find out from God which method He is planning to use to disciple, change, or influence *our* nation. He can use all of the above or just one method to influence an entire nation.

By now you may have a glimpse of what the gospel of the kingdom is all about. Jesus said when the gospel of the kingdom is preached in the entire world as a witness to all the nations and then the end will come (Matthew 24:14). I believe the Holy Spirit gave me this book to educate the body of Christ on what is the gospel of the kingdom.

If you study the book of Acts you will see that the apostles went around and preached the gospel of the kingdom. Below are some of the evidences.

Peter Preached the Kingdom of God

What I did not understand for a long time was the message Peter preached on the day of Pentecost. I wondered why he didn't mention anything about the kingdom of God in his message. Why was it only about repentance and baptism? I was ignorant and blinded by the religious spirit for a long time, and that is why I did not see anything about God's kingdom in his message. To be honest, Peter spoke about repentance and baptism only after people asked him what they should do, after they heard his preaching. The theme of the message he preached prior to that was about David and his throne, and how God raised Jesus to sit on that throne. He preached the kingdom of God from a historical perspective and showed that Jesus is the fulfillment of the prophecies and promises God gave to David.

Peter preached more about the kingdom of God in that one message than anyone else in the entire book of Acts. He referred to David and his throne several times. What does David have to do with the day of Pentecost? Or the arrival of the Holy Spirit? Or the inauguration of the church? Why would Peter refer to David in the first message ever preached in the Church Age? This gets very interesting. There are ten references to David and nine references to Abraham in the book of Acts.

Remember, Jesus is the Son of David, the legal heir to his throne. God promised David an eternal throne and a kingdom (2 Samuel 7:12-16; Luke 1:31-33).

> When your days are fulfilled and you rest with your fathers, I will set up your seed after you, who will come from your body, and I will establish his kingdom. He shall build a house for My name, and I will establish the throne of his kingdom forever. I will be his Father, and he shall be My son. If he commits iniquity, I will chasten him with the rod of men and with the blows of the sons of men. But My mercy shall not depart from him, as I took *it* from Saul, whom I removed from before you. And your house and your kingdom shall be established forever before you. Your throne shall be established forever (2 Samuel 7:12-16).

Jesus was called the Son of David throughout the Gospels. The Holy Spirit gave Peter a revelation about that when He stood up to preach. It had everything to do with God's eternal kingdom.

THE GOSPEL OF THE KINGDOM

When those Jewish people heard that message, they were cut to the heart and ran to him. Jesus said that from the day of John the Baptist, the kingdom of God was being preached and everyone was pressing into it. Three thousand people ran to Peter to get into the kingdom that day.

> Men and brethren, let me speak freely to you of the patriarch David, that he is both dead and buried, and his tomb is with us to this day. Therefore, being a prophet, and knowing that God had sworn with an oath to him that of the fruit of his body, according to the flesh, He would raise up the Christ to sit on his throne, he, foreseeing this, spoke concerning the resurrection of the Christ, that His soul was not left in Hades, nor did His flesh see corruption. This Jesus God has raised up, of which we are all witnesses. Therefore being exalted to the right hand of God, and having received from the Father the promise of the Holy Spirit, He poured out this which you now see and hear. For David did not ascend into the heavens, but he says himself:
>
> "The Lord said to my Lord,
> 'Sit at My right hand,
> Till I make Your enemies Your footstool'"
> (Acts 2:29-35).

It is interesting to look at how each of the Gospels presents the entry of Jesus into Jerusalem. When the people shouted, "Hosanna in the highest" or "Hosanna to the Son of David," Mark recorded it with David's kingdom, which we do not see in the other Gospels.

> Then those who went before and those who followed
> cried out, saying:
>
> "Hosanna!
> Blessed *is* He who comes in the name of the Lord!
> Blessed *is* the kingdom of our father David that comes in

the name of the Lord!
Hosanna in the highest!" (Mark 11:9-10).

In His triumphal, or royal, entry into Jerusalem, He was fulfilling one of the major prophecies in the Old Testament because He actually was their King.

> Rejoice greatly, O daughter of Zion! Shout, O daughter of Jerusalem! Behold, your King is coming to you; He *is* just and having salvation, Lowly and riding on a donkey, a colt, the foal of a donkey (Zechariah 9:9).

Clearly God did not "insert" the church into His original plan; the church had been part of His plan all along.

Philip Preached the Kingdom of God to the People of Samaria

> But when they believed Philip as he preached the things concerning the kingdom of God and the name of Jesus Christ, both men and women were baptized (Acts 8:12).

Paul Preached the Kingdom of God and Spoke About Entering It

> Strengthening the souls of the disciples, exhorting *them* to continue in the faith, and *saying*, "We must through many tribulations enter the kingdom of God" (Acts 14:22).

> And he went into the synagogue and spoke boldly for three months, reasoning and persuading concerning the things of the kingdom of God (Acts 19:8).

> And indeed, now I know that you all, among whom I have gone preaching the kingdom of God, will see my face no more (Acts 20:25).

> So when they had appointed him a day, many came to him at *his* lodging, to whom he explained and solemnly testified of the kingdom of God, persuading them concerning Jesus from both the Law of Moses and the Prophets, from morning till evening (Acts 28:23).
>
> Then Paul dwelt two whole years in his own rented house, and received all who came to him, preaching the kingdom of God and teaching the things which concern the Lord Jesus Christ with all confidence, no one forbidding him (Acts 28:30-31).

When there are that many references to the apostles preaching the kingdom of God, it is difficult to understand why so-called theologians have a problem approving the message of the kingdom today. It has always been the religious system and the religious spirit that opposes the message of the kingdom of God. When you see someone who does not like the message of the kingdom, it is evidence that a religious spirit is operating in that person. When Jesus was here on earth, the Gentiles and the sinners did not oppose Him or what He preached; It was the religious leaders who opposed Him and did not like what He preached. Some things have not changed.

I believe you have been blessed by reading this book. You may have to read it more than once to receive everything. Read it and study it until it becomes part of you. Use it for Bible study groups and teach others. When you teach something, it helps you to learn it better. I encourage you to order a copy for your friends and relatives. To order more copies of this book or any of my other works, please visit www.thekingdomnetwork.org.

Let the Revolution Begin!

More Books & Resources

DISCIPLING NATIONS SERIES

Kingdom Mandate (for any donation)
Discovering the Lost Kingdom (Volume 1) $14.00
Purpose, Calling, and Gifts (Volume 2) $15.00
God's Original Design (Volume 3) $20.00
Seeing, Entering, and Manifesting the Kingdom of God (Volume 4)$20.00
The Ekklesia (Volume 5) $30.00
The Gospel of the Kingdom (Volume 6) $20.00
Power and Authority of the Church (Volume 7) $15.00
Kingdom Family (Volume 8) $15.00
The Birthing of a Kingdom Nation (Volume 9) $20.00
What Happened to God? (Volume10) $20.00
7 Dimensions and Operations of the Kingdom of God (Volume 11) $15.00
Kingdom Economy (Volume 12) $15.00
Kingdom Government (Volume 13) $15.00
Releasing Kings and Queens to their Original Intent (Volume 14) $10.00
Kingdom Secrets to Restoring Nations Back to God (Volume 15) $20.00
Keys to Fulfilling Your Kingdom Assignment (Volume 16) $15.00

KINGDOM LIVING SERIES

The Three Most Important Decisions of Your Life $15.00
Recognizing God's Timing for Your Life $12.00
Overcoming the Spirit of Poverty $10.00
Seven Kinds of Believers $10.00
7 Dimensions of God's Glory $5.00
7 Dimensions of God's Grace $10.00
7 Kinds of Faith $7.00

HEALING OF THE NATIONS SERIES

Principles of Self Governance $20.00

KINGDOM BOOKS FOR KIDS

Genesis 126 Three Volume Book set for boys $25.00
Genesis 126 Three Volume Book set for boys $25.00
Genesis 126 Coloring Books for Boys $15.00
Genesis 126 Coloring Books for Girls $15.00

GENESIS 126 TEACHER'S MANUAL

Level 1 6-8 years $15.00
Level 2 8-10 years $15.00
Level 3 10-12 years $15.00

TO PLACE AN ORDER:

www.TheKingdomNetwork.org
Phone: 1-800-558-5020
Email: info@TheKingdomNetwork.org

About the Author

Abraham John is an internationally-known author and conference speaker. His calling is to preach the gospel of the kingdom in every nation and to equip the body of Christ to administer God's kingdom on earth to disciple nations. He has been to seventy countries, ministering in churches and conferences, and has authored more than forty books on the subject of the kingdom of God. *Discovering the Lost Kingdom, Recognizing God's Timing for Your Life, The Power and Authority of the Church, and Kingdom Secrets to Restoring Nations Back to God* are a few of his best-selling books. He is the founder and president of Maximum Impact Ministries (www.maximpact.org).

Abraham has been graced with an apostolic and governmental calling to put things back into God's original order and design. His passion is to see the body of Christ united and the true church manifest on earth. The Holy Spirit has given him the key to crack the purpose code, and one of the unique anointings upon his life is to help people identify their individual calling and gifts and release them to fulfill their destiny.

His teaching and practical training are tools to help the body of Christ restore and disciple nations. He has been a guest on several TV shows including Praise the Lord on TBN and other local channels. His Facebook live shows reaches thousands of people every week. If you would like to invite him to minister in any of your meetings please contact the ministry by email info@thekingdomnetwork.org or by phone 1 800 558 5020.

Are you struggling to discover your **PURPOSE ?**
You are not supposed to fit in but stand out !

Sign up today for the
FREE Online Kingdom Course

DISCOVERING

THE LOST KINGDOM

In this course you'll DISCOVER:

>> Your true identity and purpose
>> What God is doing on the earth and how you can partner with Him in it
>> Why God created the earth and put us on this planet
>> And much more ...

Why are people becoming more and more disinterested in **church and religion** globally?
Join the course, and discover
what your soul has been searching for all along.

FREE BOOK AND STUDY GUIDE

Other courses available
>> DISCOVERING PURPOSE, CALLING AND GIFTS
>> SEEING, ENTERING AND MANIFESTING THE KINGDOM
>> GOD'S ORIGINAL DESIGN
>> The Ekklesia
>> The Next move of GOD
   And more ...

Register Now @ **www.TheKingdomUniversity.org**

Welcome to
KINGDOM DELIVERANCE
— WORKSHOP —

Are you tired of waiting and looking for breakthroughs? Kingdom of God has the answer.

This kingdom deconstruct workshop is divided into EIGHT major categories which deal with the eight major areas of our life. Each one is connected to the next, and so if one of these areas dysfunctions, it will affect all other areas of your life.

1. Relationship with the Father
2. Spiritual Healing
3. Emotional Healing
4. Recognizing Purpose and Calling
5. Identifying and Mastering Natural and Spiritual Gifts
6. Finances—Learning to Live in Kingdom Economy
7. Healing Relationships
8. Physical Health

Take action now. Order all 8 workshop manuals today !

Thank you so much for taking the courses from The Kingdom University. Taking a course is only the first step. We are pleased to present you with the next step—that of going through the process to get rid of all the extra weights that have been slowing and hindering you from fully living out your kingdom assignment.

Call 1 800 558 5020   www.TheKingdomNetwork.org

www.ingramcontent.com/pod-product-compliance
Lightning Source LLC
Chambersburg PA
CBHW070131080526
44586CB00015B/1639